LIBERTY!
ÉGALITÉ!
¡INDEPENDENCIA!:

Print Culture, Enlightenment, and Revolution
in the Americas, 1776–1838

LIBERTY! ÉGALITÉ! ¡INDEPENDENCIA!:

Print Culture, Enlightenment, and Revolution
in the Americas, 1776–1838

*Papers from a Conference at the
American Antiquarian Society in June 2006*

The James Russell Wiggins Lecture
'We declare you independent whether you wish it or not':
The Print Culture of Early Filibusterism

DAVID S. SHIELDS

&

Conference papers by

MARISELLE MELÉNDEZ, ERIC SLAUTER, DAVID GEGGUS,
ALYSSA GOLDSTEIN SEPINWALL, KAREN STOLLEY,
ELIZABETH MADDOCK DILLON, NANCY VOGELEY,
SANDRA M. GUSTAFSON, AND MICHEL DUCHARME;
AND AN INTRODUCTION BY CAROLINE F. SLOAT

*This publication includes the twenty-fourth annual
James Russell Wiggins Lecture in the History of the Book
and the papers delivered at the conference.*

The James Russell Wiggins Lecture in the History of the Book in American Culture, inaugurated in 1983, is an annual activity of the American Antiquarian Society through its Program in the History of the Book in American Culture. The lectureship honors the memory of James Russell Wiggins, of Brooklin, Maine, former editor of the *Washington Post*, former United States ambassador to the United Nations, and, until his death in 2001, editor of the *Ellsworth* (Maine) *American*. The president of the American Antiquarian Society from 1970 to 1977, Wiggins was a longtime student of the history of printing and journalism and an articulate spokesman for the freedom of the press. The lectureship was endowed with gifts to the Society from his friends and admirers.

Library of Congress Cataloging-in-Publication Data

Liberty! Egalité! Independencia! : print culture, enlightenment, and revolution in the Americas, 1776–1838 : papers from a conference at the American Antiquarian Society in June 2006 [and] the James Russell Wiggins Lecture, "We declare you independent whether you wish it or not" : the print culture of early filibusterism / David Shields & conference papers by Mariselle Meléndez . . . [et al.] ; and an introduction by Caroline F. Sloat.
    p. cm.
   Reprinted from the *Proceedings of the American Antiquarian Society*, v. 116, pt. 2 (Oct. 2006).
   Includes bibliographical references and index.
   ISBN 978-1-929545-46-9 (alk. paper)
   1. America—Intellectual life—18th century—Congresses. 2. America—Intellectual life—19th century—Congresses. 3. America—Politics and government—18th century—Congresses. 4. America—Politics and government—19th century—Congresses. 5. Enlightenment—America—Congresses. 6. Revolutions—America—History—Congresses. 7. Books and reading—Political aspects—America—History—Congresses. 8. American literature—Revolutionary period, 1775–1783—History and criticism—Congresses. 9. American literature—1783–1850—History and criticism—Congresses. 10. Liberty in literature—Congresses. I. Shields, David S. II. Meléndez, Mariselle, 1964– III. American Antiquarian Society. IV. American Antiquarian Society. Proceedings of the American Antiquarian Society.
   E20.L53 2007
   970.05—dc22

Table of Contents

Introduction   7
CAROLINE FULLER SLOAT

'We declare you independent whether you wish it or not':
The Print Culture of Early Filibusterism   13
DAVID S. SHIELDS

Fear as a Political Construct: Imagining the Revolution
and the Nation in Peruvian Newspapers, 1791–1824   41
MARISELLE MELÉNDEZ

Written Constitutions and Unenumerated Rights   57
ERIC SLAUTER

Print Culture and the Haitian Revolution:
The Written and the Spoken Word   79
DAVID GEGGUS

The Abbé Gregoire and the Atlantic Republic of Letters   97
ALYSSA GOLDSTEIN SEPINWALL

Writing Back to Empire:
Juan Pablo Viscardo y Guzmán's 'Letter to
the Spanish Americans'   117
KAREN STOLLEY

Caribbean Revolution and Print Publics:
Leonora Sansay and 'The Secret History of the
Haitian Revolution'   132
   ELIZABETH MADDOCK DILLON

Llorente's Readers in the Americas   155
   NANCY VOGELEY

Daniel Webster and the Making of Modern Liberty
in the Atlantic World   175
   SANDRA M. GUSTAFSON

Closing the Last Chapter of the Atlantic Revolution:
The 1837–1838 Rebellions in Upper and Lower Canada 193
   MICHEL DUCHARME

Index   211

Introduction

CAROLINE FULLER SLOAT

The 2006 conference, LIBERTY/ÉGALITÉ/INDEPEN-DENCIA: Print Culture, Enlightenment, and Revolution in the Americas, 1776–1838, was the second in a series of three authorized by the Society's Council as a complement to the annual James Russell Wiggins Lecture in the History of the Book in American culture. The Wiggins Lecture is delivered by the conference convener, who organizes additional sessions around a selected theme. The first conference 'Histories of Print, Manuscript, and Performance in America' was organized for 2005 by Sandra Gustafson, English, University of Notre Dame. Her Wiggins Lecture, 'The Emerging Media of Early America,' appeared in *Proceedings of the American Antiquarian Society*, volume 115, part 2.

When David Shields proposed a conference focused on the history of the book in the Americas, it was a suggestion that mirrored the aspirations of the American Antiquarian Society's founder Isaiah Thomas. In the original bylaws of 1812, he envisioned that the collections of the Society would include 'books of every description, including pamphlets and magazines, especially those which were early printed either in South or North America.' To foster this interest, individuals residing in South America were routinely elected to the Society in its early years. Among those elected was Simón Bolívar, in October 1829, although he died at the end of the following year and there is no record of his having accepted his election.

CAROLINE FULLER SLOAT is the Society's director of scholarly programs.

The Society's South American collections were strengthened as titles became available. A boost came in the form of the Isaac and Edward L. Davis Fund, established in 1868 for the purchase of materials relating 'to that portion of North America lying south of the United States.' Stephen Salisbury III (1835–1905), who became the Society's president in 1887 and was its greatest benefactor in life and in death (when his bequest of $200, 000 enabled the Society to build the current Antiquarian Hall), was passionately interested in the archaeology of South and Central America. Salisbury was instrumental in helping to develop the collection by giving early imprints from Mexico and Central America, a subject area that now also includes his own manuscripts of travel and participation in archaeological excavations. Salisbury's interest in archaeology was sparked during his first visit to the Yucatan Peninsula in 1862. Papers on archaeological expeditions to the Yucatan, many sponsored by Salisbury, were published in earlier volumes of the *Proceedings of the American Antiquarian Society*. Essays written by him include 'Dr. LePlongeon in Yucatan,' (1877) and 'Terra Cotta Figure from Isla Mujeres,' (1878). Salisbury further developed this study in three books on the Mayan culture, *The Mayas and the Source of Their History* (1877), *Maya Archaeology and Notes on Yucatan* (1879), and *Maya History and Mexican Copper Tools* (1880). Later, during the early years of Clarence S. Brigham's tenure as librarian of the Society (librarian 1908–30; director 1930–59), all of the works of the Chilean bibliographer José Toribio Medina (1852–1930) were acquired, as well as a large collection of Mexican almanacs and imprints. While South America is not a primary collecting focus of the Society and, indeed, certain parts of the collection have been distributed to other centers, specific subject areas continue to be collected.[1]

1. To be able to maintain collections at a level useful for serious research, in 1968 the AAS Council reaffirmed a developing practice that the range of collecting would include the former French and English parts of North America from the period of settlement by Europeans through 1876. As a result, many European and South American imprints went to Brown University and newspapers to the University of Connecticut. Additions to the collection are now restricted to West Indian imprints and to books and pamphlets dealing

AAS interest in Canadiana extends to printed materials relating to the history of New France and British North America from the period of European settlement through 1876. The collection reflects the geographical, cultural, and historical links between French and English-speaking Canada and the United States. Journals of early discovery and exploration, nineteenth-century guidebooks, illustrated reports of expeditions, biographies, essays in Canadian folklore and literature, and federal and provincial government documents are a part of this rich and diverse collection. Family histories relevant to Loyalist studies, maps and lithographs of Canadian cities, early Canadian newspapers, nineteenth-century almanacs, and scholarly periodicals are also part of the collection. Most relevant for this conference is the collection of documentary series such as those published by the Champlain Society. *The Rebellion of 1837 in Upper Canada* focuses on one of the central events of Ontario's early history, and AAS holds several other works about that armed insurrection in Upper and Lower Canada. Among the primary sources on the patriot uprising are several rare personal narratives by political prisoners who were transported to the British penal colony in Van Dieman's Land following the rebellion of 1837–38.

The conference topic provided an opportunity to showcase highlights of the collection. An exhibition curated by Joanne Chaison, AAS research librarian is the source for the illustrations selected for the essays based on the conference talks.

The papers read and discussed at the 2006 conference were premised on the intellectual connections resulting from the circulation of written works throughout the Atlantic World. They charted the circulation of print and communications in Caribbean and South

---

with Central and South America and the West Indies (generally relating to history, relations with the United States, or description and travel) that were printed in the United States before 1877. Secondary works are added in areas such as social, political, and economic histories of the West Indies and relations between the United States and Mexico during the period of westward expansion.

American revolutions and considered the impact of materials that originated in Europe and North and South America on other imperial and colonial contexts. David Shields's Wiggins Lecture, '"We declare you independent whether you wish it or not": The Print Culture of Early Filibusterism,' looked at a long tradition of soldiers of fortune passionately committed to the export of revolution, operating from the Old World and the New. He identified the operative binary for these adventurers' appropriation of communication forms not as public-private but as public-secret. 'Publicity,' he claims, 'was the hallmark of American nationalist adventures or adventures invoking a cosmopolite liberty.' Secrecy is understood as a sign that the adventure was under the aegis of an Old World imperial power.

In the New World, there were abundant texts associated with the founding of the United States. Among them, are the Declaration of Independence, the Constitution, and the Bill of Rights. The paper by David Armitage is not reproduced in this volume, but his recent book *The Declaration of Independence: A Global History* (Harvard University Press, 2007) speaks directly to this point and includes many examples of such declarations. Writing on constitutions and rights, Eric Slauter notes that between 1776 and 1826, of the nearly sixty constitutions drafted in the new states of the Americas, twenty were in Latin America.

Mariselle Meléndez traces the role of five newspapers published in Lima showing how they were used first by the colonial authorities to respond to the American and French revolutions and some thirty years later by creole intellectuals in support of independence. David Geggus describes the surprising richness of newspaper archives and other printed sources relating to the abolition of slavery and the Haitian Revolution. Local journalism and expatriate writings in both the United States and France, falsified documents, rumor and written sources, the use of free colored scribes by illiterate slave leaders—are central to uncovering the intentions of the black insurgents.

Four of the papers considered the works of influential republican writers whose writings and relationships with other authors and intellectuals spurred the shaping of their ideas about the kind of polity might emerge and flourish after independence.

Alyssa Goldstein Sepinwall studies the friendship between Abbé Grégoire and Joel Barlow that was based on agreement about republicanism and foundered because of irreconcilable differences. Karen Stolley interprets Viscardo's 'Letter to Spanish Americans' (1791). Leonora Sansay's largely unknown novel about a failing marriage is in Elizabeth Maddock Dillon's interpretation, up to a point, a critique of the colonial fantasy of white superiority over black incapacity. But as the novel unfolds, Sansay identifies the existence of a third category—the white creole—who is identified with the colonial rather than the European white culture. Nancy Vogeley's examination of Llorente ties French printing and trade routes that introduced European writers and ideas to Mexico during its time of nation-building between 1821 and 1824, when its first constitution was written. Llorente's contribution, derived from his understanding of Spanish America's Catholic history and the role he considered most appropriate for religion in the new state, has been underplayed in interpretations of Mexican independence and statehood.

The paper delivered by Karen Racine (history, University of Guelph), 'Proxy Pasts: The Use of British Historical References during the Spanish American Independence Era' is not included in this volume. In it, she outlined ways in which English ideas of liberty as expressed during its Civil War and the Protectorate of Oliver Cromwell inspired Spanish American reformers.

Essays by Sandra Gustafson and Michel Ducharme show two of the ways in which this era of independence, republicanism, and liberty can be shown to have come to an end. Gustafson traces Daniel Webster's reorientation of constitutional thinking in the United States with the rise of Garrisonian abolitionism and the threat of Southern secession in the 1830s, while Ducharme takes a close look at the Canadian revolutionary uprisings of 1837 and 1838. The conference viewed the circulation of writings and ideas throughout the Atlantic World when liberty, equality, and independence were on the minds of many. It provided an opportunity for books, letters, public documents, and treaties to be put into conversation with each other revealing connections, sometimes unexpected, in thought and sentiment.

Acknowledgments

The American Antiquarian Society acknowledges with gratitude the generous financial support of the journal *Early American Literature* in making this conference and publication possible. The conference program was developed by a committee consisting of David S. Shields (American literature, University of South Carolina), chair; Mariselle Meléndez (Latin American literature, University of Illinois at Urbana-Champaign); Karen Stolley (Spanish, Emory University); and Ralph Bauer (English, University of Maryland). The Society is most grateful to Shields for his vision and leadership of the conference and to the committee that worked with him. Special thanks are due to Joanne Chaison, AAS research librarian, who worked with Jaclyn Donovan Penny, Georgia Barnhill, and Elizabeth Pope to select representative items from the collection for display in the Council Room during the conference. Finally, as Shields noted in his closing remarks, this symposium was the last of a long series of AAS scholarly events organized by Vice President for Collections and Programs John B. Hench. For the past thirty years, Hench has represented AAS to the academic community, and on behalf of all who have benefited from his vision, the participants gave him the accolade he so richly deserved.

'We declare you independent whether you wish it or not': The Print Culture of Early Filibusterism

DAVID S. SHIELDS

H OW DID THE MOST VOLATILE CITIZENS of the early republic organize their communications? I don't mean the rural rioters of the Whiskey Rebellion or Shays's Insurrection, rather, that more adventurous, more dangerous group—those soldiers of fortune and partisans of liberty who exported revolution from the thirteen United States, troubled the American territories of Spain, France, England, and the Native Nations, and set up republics or realms by force of arms or popular fiat.

From the 1780s through the 1850s, three generations of men, intoxicated by the doctrines of liberty, or pathologically fixated upon getting glory on the scale of Washington or Napoleon, or simply reveling in the possibility of acting in spaces mental and geographical beyond the constraints of morality and law, formed combinations and conspiracies to set up separate states, new republics, or territorial fiefdoms. During the Narciso Lopez ventures to

This paper was delivered as the Twenty-Fourth Annual James Russell Wiggins Lecture in the History of the Book in American Culture on June 16, 2006. It was the keynote address, opening the 2006 Conference of the Society's Program in the History of the Book in American Culture. In his introductory remarks, David Shields dedicated the lecture to John Hench, 'the public face of the American Antiquarian Society for many researchers for the past quarter century,' in recognition of his service on the occasion of his retirement.

13

Fig. 1. *Atlante Dell'America Contenente le Migliori Carte Geographiche, e topografiche delle Principali Cittá, Laghi, Fiumi, e Fortezze del Nuovo Mondo* (Livorno, Italy, 1777).

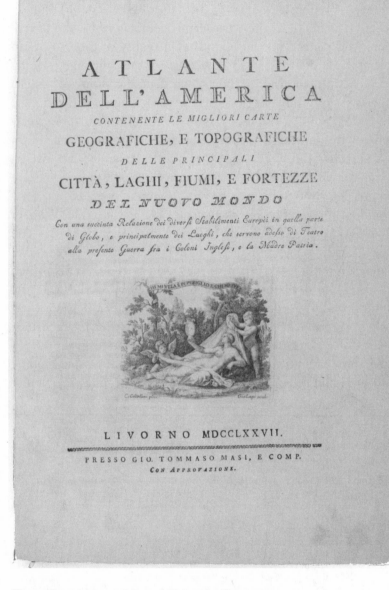

ATLANTE
DELL'AMERICA

CONTENENTE LE MIGLIORI CARTE

GEOGRAFICHE, E TOPOGRAFICHE

DELLE PRINCIPALI

CITTÀ, LAGHI, FIUMI, E FORTEZZE

DEL NUOVO MONDO

Con una succinta Relazione dei diversi Stabilimenti Europèi in quella parte
di Globo, e principalmente dei Lueghi, che servono adesso di Teatro
alla presente Guerra fra i Coloni Inglesi, e la Madre Patria.

LIVORNO MDCCLXXVII.

PRESSO GIO. TOMMASO MASI, E COMP.
CON APPROVAZIONE.

Fig. 2. Frontispiece, *Atlante dell'America Contenente.*

Cuba in the 1850s, newspapers coined a name for this sort of adventurer—'Filibuster'—derived from the Dutch term filibustier—freebooter.[1] It linked the American adventurers with the buccaneers who danced on the bounds of illegality in the Caribbean during the late 1600s. In 1794, because of the campaign by Citizen Genêt, the minister of the French Republic, to incite western Americans and Indians to conquer Spanish Louisiana for France, the United States Congress passed a Neutrality Act. It criminalized as a misdemeanor 'the organization of a military expedition by a person within the United States territory aimed at a foreign dominion with which the United States was at Peace.'[2] The Act did not deter the practice. The early republic saw a bizarre proliferation of adventures in the wake of Genêt's crusade: William Blount's conspiracy—Aaron Burr's march on New Orleans—The East Florida Revolution[3]—O'Fallon's Yazoo settlement[4]—The Natchez republic[5]—William Bowles's Muskogee republic (which was also a one-day kingdom),[6] the Republic of West Florida—The Gutiérrez-McGee venture in Texas. The Act did, however, cause a striking divergence in modes of expression employed by filibusters: one set of adventurers openly declared their projects and ideals, defying the Neutrality Act as a hobble to the international spread of liberty; the other occulted their communications, cultivating

1. Robert E. May, *Manifest Destiny's Underworld, Filibustering in Antebellum America* (Chapel Hill: University of North Carolina Press, 2003), xi, 3–4, 53–54, 299, 323.

2. Act of June 5, 1794, Chap. 50, section 5, 1. Stat. 381 384.

3. James G. Cusick, *The Other War of 1812: The Patriot War and the American Invasion of Spanish East Florida* (Gainesville: University of Florida Press, 2003).

4. John Carl Parish, 'The Intrigues of Dr. James O'Fallon,' *Mississippi Valley Historical Review* 17 (September 1930): 230–63. I will not be discussing this venture, but O'Fallon was connected with George Rogers Clark at one juncture in a filibuster to deliver the interior to the French.

5. Provoked by a religious conflict between Anglo-Protestants and Roman Catholics in the wake of the Pinckney Treaty in 1796, a Committee of Safety asserted control in Natchez, supplanting the government of Goyoso until the formal installation of United States authority late in 1797.

6. J. Leitch Wright, *William Augustus Bowles, Director General of the Creek Nation* (Athens: University of Georgia Press, 1967). See also the discussion of Bowles and Alexander McGillivray, in Claudio Saunt, *A New Order of Things: Property, Power, and the Transformation of the Creek Indians, 1733–1816* (New York: Cambridge University Press, 1999), 85–88, 205–13.

conspiratorial secrecy. My initial claim today is that when secrecy cloaked a filibuster adventure, the invasion or insurrection was for the benefit of an Old World imperial power, not the United States. Publicity was the hallmark of American nationalist adventures or adventures invoking a cosmopolite liberty.

How did these two cohorts organize their communications? Conspiratorial adventures employed manuscript writing in the forms of secret correspondence among participants and secret plans communicated to the diplomatic offices of governments seen as potential backers of territorial takeovers. They also employed verbal rumor. American nationalist adventurers presented written (later printed) warrants for their actions modeled on the penumbra of texts surrounding the founding of the United States. In the communicative practices of filibusterism—in the communicative culture of the most volatile citizens of the early republic—one discovers the operative horizon of imagined publicity and of secrecy in the early republic.

In the early autumn of 1810, Secretary of State Robert Smith placed a document on President James Madison's desk that proved diplomatically inconvenient: The Declaration of Independence of the Republic of West Florida. Madison wished to annex West Florida to the United States. He had been talking wish into fact in his dealings with the Napoleonic regime in Spain, insisting that the territory had been included in the Louisiana Purchase.[7] When he was Secretary of State under Jefferson, Madison had sent William Wykoff into West Florida to stir up support for annexation among the Anglo inhabitants. The sentiments that Wykoff unleashed, however, took an extravagantly independent turn.[8] In the summer of 1810, residents formed secret committees of correspondence, called three public conventions petitioning the Spanish administration for redress of grievances,

7. Richard R. Stenberg, 'The Boundaries of the Louisiana Purchase,' *Hispanic American Historical Review* 14 (1934): 32–33.

8. Wanjohi Waciuma, *Intervention in Spanish Floridas: A Study in Jeffersonian Foreign Policy* (Boston: Branden Press, 1976).

organized a makeshift army, designed a lone-star flag, and on the 23rd of September conquered the Spanish fort in Baton Rogue. On the 26th John Rhea issued the Declaration of Independence.[9] A month later, a constitution had been fashioned and a copy dispatched to the United States Secretary of State; a president elected (the former United States minister to the French Republic, Fulwar Skipwith); a legislature convened; and plans made to seize Pensacola and Mobile from the Spanish.[10]

Madison decided to ignore the existence of the republic and ordered the governor of the Louisiana Territory to intervene with force, for 'a crisis has at length arrived subversive of the order of things under the Spanish authorities.'[11] Madison quashed the republic with minimal public outcry. There was no press in West Florida. Every declaration, document, speech, petition, and explanation of the West Florida Revolution took place in manuscript. There were perhaps four copies of the Constitution, of which one survives, and twice as many copies of the West Florida Declaration of Independence; two survive. One cannot ignore a Revolution that reproduces itself in various expressive media. It is not too difficult to ignore a revolution that projected itself in less than two dozen pieces of paper that it had neglected to send to the gazettes.

Some maxims: in the eyes of established power, revolution always appears illegitimate; in the court of world opinion there is

9. Its text appears in Stanley Clisby Arthur, *The Story of the West Florida Rebellion* (St. Francisville, La.: The Democrat, 1935), 113–14. This account suffers from a parochial understanding of the diplomatic context of the outbreak. Isaac Joslin Cox, *The West Florida Controversy, 1798–1813* (Baltimore: The Johns Hopkins University Press, 1918) is the classic introduction to the revolution and annexation, providing texts of many of the primary materials.

10. The correspondence of the revolutionaries and the proclamations of President Skipwith are printed in 'The West Florida Revolution of 1810, as told in the Letters of John Rhea, Fulwar Skipwith, Reuben Kemper, and Others,' *Louisiana Historical Quarterly* 21 (1938).

11. James Madison, Presidential Address to Congress. See 'Madison and the Collapse of the Spanish-American Empire: The West Florida Crisis of 1810' in Robert A. Rutland et al., eds., *The Papers of James Madison, Presidential Series* (Charlottesville: University of Virginia Press, 1984–), 2: 305–20

no venue, no procedure for determining a revolution's legitimacy or illegitimacy; at best the candid world concerns itself with the question whether a revolution was warranted or not. The American Revolution projected a penumbra of printed texts that supplied warrants[12] for dissolving the political relation between the colonies and Great Britain and asserting sovereignty. The Revolution's literature provided a pattern for any insurrectionary group to stamp its actions as warrantable. The problem with the Revolution of West Florida was that its projectors contented themselves with miming the gestures of virtuous revolution, thinking that copying a warrant was enough. They failed to grasp the larger lesson of the American Revolution. Having a warrant and doing what is warranted simply constitute the first moments in the assertion of sovereignty. One has to advertise that fact to as broad a public as can be invoked, by print and whatever other expressive means come to hand. Some who participated in the short life of the republic learned this lesson. When Reuben Kemper[13] and his Floridian band joined the 1812 Guitierrez filibuster in Texas, he took with him Florida's lone star flag,[14] and a conviction that the press must amplify their actions in the disputed territory and throughout the continent.

History of the Book scholarship has increasingly asked about the social and cultural conditions that bring certain communications into print, others to manuscript circulation, and still others to oral delivery. In the 2005 AAS Conference of the Program on the History of the Book in America, Sandra Gustafson promoted an exploration of the various performative registers within which

---

12. A warrant is an assurance, often written, of the reasonable grounds for a course of action, or an authorization for action by a grantor. Alvin Plantinga, the epistemologist, has supplied the current influential philosophical formulation: 'that quantity enough of which, together with true belief, yields knowledge.'

13. Andrew McMichael, 'The Kemper "Rebellion": Filibustering and Resident Anglo American Loyalty in Spanish West Florida,' *Louisiana History* 43 (2002): 133–65.

14. The first Texas Revolution had a green flag. The lone star flag that Kemper brought however imprinted itself on the Anglo population. It was adopted as the flag of the Republic of Texas a decade later. It would enjoy later incarnations in the 1850s Cuban ventures and as the 'bonny blue flag' of Mississippi.

communications operate.[15] We've glimpsed in the West Florida insurrection the ritual repetition of the actions, institutions, and articulations of the American Revolution. The performances show that the *vox populi* spoke the people's will more immediately in West Florida than the Neutrality Act. But what of the filibusters who cultivated secrecy? What were the premises of their ways of communicating? I've suggested that a hush-up meant a transatlantic organization; a publicity campaign, a hemispheric organization. But more than this—if the public filibusters adverted to the power of the *vox populi*, the secret filibusters adverted to the influence of that great counterforce to popular sovereignty, diplomatic policy.

Consider the conspiracy by United States Senator William Blount in 1797. He attempted to organize frontier armies composed of Native Americans, Anglo settlers in Louisiana, and recruits from New York, Pennsylvania, Tennessee and Kentucky to attack Spanish outposts at New Madrid, New Orleans, and Pensacola in order to seize the Mississippi basin and Florida for the British. (The Louisiana Territory came under the jurisdiction of Spain by secret treaty at the end of the Seven Years War in 1763 and remained so until its retrocession to France by secret diplomatic treaty in 1800.) The accidental discovery of Blount's plan occasioned the first impeachment hearing and expulsion in the annals of the United States Senate.[16] Blount's co-conspirators included John Chisholm, prototype of the 'ring-tailed roarer' of frontier literature; Dr. Nicholas Romayne,[17] a

15. Conference: 'Histories of Print, Manuscript, and Performance in America,' June 10–12, 2005. http://www.americanantiquarian.org/phbac.htm. Gustafson delivered the 2005 James Russell Wiggins Lecture at the conference. See Sandra M. Gustafson, 'The Emerging Media of Early America,' *Proceedings of the American Antiquarian Society* 115 (2006): 205–50.

16. Buckner F. Melton, Jr., *The First Impeachment: The Constitution's Framers and the Case of Senator William Blount* (Macon, Ga.: Mercer University Press, 1998). See also Frederick J. Turner, ed., 'Documents on the Blount Conspiracy, 1795–1797,' *American Historical Review* 10 (1905): 574–606.

17. William B. Eigelsbach, 'The Blount Conspiracy: Notes of Samuel Sitgreaves on the Questioning of Dr. Nicholas Romayne on July 13 and 14, 1797, Before the House Impeachment Committee,' *Journal of East Tennessee History* 66 (1994): 81–96.

New York physician who retained his English citizenship; and James Carey, an Indian interpreter who roamed the Southeast. Each was convinced that the maintenance of the Louisiana territory in the slack hands of enfeebled Spain would lead to French control and a disciplinary dominion that would produce economic mayhem for Anglo settlers of the interior. Each had become disillusioned with the United States government policy in regard to the West: Blount because the prospect of a French takeover of Louisiana threatened a vast landscape of speculative land deals upon which his fortune depended and because the rapprochement with Spain inaugurated by the Pinckney Treaty (1795) appeared to him a guarantee of eventual French control of the Mississippi; Chisholm for denying a petition for citizenship from a group of British settlers in territory of dubious American jurisdiction; Romayne out of an English patriotic disdain for American policy.

Samuel Flagg Bemis once observed that, 'The very nature of an intrigue of this kind is to leave as little documentary evidence as possible.'[18] He was wrong. The *sine qua non* of secret conspiracy is correspondence—whether the cipher letter or the privately conveyed and retained missive. It was the exposure of one such letter between Blount and Carey that brought the secret plan into ruin and Blount's career and fortune into dust. It would also be the infamous cipher letter received by General James Wilkinson, purportedly from Aaron Burr, that occasioned the collapse of Burr's Quixotic attempt to create an independent Western nation extending into Mexico.[19]

The secrecy of conspiratorial letters after the passage of the Neutrality Act was a reaction to the openness of letters and missives circulated by Citizen Genêt and his associates enlisting citizens of the

18. Samuel Flagg Bemis, *Pinckney's Treaty* (1926; reprint Wesport, Conn.: Greenwood Press, 1973), 143.

19. Mary Jo Kline and Joanne Wood Ryan, *Political Correspondence and Public Papers of Aaron Burr*, 2 vols. (Princeton: Princeton University Press, 1983), 2:921. The editors argue that the letter was written by Jonathan Dayton. The letter and its cipher are available on the University of Kentucky Law School website documenting the Aaron Burr Treason trial: http://www.law.umkc.edu/faculty/projects/ftrials/burr/burrletter.html.

United States and others to participate in the armed liberation of Spanish Louisiana. Circulated by the public post and readily open to surveillance,[20] these letters sought acquiescence for Governor Isaac Shelby to recruit in Kentucky for the invasion of Louisiana,[21] commissioned George Rogers Clark to lead an invasion army, and inspired the formation of Democratic-Republican clubs. The French Girondiste ministers, such as the ex-journalist Citizen Mangourit in Charleston, prepared public letters to be read aloud, dispensed letters of marque for America sea captains willing to attack Florida, and composed a letter of address to the Creeks and Cherokees inviting them to overthrow the tyranny of Spanish exploiters:[22] 'The liberty that the French have won commands them to love the Indians because they are men and free beings . . . The equality that the French admit was the first gift made to man, where did they find it, Indians? In your institutions . . . who has opposed the equality of free men? The Kings of Europe, the King of France. They treated you as savages . . . The French nation, whose citizens are as innumerable as the trees of your forests and the sands of your rivers, is waging a war without quarter against kings and nobles . . . Friends of equality have joined, are joining, and will join the French Nation in this holy war of virtue against vice. You join also. I have spoken.'[23]

Addresses and preparations so public could not escape the attention of the Spanish. Their diplomatic objection to President Washington insisted that toleration of open incitement to war was tantamount to an act of aggression. To avoid war,

20. For the postal system's difficulties maintaining the privacy of correspondence, see Richard R. John, *Spreading the News: the American Postal System from Franklin to Morse* (Cambridge: Harvard University Press, 1995), 43.

21. Archibald Henderson, 'Isaac Shelby and the Genêt Mission,' *Mississippi Valley Historical Review* 6 (1920): 451–69.

22. Richard K. Murdock, 'Citizen Mangourit and the Projected Attack on East Florida in 1794,' *Journal of Southern History* 14 (1948): 522–40. Mangourit composed an open letter to Native Americans urging their rebellion from Spanish rule. This printed text was to be read aloud to various tribal groups encountered by Mangourit's agents.

23. R. R. Palmer, 'A Revolutionary Republican: M. A. B. Mangourit,' *William and Mary Quarterly*, 3rd ser. 9 (1952): 488.

Washington had Genêt recalled and insisted upon passage of the Neutrality Act.

Correspondence could not be obtruded upon the public without the risk of criminal prosecution. In the English-speaking world since the late seventeenth century, revolutions and conspiracies had begun in the treasonous correspondence of a circle of the aggrieved. In the Glorious Revolution, the extra-parliamentary initiatives that led to the bloodless coup removing King James II, were organized by a network whose secret communications and actions were lauded after the installation of William and Mary as monarchs of England. In the Glorious Revolution in America, Jacob Leisler in New York and the Mathers in New England established committees of correspondence. This example was adopted by the patriots of the American Revolution. Sam Adams's communicative methods were particularly interesting. He used the Freemasonic model of dual modes of expression: esoteric communications and actions were entrusted to the Sons of Liberty, while exoteric communications—public statements such as *The Rights of the Colonists*—appeared in print and manuscript as a *Report of the Committee of Correspondence of the Boston Town Meeting, Nov. 20, 1772*.[24] Often membership in the two organizations was concurrent.

Correspondence was necessary whether one's insurrection was overt or occult. In conspiracies it was particularly necessary. When incrimination is a prospect, there must exist among the community of plotters vehicles that reinforce trust. For all the practical utility of letters in articulating projects and instructing followers from afar, their greatest utility lay in their incarnation of contractual obligation. Exchanged letters were signed, and thus were mutually incriminating. Theoretically, the potential that one's colleague could expose him imposed a discipline on his concerted actions. Practically, this proved the undoing of many a

24. Harry Alonzo Cushing, *The Writings of Samuel Adams*, 4 vols. (Boston: G. P. Putnam, 1904), 2:350–59. Much of Volumes two and three of Adams's writings transcribes communications to various committees of correspondence.

scheme.[25] General James Wilkinson, commander in chief of the United States Army, and correspondent in Aaron Burr's plot, also happened to be a paid agent of the Spanish ministry.[26] His loyalty to the providers of a regular 'pension' proved deeper than his investment in Burr's schemes. When Wilkinson had the cipher letter in hand, he forwarded it to Washington, D. C.

The evidentiary character of conspiratorial letters had positive as well as negative valences. They could show potential recruits the conspicuousness of participants in a scheme. Aaron Burr was a potent name to conjure with. So was General Wilkinson. But their greatest power was when they were shown to potential foreign backers. When Chisholm went to England to secure backing for the Blount filibuster, he carried papers indicating who the parties to the adventure were and what they intended. To Whitehall the letters showed the actual existence of a network of actors.

What do conspiratorial letters say? Let us examine Senator Blount's to Carey, April 21, 1797:

> Dear Carey: I wish to have seen you before I returned to Philadelphia; but I am obliged to return to the session of Congress, which commences on the 15th of May.
>
> Among other things that I wished to have seen you about, was the business Captain Chesholm mentioned to the British Minister last Winter in Philadelphia.
>
> I believe, but am not quite sure, that the plan then talked of will be attempted this fall; and if it is attempted, it will be in a much

25. The American Revolution was no different than other conspiratorial insurrections in this regard. A richly-developed scholarly literature concerning the secret correspondence of the founders exists, treating matters from cryptography in letter writing to secret diplomacy and espionage. Highlights of this literature include Edmund Cody Burnett, 'Ciphers of the Revolutionary Era,' *American Historical Review* 22 (1917), and Ralph E. Weber's general history, *Masked Dispatches: Cryptograms and Cryptology in American History, 1775–1900* (Washington, D.C.: Center for Cryptologic History, National Security Agency, 1993), which details the code used by the Continental Congress to communicate with its agents overseas. For European practices and a discussion of the methods governments used to practice surveillance on mail, see James W. Thompson and Saul K. Padover, *Secret Diplomacy: Espionage and Cryptography, 1500–1815* (New York: Frederick Ungar, 1965).

26. Buckner F. Melton, Jr., *Aaron Burr: Conspiracy to Treason* (New York: John Wiley, 2002), 104, 114, 120–22, 139–40.

larger way than then talked of; and if the Indians act their part, I have no doubt but it will succeed. A man of consequence has gone to England about the business, and if he makes arrangements as he expects, I shall myself have a hand in the business, and probably shall be at the head of the business on the part of the British. You are, however, to understand, that it is not yet quite certain that the plan will be attempted; yet, you will do well to keep things in a proper train of action, in case it should be attempted, and to do so, will require all your management, because you must take care, in whatever you say to Rogers, or any body else, not to let the plan be discovered by Hawkins, Dinsmore, Byers, or any other person in the interest of the United States or Spain.

If I attempt this plan, I shall expect to have you, and all my Indian country and Indian friends, with me.[27]

What is striking about this letter is the allusive pressure of the unspoken here—a constant reminder of the reader's complicity in a 'plan' already shared. There is a blandness, a manner of communicating information (for instance that Chisholm is currently in England securing backing) in veiled, undramatic terms. This, of course, bespeaks that awareness among conspirators of the illegality of what they were doing—guilt guised as prudence.

Genêt's Conspiracy, Blount's Conspiracy, Burr's Conspiracy, and William Bowles's plan for a Creek empire called Muskogee all depended upon an army of frontier adventurers and Native Americans moving against the scattered network of Spanish outposts in Louisiana and Florida. How did they gain recruits for their secret wars? Genêt's tactics—organizing networks of voluntary associations and making popular appeals and reading public letters—had been outlawed. Sending private letters to knots of prospects had little merit. The kinds of circumlocution and allusion in the Blount letter were not designed to inspire a man to grab his long rifle. There had to be an oral performance. Those persons charged with recruiting volunteers were tasked with filling the back country with rumors to provoke indignation and disquiet

27. Melton, *The First Impeachment*, 145.

among settlers and the native population. Romayne in the Blount plot wrote that stories should be spread that the Spanish were on the verge of ceding Louisiana to France. This would 'inflame the minds of the people in a certain way, so as not to let out any of the plan, and yet put things in such a situation as will make our plan, when it takes place, appear as the salvation of the people.'[28] Burr's theory of rumor-mongering went a step beyond that of Romayne and Blount. He floated several contradictory schemes, each suited to the particular audience he found himself with, stirring the widest sense of possibility, but making news gatherers in the center of power incapable of charging him with any particular illegal course of action, because the sum of the record was contradictory to the point of incoherence. He was going to seize Mexico. He was going to march on Washington, D.C., seize the president and the banks,[29] he was going to seize Louisiana and set up an independent kingdom, he was going to seize New Orleans and Mexico City and hand them over to the British. When rumors become so inchoate that they seem nonsense, the seriousness of the threat that a plotter poses becomes less credible, defenses less vigilant. The fog of talk enabled Burr to raise a flotilla, field a troupe, advance down the Mississippi, even resist by arms an officer of the government without the President acting on the barrage of epistolary warnings and newspaper tales informing him of Burr's sayings and doings.[30]

The abundance of contradictory claims eventually proved beneficial to Burr in his trial upon violating the Neutrality Act.[31] It contributed to the appearance that there was no concerted design, even when his flatboats of filibusters were moving down the waterways of Middle America. Burr was acquitted.

28. *Annals of Congress* 2343, 2352–54 (1797).

29. This rumor, meant to misinform Carlos Martinez de Yrujo of Burr's ambitions on Spanish territories and possibly secure money from the Spanish crown, was floated by Jonathan Dayton, Burr's protégé. Melton, *Aaron Burr*, 92–93.

30. Thomas Perkins Abernathy, *The Burr Conspiracy* (New York: Oxford University Press, 1954), 26–44.

31. Burr beat the treason charge of his first trial because the prosecution could not procure the two witnesses—stipulated by the Constitution—who could connect Burr with the incident in which his force resisted arrest by an officer of the government.

We know more about the conspiratorial conversation campaigns waged in the public houses of the West than about any other talk in the frontier territories during the first decades of the republic. With Ken Starr profuseness, the Senate hearings on Blount, and the trial proceedings of Aaron Burr[32] contain dozens of accounts of Chisholm, or Romayne, or Burr, or some other plotter listening to complaints by locals in a backcountry tavern, and entering the stream of conversation, suggesting that the United States would not long be master and that doings were afoot. If the tavern talk was peaceful, injecting rumors of a Spanish closure of New Orleans, or of a French takeover could stir up angst, which could then be sauced by complaints about the United States government's indifference to securing the port upon which the economic future of the interior rested. The Senate records contain quasi-verbatim transcripts of exchanges. Words spoken at the dark end of the bar could find their way into print—in Congressional proceedings, in court reports, and in newspapers, particularly, but not exclusively—after a smoking letter had brought a plot to light.

Nigel Smith, the great literary historian of the English Commonwealth period, concluded that newspapers—mercuries—came into being to countermand the promiscuous representations of rumor with a firmer account of affairs in the realm.[33] The press did not function in this way, however, in the Blount, Burr, West Florida, or other early filibusters. Correspondents in those areas did not write to editors to voice their misgivings; they wrote to the president or the secretary of state, who as a rule did not share these reports with the papers. What the papers did do with a peculiarly non-partisan zeal was to expose what had been secret, once the secret had been exposed. They operated in a sympathetic

---

32. T. Carpenter, *The Trial of Col. Aaron Burr*, 3 vols. (Washington City: Westcott & Co. 1808). David Robertson, *Reports of the Trial of Colonel Burr (late Vice President of the United States) for Treason and for a Misdemeanor*, 2 vols. (Philadelphia: Hapkins and Earle, 1808).

33. Nigel Smith, *Literature and Revolution in England, 1640–1660* (New Haven: Yale University Press, 1997), 54–69.

tension with the process of investigation and exposure superintended by the United States Senate and courts. The manuscript Senate record was not the basis of reportage. Documents that appeared in the several separate reports published by Congress in 1797 and 1798 did appear in the newspapers.[34] What the papers recorded beyond the government account were the comments of members from the floor and the testimonies of sworn witnesses (i.e., the oral examination) supplementary to the findings. The major papers at the seat of government—the *Philadelphia Gazette, Claypoole's American Daily Advertiser, Gazette of the United States, Aurora, Universal Gazette*—provided this with varying amounts of editorial comment and partisan critique while posing numbers of questions not treated in Congress. A network of papers, from New Bern, North Carolina, to Boston, republished the stories from the Philadelphia papers; northern papers—*Boston Gazette, Connecticut Courant, Independent Chronicle, Massachusetts Mercury*, and *Newport Mercury*—were markedly more editorial in their commentary.

What most startles about the newspaper's treatment of secret plots was their entire avoidance of making an independent inquiry. In other realms of public activity—commerce, exploration, military exercises, diplomatic affairs—newspapers sought and published private correspondence. When it came to secret ventures and conspiracies, there was a thoroughgoing reliance on intelligence secured by organs of government. It was as if the publication of secret matters, because of their peculiar tension with the

34. *Proceedings on the Impeachement of William Blount, a Senator of the United States from the State of Tennessee, for High Crimes and Misdemeanors* (Philadelphia: Joseph Gales, 1799); *Deposition of Gen. Elijah Clark, of the State of Georgia* (Philadelphia: Joseph Gales, 1798); *Letter from the Chevalier d'Yrujo* (Philadelphia: Joseph Gales, 1798); *Report of the Committee of the House of Representatives of the United States, Appointed to Prepare and Report Articles of Impeachment against William Blount, a Senator of the United States* (Philadelphia: John Fenno, 1797); *Further Report from the Committee, Appointed . . . to Prepare and Report Articles of Impeachment Against William Blount* (Philadelphia, 1798); and *Further [Supplementary] Report from the Committee* (Philadelphia, 1798). The Articles of Impeachment were published in *Further Report of the Committee, Appointed on the Eighth of July Last, to Prepare and Report Articles of Impeachment Against William Blount* (Philadelphia: John Fenno, 1778); *Further Report of the Managers Appointed to Conduct the Impeachment against William Blount* (Philadelphia, 1798); and *A Bill Regulating Certain Procedures in Cases of Impeachment* (Philadelphia: John Fenno, 1798).

prerogatives of the public sector, was viewed the proper and special concern of the government.

One undertheorized feature of the communication of the early republic is the relation of the secret to the public. Public sphere theorists, even those influenced by the multiple publics models propounded by Lawrence Klein and others,[35] usually view the fundamental structural tension of the communicative realm to be that between public and private, with the private understood to comprehend anything from the private conscience of post-Reformation theology, to the personal interest of classical liberal ideology, to the *res domestica* that stood distinct from the *res publica*. When the realm of the secret did come into view as a separate zone of activity distinct from the private, it has appeared as a delusional vapor, haunting the cities and suburbs of the early republic with scheming Jesuits, godless Freemasons, and occult cosmopolites of the Illuminati.[36] This bogey spotting seems necessary to republican thinking.[37] Since Richard Hofstadter sketched the 'paranoid style' of American politics in the days of Barry Goldwater,[38] scholars have invoked the sphere of the secret as a theoretical space governed by fantasies of conspiracies. In truth, where the republic existed most concretely, in the settled seaboard states of the republic, the secret cabal, army, sect, or conspiracy may have been phantasmal. But where the republic was itself phantasmal, in the West, where civil governments, boundaries, and communities were so

35. Lawrence Klein, 'Gender and the Public/Private Distinction in the Eighteenth Century: Some Questions About Evidence and Analytic Procedure,' *Eighteenth Century Studies* 19 (1995): 97–109.

36. David Brion Davis, 'Some Themes of Counter-Subversion: An Analysis of Anti-Masonic, Anti-Catholic, and Anti-Mormon Literature,' *Mississippi Valley Historical Review* 47 (1960): 205–24. Bernard Bailyn, 'A Note on Conspiracy,' *The Ideological Origins of the American Revolution* (Cambridge: Belknap Press of Harvard University Press, 1967). Gordon Wood, 'Conspiracy and the Paranoid Style: Causality and Deceit in the Eighteenth Century,' *William and Mary Quarterly*, 3rd ser. 39 (1982): 401–40.

37. See Ed White, 'The Value of Conspiracy Theory,' *American Literary History* 14 (2002): 1–31.

38. Richard Hofstadter, *The Paranoid Style in American Politics and Other Essays* (Chicago: University of Chicago Press, 1964).

amorphous as to scarcely merit the name, conspiracy there was concretized, and the secret combination became an enduring structure of political practice.[39]

Secrecy was also the life blood of diplomacy. The aspirations of sovereign states about territory, and the agreements of nations about their disposition toward other states were matters best preserved in privacy.[40] The great fear of the people in Florida, Louisiana, and Texas was that decisions about who would rule, who would have trade access to the river systems, and who would adjudicate property claims would be determined regardless of their wishes by closeted men in some European capital. This was the fear that conspirators played upon when rousing westerners to arms, even when the conspirators were in the service of the diplomacy of some foreign power. The conspiratorial filibusters generated an extraordinary secret literature of plans kept in the private archives of various European departments of state. No one in the United States doubted that the secret vaults of Whitehall harbored minister Robert Merry's reports of Burr's proposals and Chisholm's outline of the Blount conspiracy, stashed with other documents such as Francisco de Miranda's proposal for a conquest of Mexico during the Nootka Sound Affair or Sir John Dalrymple's more comprehensive blueprint for conquering Central and South America.

But what of Revolutionary France? Did Genêt's publicity mean diplomatic transparency? Hardly. The foreign office secret archive for the 1790s is astonishingly rich. Le Clerc Milfort, a Spanish agent, who turned French agent in the Creek territory, composed an imposing shelf of plots for the French takeover of

---

39. Of literary and cultural scholars, Ed White has most creatively taken up the tensions between the discursive worlds and forms of the urban coast and the back country. See *The Backcountry and the City: Colonization and Conflict in Early America* (Minneapolis: University of Minnesota Press, 2005).

40. In diplomacy transparency has rarely been deemed a practicable course of action. Despite radical republicans' ideological objections to secret arrangements, the diplomatic practice of the United States from the era of the Revolution always made use of clandestine deals, encrypted messages, and hidden agendas. Walter MacDougall, 'Back to Bedrock: The Eight Traditions of American Statecraft,' *Foreign Affairs* 76 (March/April 1997).

Spanish Louisiana between 1795 and 1800.[41] There is also the anonymous French memorandum addressed to the French minister to the United States that Lord Dorchester in 1787 intercepted in Canada, outlining a French takeover of Louisiana. The Girondist government had a copy of General George Rogers Clark's and Dr. James O'Fallon's plan for a French takeover of New Orleans as early as 1792, conveyed to J. P. Brissot de Warville through Thomas Paine, before Genêt sailed for America. Brissot in that same moment was considering Francisco Miranda's proposal for a revolution throughout Spanish America. Miranda, having failed to garner English support for his liberation of Spanish America, crossed the Channel and intoxicated the Girondistes with visions of a revolution in Hispanic America.[42] Gilbert Imlay, Joel Barlow, and Thomas Paine—all resident in Paris in 1792—and all sympathizers in the Revolution—contributed their ideas for a French liberation of the interior from Spanish tyranny. Perhaps the most interesting document is an anonymous 1792 plan for a takeover.[43] It recommended that Genêt be the provocateur of insurrection, that the various inland settlements at Cumberland, Marietta, and Scioto serve as recruitment centers, and that General James Wilkinson (not Clark) be appointed chief of the expedition. The writer also suggested that H. H. Brackenridge be contacted as a possible leader. This plan is almost certainly the work of Joel Barlow.[44] The American Jacobin novelist Gilbert Imlay in that same year composed a proposal for a French expedition to secure the interior.[45] Another American in

41. E. Wilson Lyon, 'Milfort's Plan for a Franco-Creek Alliance and the Retrocession of Louisiana,' *Southern Historical Journal* (1938): 72–87.

42. Karen Racine, *Francisco de Miranda: A Transatlantic Life in the Age of Revolution* (Wilmington, Del.: SR Books, 2002), 134–37.

43. 'Plan proposé pour faire une revolution dans las Louisiane,' *Annual Report of the American Historical Association* 1 (1896): 945–53. This volume contains texts of most of the French secret archive.

44. Barlow's deep involvement with the ill-fated Scioto land company, his advocacy in other places of a revolutionized hemisphere (a visionary possibility bruited momentarily in the plan), and his connection with Brackenridge strongly argue for his authorship.

45. Gilbert Imlay, 'Observations,' *Annual Report of the American Historical Association* 1 (1896):952–54.

Paris, Stephen Sayre, proposed an expedition concerted with Miranda's, liberating Mexico and Louisiana simultaneously. It proposed that Barlow himself, Beauspoils (a military officer), and Lyonnet (a former resident of New Orleans) be sent to Philadelphia as a cell to prepare by ideological agitation for Miranda's arrival and a general uprising of Spanish America.[46] The French government accepted parts of Sayre's recommendation: a cell was established in Philadelphia, but it was composed of four Frenchmen. It immediately began generating propaganda, distributing a broadside address through Louisiana entitled 'Liberty. Equality. The Freemen of France to their Brothers in Louisiana.'[47] It declared: 'Now is the time to cease being the slaves of a government, to which you were shamefully sold; and no longer to be led on like a herd of cattle, by men who with one word can strip you of what you hold most dear—liberty and property.'[48]

The French revolutionary government's commitment to broadcasting sedition in the Spanish empire explains the Spanish response. In Mexico the institution long tasked with ferreting out sedition—The Holy Office of the Inquisition—was deployed against the infiltration of revolution.[49] Prohibitions were declared upon Paine's 'The Rights of Man.' Also prohibited was James Puglio's *El Desengagno del Hombre*, a Spanish-language survey of the Paine-Burke controversy prepared by a Philadelphia language teacher in 1794 as part of the propaganda for whatever scheme the French might set into motion. Other titles specifically proscribed during the 1790s were Volnay's *Les Ruines, ou meditations sur le revolution des Empire*; Condorcet's *Esquisse de un tableau historique des progress de l'espirit humain*; Servaign Mereghal's *History of the Revolution*, Montesquieu's *Persian Letters*; Mably's *Des droits et devoirs du citoyen*; and Costi's translation of

46. *Annual Report of the American Historical Association* 1 (1896): 954–57.

47. Archibald Henderson, 'Isaac Shelby and the Genêt Mission,' 451–69.

48. Charles Gayarre, *History of Louisiana* (New York: William J. Widdleton, 1867), 337–41.

49. Jose T. Medina, *Historia del Tribunal del Santo Officio de la Inquisicion de Mexico* (Santiago, 1905), 434–44.

Locke's *Treatise on Human Understanding*. The edicts of the Inquisitions were published periodically in the *Gazeta de Mexico*. The verdicts of various sedition trials, such as that of Esteven Morel, who directed a republican circle and was arrested with two trunks of French-language books—were not aired in the *Gazeta*.[50]

The Inquisition, for all its diligence, could not hold back the tide of circumstance that would overthrow the old imperial order. The Napoleonic invasion of Spain, the arrest of King Ferdinand VII, and the prospect of a decapitated empire gave rise to an uncertainty that insured the old political arrangement would not survive. In the summer of 1810, as Napoleon's armies closed in upon the remnants of the royal army on the Iberian penninsula, all of Spanish America was in turmoil. In Mexico it would not be an incendiary pamphlet that would spark revolution, but the preaching of a Catholic priest, Father Miguel Hidalgo y Costilla.[51] On September 16, 1810, he inaugurated a campaign, which quickly mutated from a call for Catholic purity and loyalty to Ferdinand VII, to nationalist insurrection of creoles and natives against an officialdom dominated by Spanish-born *peninsulares*. Hildalgo dispatched Jose Bernardo Maximiliano Gutiérrez de Lara to Washington, D.C., to secure aid from President Madison. While Gutiérrez was in Washington, Hidalgo's revolution was betrayed by a turncoat ally, leading to his capture and execution by monarchists. Gutiérrez came away from Washington with no concrete promise of support in his plan to reactivate Padre's Hidalgo's rising.

I will not enter the argument as to whether the Gutiérrez-McGee revolt was a duplicitous exercise in America imperialism[52]

50. For a history of the bannings, see John Rydjord, 'The French Revolution and Mexico,' *Hispanic American Historical Review* 9 (1929): 61–65.

51. Hugh M. Hamill, *The Hidalgo Revolt: Prelude to Independence* (Gainesville: University of Florida Press, 1966). See also, Odie B. Faulk, *The Last Years of Spanish Texas, 1778–1821* (The Hague: Mouton, 1969).

52. Isaac Cox, 'Monroe and the Early Mexican Revolutionary Agents,' Annual Report of the American Historical Association, 1 (Washington: American Historical Association., 1913): 199–215. Frank Lawrence Owsley, Jr., and Gene A. Smith, *Filibusters and Expansionists: Jeffersonian Manifest Destiny, 1800–1821* (Tuscaloosa: University of Alabama Press, 1997). John J. Carter, *Covert Operations as a Tool of Presidential Foreign Policy in American History from 1800 to 1920: Foreign Policy in the Shadows* (New York: Mellen Press, 2000), 29–42.

or a multi-ethnic, auto-dynamic revolution.[53] My own sense favors the latter, though it is apparent that Madison's minister to Latin America, Captain William Shaler, on several occasions violated the United States Neutrality Act in favor of Gutiérrez. My interest is in the wholehearted commitment to publicity found among the leaders of the rising—Gutiérrez, August McGee, Reuben Kemper, and Alvarez de Toledo. Because the revolution was a battle with the Mexican monarchists for the hearts and minds of an amorphous population composed of Tejanos, Anglos, Nativos, and French settlers, publicity abounded. Shaler first violated American neutrality when he supplied $100 to finance printing of four of Gutiérrez's proclamations for distribution throughout the territory:[54] to 'Officers, Soldiers, and Inhabitants of San Antonio de Béxar,' to 'Compatriots . . . in the Province of Texas,' to the 'people of Mexico,' and to the 'American volunteers—a praise and a promise of honor and riches for service.' The revolutionaries flooded the countryside with pamphlets, including Spanish and English versions of Alvarez de Toledo's *The Friend of Men*, a tract urging civil war and promising American intervention. This piece, addressed to the editor of the republican newspaper, the *Aurora*, was published in Philadelphia in 1811 by Bradford and Inskeep, the favorite printer of political radicals and filibusters.[55] Other items were published in Natchitoches, apparently funded by 'The Club of Mexico,' a group of New Orleans merchants of republican persuasion who had commercial ambitions in Mexico.

53. J. C. A. Stagg, 'The Madison Administration and Mexico: Reinterpreting the Gutiérrez-Magee Raid of 1812–1813,' *William and Mary Quarterly*, 3rd ser. 59 (2002): 409–49.

54. These proclamations were probably published as broadsides in Alexandria, Louisiana. Richard C. Gronert notes that the first was published in the *Alexandria Herald* as well. 'United States and the Invasion of Texas, 1810–1814,' *The Americas* 25 (1969): 294. This article misinterprets the adventure by erroneously believing that Shaler was a clandestine agent and the filibuster a secretive venture. The Guitiérrez venture was characterized by its wholly public character and Shaler by his role as a credentialed government emissary to the Spanish American states.

55. For the circumstances of this pamphlet's publication, see Harris Gaylord Warren, 'Jose Alvarez de Toledo's Initiation as a Filibuster, 1811–1813' *Hispanic American Historical Review* 20 (1940): 60. n.15.

The idealism of these revolutionary proclamations was belied by Gutiérrez's summary execution of the governor of Texas and other officers after Kemper seized San Antonio—an action that digusted Kemper and the Anglo contingent of the army, leading to mass desertions. President Monroe, after reading a letter written from Natchitoches by an eye-witness correspondent describing the massacre in the June 2, 1813, issue of the Baltimore newspaper, *American and Commercial Daily Advertiser,* called Shaler to task for supporting Gutiérrez.[56]

One wonders whether Gutiérrez's issuance on April 16, 1813, of the Texas Declaration of Independence from Spain was a gesture to repair the alienation of Shaler and the Anglo Texans. Gutiérrez knew of Shaler's reverence for the American Declaration and its principles and no doubt had heard of Shaler's communicating the document to the circle of liberal families in Santiago, Chile, while stationed there in 1802.[57] Whatever good effect the declaration may have had was completely eradicated shortly thereafter by the constitution formulated by a committee of seven Guittierez appointees.[58] This document made Gutiérrez a dictator-governor. Shaler then abandoned his neutrality and engineered the removal of Guitierrez as head of the revolutionary movement. Shaler assisted in the founding of the first two Texan papers: the broadside *Gaceta de Texas,* which had a run of one issue, and *El Mexicano,*[59] both of which contained diatribes against Gutiérrez's actions. A press was carted from Natchitoches to San Antonio and overseen by a cosmopolitan Venezuelan printer. By the end of June 1813, public opinion had been moved enough

56. Stagg, 'The Madison Administration and Mexico,' par. 50.

57. Roy F. Nichols, 'William Shaler, New England Apostle of Rational Liberty,' *New England Quarterly* 9 (1936), 73, details Shaler's time in Chile, where he left a Spanish translation of the Declaration of Independence and an English language copy of the United States Constitution.

58. Garrett, 'The First Constitution of Texas, April 17, 1813,' *Southwestern Historical Quarterly* 40 (1937): 290–308.

59. We should note that the change in title moves the question from local self-determination to the national fate of Mexico—not the sort of move that someone would make to prepare the locale for annexation to the United States.

that when Gutiérrez, spooked by a false alarm, ordered the aban-
donment of San Antonio, the citizenry determined a change was
in order. Shaler's candidate for a replacement was Alvarez de Toledo, a Cuban-born Hispanic radical, whose repute depended almost entirely upon his mastery of the pen and the press. Toledo,
however, soon demonstrated a lack of mastery at wielding men
and arms.

The Texas Constitution was the crucial document of the revolution that occasioned a rupture between the Mexican leaders of
the revolt and its American well-wishers. The constitution, which
made no pretence of speaking for the people, thus violated the
most authoritative construction of political warrant cherished by
Americans. As Gordon Wood has indicated, written constitutions
were the articulations of the mythically potent, expressive will of
the people. As Peter Onuf has argued, the prevailing understanding of state sovereignty in America required that frontier people
seeking statehood must articulate themselves as integral territorial communities possessed of distinct and irreducible rights.[60] A
constitution composed by a convention of settler-citizens provided this. Without such a procedure and a compact, no new
order under God was declared, no ethnogenesis by fiat, no defen-
sible warrant for political being.

In Anglo-America a written constitution was the social compact
of the people. Its authority supplanted unwritten custom and state
prerogative. It declared association. The thirteen original state
constitutions performed this task primordially, but the creation of
polities beyond the thirteen was fraught with legal difficulties because of the competing claims of states for western territories.
The model for all filibuster constitution-making was set by the
patriots who attempted to form states on the frontier in the
1780s. While Vermont's declaration of its own sovereign status
in its 1776–77 declaration of independence and constitution

---

60. Peter Onuf, 'Towards Federalism: Virginia, Congress, and the Western Lands,'
William and Mary Quarterly, 3rd ser. 34 (1977): 360–61.

serves as a discursive model, the developed strategy of obtrusive publicity began with the creation of the Free State of Franklin, what is now Tennessee, in 1784.

In that year, when the legislature of North Carolina passed a bill ceding its claims to western lands to the United States as compensation for war debts, a group of settlers in the fertile, western lands of the Wautauga gathered together and formed an independent polity. They drafted a provisional constitution and composed a declaration of independence from North Carolina—'A Declaration of Rights' and 'The Constitution and Form of Government'—'agreed to and resolved upon by the representatives of the Freemen of the State of Franklin, elected and chosen for that particular purpose, in convention assembled, at Jonesborough, the 17th December, Anno Dom. 1784.'

The movement to create an independent polity west of the Appalachians was at root a practical matter. One message that the pre-Revolutionary regulator agitations had taught frontier settlers was that seaboard oligarchies were in no great hurry to extend the institutions of civil society into the interior. One had to make one's own order.

The constitution of Franklin evinced a detailed familiarity with several state Constitutions—especially Vermont's, Pennsylvania's, and North Carolina's.[61] Copies prepared by a frontier scrivener were distributed through the general population in manuscript through militia companies, the frontier's most articulate institutions of civil order. (Indeed, they formed the basis of representation in the legislature.[62]) Franklin asserted its rights and sovereignty against the claims of another state: we 'declare ourselves independent of North Carolina.' North

61. 'The Constitution of the State of Franklin,' Appendix A, in Samuel Cole Williams, *History of the Lost State of Franklin* (New York: Press of the Pioneers., 1933), 339–47.

62. Copies were dispatched to the North Carolina governor, legislature, the United States Senate, and the president of the United States. They provoked a manifesto war with the North Carolina government, a debate within the United States Congress when they requested admission as an independent state, and a model for populations that wished to assert sovereignty outside of the usual provisions of United States government and international law.

Carolina repealed its act of secession. The United States Senate came within a hair's breadth of admitting the state, but declined because of the western separatists in the Kentucky territory. The precedent of persons declaring independence and organizing governments without the superintendence of the United States government risked anarchy of another sort. Franklin's publication barrage nearly secured what its citizens wished. Their isolated situation enabled the Free State to operate as the effective government for three years, despite the opposition of the North Carolina government.

With their independence contested, the citizens of Franklin convened to draft a permanent constitution composed by the Reverend Sam Houston, uncle of the future governor of Tennessee and founder of the Texas Republic. Their response in the face of non-recognition by North Carolina and Congress was to make the voice of the people sound more resonantly through the fabric of government. Houston looked to the most radical of the republican state constitutions in its institutionalization of the people's voice in government—that of Pennsylvania. Like the Pennsylvania constitution, the proposed second constitution of Franklin declared that the people participate directly in legislation. Every bill put before the legislature was to be printed (although there was no press in the territory at that time) and distributed gratis to the voting populace for comment. After the voice of the people had commented, at the next legislative session the bill could be put to a vote.

The convention voted down Houston's draft constitution, not because of its hyper-publicity, but because of its religious and moral requirements for office holders. Franklin was in a state of political turmoil when North Carolina forces marched into it, defeated Governor Sevier's Franklin State militia, and reasserted control over the territory. In 1790 North Carolina again ceded the western territory to the United States government—this time under the federal Constitution. George Washington appointed William Blount governor of the territory.

I began this meditation by pointing to the division between public and secret modes of communication in these early American political adventures. I close by noting that in this literature one encounters the horizons of publicity and—not privacy—but secrecy. In the failed second constitution of Franklin we find a vision of public life in which the press was to be an engine that makes the people co-equal with the government, annihilating the private-public divide. In the rumors, verbal misinformation campaigns, secret letters, and encrypted plans of conspirators, we find that force most inimical to the *vox populi*, the ambition of the adventurer who seeks to force change regardless of the will of the people. The secret conspiracies, once exposed, formed a peculiar spectacle. One wonders why so frequently officers of the government—persons entrusted with high office in the United States—Vice President Burr, generals George Rogers Clark and James Wilkinson, governors Sam Houston of Tennessee and John Quitmann of Mississippi, senators Blount of Tennessee and Adair of Kentucky—did not content themselves with service to the people of the United States, but surrendered to the secret promptings of their imaginations to seek a more dangerous glory of a more ancient and selfish kind. Print culture no doubt played a role in this too, supplying the promises from historical literature of pomp and personal glory that made the idea of harmonizing one's voice with the choir of the people seem insipid. No doubt the old books that preserved ancient vanities made these men put by the solid achievements of the Revolution and like Napoleon dream the old dream of being emperor, autarch, conquerer, and king.

Fear as a Political Construct: Imagining the Revolution and the Nation in Peruvian Newspapers

MARISELLE MELÉNDEZ

FEAR HAS BEEN DEFINED as 'an unpleasant emotion caused by the threat of danger, pain or harm' or as an emotion which causes us 'to be in apprehension of evil; to be afraid; to feel anxiety; to be uncertain; to doubt.' Fear has historically been associated with the possibility of a state of disorder which appeals in many cases to future consequences. Fear is the sense that emerges prior to an action and that guides those in power to establish political mechanisms to stop the possibility that a situation could become out of their control. As Thomas Hobbes stated in *De Cive* (*The Citizen*,1651): 'I comprehend in this word fear a certain foresight of future evil; neither do I conceive flight the sole property of fear, but to distrust, suspect, take heed, provide so that they may not fear, is also incident to the fearful.'[1]

Based on the notion of fear as a mental state denoting uncertainty, apprehensiveness, and anxiety, this article examines how the idea of the revolution as a political construction and as a symptom of fear was perceived and circulated by colonial authorities

---

1. Thomas Hobbes, *De Cive*, Charles T. Wood, trans. (Garden City, N.Y.: Anchor Books, 1972) 24.

MARISELLE MELÉNDEZ is associate professor of Spanish, University of Illinois at Urbana-Champaign. She was a member of the planning committee for the '*Liberty/Égalité/ Independencia*' *Conference*. She thanks Elise Bartosik-Vélez (Dickinson College) for her helpful suggestions on the translations of the primary texts.

and creole intellectuals in such Peruvian newspapers as the *Mercurio peruano* (1791–95), *El peruano* (1811–13), *El censor de la revolución* (1820), *El pacificador del Perú* (1821), and *Gaceta del Gobierno del Perú* (1823–25). I explore the relationship of these conceptualizations of fear to the manner in which national preoccupations were interpreted as a result of the important historical events taking place at the time. This essay focuses specifically on how, in some instances, the French Revolution (1789–99) and the American Revolution (1775–83) were perceived by Spanish authorities at the end of the colonial period; and on how these movements were interpreted by those involved in the process of Peruvian independence when the time came to define themselves as a nation. I aim to demonstrate the centrality of fear as a political idea and cultural construct in the marketing of these revolutions to readers of those Peruvian newspapers. It is within this context, as Corey Robin has argued, that fear emerges as a contradictory 'political tool,' which may be productive for those in power, but may also become 'an obstacle and a stumbling block' in the pursuit of a foundation for politics.'[2]

Circulating Fear: The Idea of the Revolution

The *Mercurio peruano* was founded by the Sociedad Académica de Amantes del País (Academic Society of Lovers of the Country), a group of young intellectual creoles, mainly from Lima, whose range of expertise included medicine, commerce, science, geography, religion, literature, and law. The name chosen for their association was intended to emphasize their aims to educate their country and demonstrate their passionate love for it. The founders obviously perceived themselves as spokesmen for their native country and as the chosen few in charge of educating their homeland and the rest of the world.

2. Corey Robin, *Fear: The History of a Political Idea* (New York: Oxford University Press, 2004), 16, 252.

The *Mercurio peruano* published nineteen articles about the French Revolution. Fifteen of them were related to the beheading of the French king on the guillotine. According to Claudia Rosas Lauro, these writings were intended to teach the Peruvian people about the dangers of the revolution and to warn them that something similar could occur in Peru.[3] The acts related to the insurrection of the Inca Tupac Amaru in 1780–81 were then still a vivid memory for many of the Spanish authorities. This political propaganda against the revolution also aimed to gather sympathy for Spain in its war against France by requesting donations to support the costs of such war.[4] Although I agree with Rosas Lauro, it is pertinent to ask how the discussion of the French Revolution fit within the cultural and political agenda set forth in their prospectus for *Mercurio peruano* by the creoles in charge. What voice are we really hearing in these particular writings? The editors had contended that their newspaper would depart from coverage of events in other parts of the world in order to focus primarily upon news of their own homeland: 'that we are more interested in what happens in our Nation than what happens to the Canadian, the Laplander or the Muslim.'[5]

It is important to point out that the majority of the news published in the *Mercurio* and related to the French Revolution was not authored by Peruvians themselves. For example, published in the newspaper were royal decrees, excerpts taken from *La Gazeta de Madrid* (*Madrid Gazette*), declarations against France on behalf of the Spanish king, and copies of letters from the French queen. In the case of the royal decrees,

---

3. Claudia Rosas Lauro, 'El miedo a la revolución. Remores y temores desatados por la Revolución Francesa en el Perú, 1790–1800' in Claudia Rosas Lauro, ed., *El meido en el Perú, Siglos XVI al XX* (Lima: Pontificia Universidad Católica, 2005), 139.

4. Rosas Lauro, 'El miedo a la revolución,' 143.

5. *Mercurio peruano*, 1, no. 1 (January 2, 1791). All translations from Spanish into English are my own, unless otherwise specified. The edition I have used is *Mercurio Peruano, Prospecto del papel periódico intitulado Mercurio Peruano de Historia, Literatura y Noticias públicas, que á nombre de una Sociedad de Amantes del País, y como uno de ellos promete dar á luz*, Edición Faccsimilar (Lima, Biblioteca Nacional del Perú 1964).

colonial authorities described the French Revolution as the most horrific event that could happen to a civilized nation. King Charles IV of Spain, in a royal decree drafted on March 25, 1793, and published in the *Mercurio peruano* on August 15, 1793, made a direct connection between the revolution and 'disorder, impiety and anarchy,' which had contributed to the 'turbulences' and 'horrendous' events in France after the execution of Louis XVI and his wife Marie Antoinette. The decree indicated that the French Revolution had created an excuse to impose an irrational government, full of 'excessive ambition' and 'danger,' translating to instability through Europe. He declared that Spanish citizens felt 'oppressed, horrified and indignant' toward the manner in which the revolution had been conducted and that they were appalled by the fact that France had attacked their country without an official declaration of war.[6] As a result, King Charles concluded that he had no option but to declare war against France. His intention was to restore 'tranquility to Europe,' thereby contributing to 'the general well-being of humanity' as part of his duty to maintain 'paternal vigilance' over both his own territories and Europe in general.[7] This 'paternal vigilance' reflected fear and anxiety that events in France could replicate themselves in Spain and other European countries. Fear of seeing his own monarchy overthrown underlies the rhetoric of this royal decree.

The Academic Society of Lovers of the Country responded to this decree by proclaiming their support for the Spanish king in a published note. They considered the acts during and following the French Revolution to be 'the most scandalous events' in human history.[8] The brief article highlighted the insult that had been committed against the monarchy and encouraged Peruvians to support the war against France financially out of loyalty to their own king. Revolution was viewed here as a foreign affair that could lead to similar events in Spain—or possibly a movement

6. *Mercurio peruano*, 7, no. 273 (August 15, 1793): 250–51.
7. *Mercurio peruano*, 7, no. 273 (August 15, 1793): 249.
8. *Mercurio peruano*, 7, no. 273 (August 15, 1793): 254.

similar to the one that Tupac Amaru had led in 1780.[9] The editors' support for the king may have come from their own anxiety that France, might spread its military operations against Spanish possessions in the Americas, which could make them vulnerable to the same state of disorder prevalent in France at the time. Their view of the political situation in France, of course, was filtered through official versions recounted to them by Spanish authorities.

Articles reprinted from *La Gazeta de Madrid* also emphasized the notion that the French Revolution had brought instability to Europe, and as such, all citizens must fear the dangers to which they could be exposed if similar political and social events took place in their own territories. It also justified Spain's decision to declare war against France. An article reprinted from *La Gazeta* based on a speech given by the British Prime Minister William Pitt openly stated that what was being witnessed in France was a clear prelude to 'the bad things that all Europe needed to be afraid of.'[10] The revolution and the beheading of the French king were summarized by Pitt as 'the most unfair, cruel and inhuman violation that the history of centuries brings to mind.' As a result, the British minister warned the public of 'the dangers that threaten other nations' if France was not stopped or if other countries followed in France's footsteps. The French revolution was conceived in this speech as 'subversive to all social order, contrary to the experience of centuries, repulsive to morality, hostile to religion, ultimately designed to aggrieve humankind, depriving governments of the energy required to defend the public good.'[11] The reprinting of this speech in Spain and its colonies was extremely important because it offered a picture of the

9. It is interesting to note that the editors of the *Mercurio peruano* did not publish any articles related to the Tupac Amaru insurrection. It was as if they felt the need to obliterate this episode from their historical memories.

10. *Mercurio peruano*, 7, no. 273 (August 15, 1793): 255. This article was originally a speech read in London on February 2, 1793, by William Pitt, no defender of the French Revolution, and the attendant agitation in England for parliamentary reform. In this speech he warned that the situation in France could also affect Great Britain to the extent that all British citizens should remain wary of the dangers of such a revolution.

11. Mercurio peruano, 7, no. 273 (August 15, 1793):256.

revolution as an unruly act that had disrupted social order and good government and had brought decay at all levels—moral, political, and religious. The objective of this news article was to incite fear in readers, so that they would view the events related to the revolution only in terms of its supposed negative repercussions rather than any positive social and political change related to freedom and equality. As Jean Delemeau suggests, fear in its cultural dimension points to the presence of a threat that forces the individual to see enemies of all sides, whether 'inside and outside of the space which one wishes to control.' This type of fear is filtered through suspicions and denunciations, as can be observed in the aforementioned news articles. Fear is always seen as an attempt to destroy a sense of security, or what Delemeau refers to as 'an utopia of security.'[12]

Unless we conclude that the inclusion of these articles meant agreement with the views they contained, we are forced to question the extent to which the editors were acting freely or coercively. We can either agree with Rosas Lauro when she suggests that the publication of news related to the French Revolution demonstrated opposition by the creole aristocracy to the revolution, or we can question if, lacking a free press, the publication worked as a palliative to calm those who supported the monarchy and viewed its fall as a source of fear. After all, the newspaper was subsidized by the colonial government. As Carmen McEvoy reminds us, the editors of the *Mercurio* had to take into consideration the fact that their writings could be perceived as a threat to the public order and the vice-regal government, especially when many of the editors also held public offices.[13] Indeed, once the newspaper lost the economic support of the government,

---

12. Jean Delemeau, 'Miedos de ayer y de hoy,' in *El miedo: Reflexiones sobre su dimension social y cultural*, ed. Marta Ines Villa Martinez (Medellin, Colombia: Corporación Región, 2002), 17, 21.

13. Carmen McEvoy, 'Seriamos excelentes vasallos y nunca cuidadanos: Prensa republicana y cambio social en Lima, 1791–1822,' Iván Jaksić, ed., *The Political Power of the Word: Press and Oratory in Nineteenth-Century Latin America* (London: Institute of Latin American Studies, 2002) 73.

VIVA FERNANDO VII.

MINERVA

EXTRAORDINARIA.

Lima 6 de diciembre de 1808.

A NOCHE LLEGO AL PUERTO del Callao la fragata Bárbara procedente de Valparayso con el adjunto pliego del Señor presidente de Chile á nuestro excelentísimo xefe, de cuyo órden se imprime sin pérdida de tiempo para satisfaccion de los fidelisimos peruanos.

Issue 66 of *The Minerva Peruana*, December 6, 1808. This newspaper was published in Lima between 1808 and 1810. American Antiquarian Society.

the editors had to cease publication.[14] Again, the fact is that publishing the news might have worked as a double-edged sword; on the one hand, it served to incite fear within those who were witnessing the changes taking place in France from afar, while on the other, it might have provoked readers to learn more about a situation that was being presented to them through the vehicle of official voices. As Teodoro Hampe-Martinez correctly suggests, there is certain ambiguity when it comes to the views that the editors consider worth mentioning when discussing the role of this particular newspaper in Peruvian politics. From 1808 to 1819, Peru endured what has been considered by some historians a civil war. The Central Andes in general witnessed a general cycle of rebellions, revolutions and counter-revolutions that made the attaining of independence from Spain longer there than in Mexico, Venezuela, or Colombia.[15] In the midst of this political instability, *El peruano* was born.

According to its editor, Guillermo del Rio, *El peruano* belonged to all Peruvians, and its goal was to facilitate the circulation of news that could contribute to 'the path of virtue and glory' while 'contributing to their happiness.' The newspaper also aimed to remove Peruvians from 'the stagnation' that had dominated their thinking until then.[16] Still, in 1811, the French Revolution and its aftermaths remained a vivid memory for Spain and its colonies, especially considering circumstances in Spain at the time. In fact, since 1796, in its war against England (1796–1806), and in the

14. It was not until April 18, 1811, that the court of Cadiz instituted in Lima the freedom of the press or the right to publish without a previous license. Villaneuva observes that although freedom of the press was supposedly granted in 1811, the Spanish government established the Juntas de Censura the same year with the aim to examine all writings deemed subversive. '*El peruano*,' Carmen Villaneuva, ed. *Coleccion documental de la Independencia del Perú* (Lima: 1972), introduction.

15. Teodoro Hampe Martinez, 'La Revolucion Francesca vista por el *Mercurio peruano*: cambio politico versus reformismo criollo,' Colloque de Bordeaux, *Les Révolutions Ibèriques et Ibèro-Americaines à L'Aube du XIXe Siècle* (Paris: Editions du Centre Nacional de la Rechereche Scientifique, 1989); Jear Piel, 'Aproximación bibliográfica al ciclo de las revoluciones centro andinas (Peru-Bolivia),' Robert M. Maniquis, ed., *La revolución francesa y el mundo ibérico, y el mundo ibérico* (Madrid: Sociedad Estatal Quinto Centenario, 1989), 467.

16. *El peruano*, no. 1 (1811): 1.

Napoleonic wars (1799–1815), Spain found its Atlantic sailings declining and its 'colonial trade strangled.'[17] In sum, the nation was in a state of bankruptcy. For Spaniards at that juncture, Napoleon Bonaparte had become an epitome of everything that had been evil about France since the French revolution. This was sustained by 'his monstrous aggrandizement and the political turmoil that he has caused in Europe.'[18] The decision of Bonaparte to crown his brother as the new king of Spain in 1807, after Charles IV was forced to abdicate, also represented an act that Spaniards as well as Spanish Americans refused to accept.[19]

A fascinating article, titled 'Para la historia de la Revolucion de Espana' ('For the History of the Spanish Revolution'), by D. Alvaro Flores Estrada, general procurator of the Principality of Asturias, published first in 1810 in Spain and reprinted in 1811, attests to the presence of this historical event. Flores summarized the French Revolution as an event that incited 'too much enthusiasm in its beginnings, and too many bad things at the end.'[20] He added that such an event polarized people to the extent that twenty-one years later it was still difficult to conclude which group was correct: Those who vehemently opposed the revolution or those who viewed it as a necessary step toward progress. However, the author did add one reality: the Revolution left the French people 'horrified after seeing so much blood . . . tired of ten continuous years of the bloodiest war . . . fearful' of so much death, and 'tired and irritable because of all the injustices' that had taken place.[21] This type of discourse on the French Revolution can be perceived as a preventive measure. The article emphasized the negative consequences of such a historical transformation which could cause the people of a country in which it had happened to question the value of radical social change. This article

17. John Charles Chasteen, *Born in Blood and Fire: A Concise History of Latin America* (New York: W. W. Norton, 2001), 96.
18. *El peruano*, no.12 (October 15, 1811): 93.
19. Chasteen, *Born in Blood and Fire*, 97.
20. *El peruano*, no. 3 (September 13, 1811):17.
21. *El peruano* no. 3 (September 13, 1811): 18.

was also very opportunistic, especially in view of the different revolutionary movements that had taken place in Spanish American territories since 1808, whereby Spaniards and Spanish Americans were further distancing themselves from one another politically, socially, and economically. This was also after what is considered the post-constitutional period of 1812, when Peru witnessed strong political repression at all levels, including the press.[22]

Eight years later, the Peruvian patriot Bernardo Monteagudo, editor of the newspaper *El censor de la revolución* (*The Judge of the Revolution*), denounced Spain's obligation to make a decision about the future of America.[23] In an introduction to the first issue, the editor emphasized the Age of the Enlightenment as crucial in the process of intellectual, political, and scientific advances that had changed the face of the world on a global scale. Monteagudo continued that theme, in the nineteenth century, South America was fully participating in, and taking advantage of ideas circulated by the great thinkers of the Enlightenment—ideas that had radically changed the relationship of individuals with the world around them. During this period of profound changes, he argued, the revolution, and more specifically political revolutions, came to play a vital role in the development of societies. According to the editor, political revolutions constituted 'the natural pronouncements of having arrived at a moment when society discovers there are other institutions capable of making it happier and it feels capable of overcoming the obstacles facing it.'[24]

For Monteagudo, the American Revolution represented a perfect example of a successful political revolution that had a profound

---

22. McEvoy, 'Seriamos excelentes vasallos y nunca cuidadanos,' 53.

23. *El censor de la revolución*, first published on April 20, 1820, lasted until July of the same year. It was published on the tenth, twentieth, and thirtieth of each month from Santiago de Chile. It included articles the editors deemed important when discussions on the issue of the Spanish American revolution, as well as personal letters from citizens and advertisements. Many of the articles dealt with the debate over freedom of the press, including its advantages and how it was being violated by colonial authorities. It has been reprinted in *La prensa en la Independencia de Perú*, Bernardo Monteagudo, ed. (Buenos Aires: Coni Hermanos, 1910).

24. *El censor de la revolución*, no. 1 (1820), 2.

impact on the rest of the Americas. The editor considered this revolution, along with the French and others that had begun to occur in South America, to be positive movements toward freedom and progress, and the only venues to stop the despotism that had been so prevalent in South America. Not even 'fanatic fear' or 'extreme ignorance' could stop the revolution from reaching to the rest of South America. Peruvians, in particular, were 'determined to follow the spirit of the century and the order of nature which call us to establish a liberal and fair government.'[25] In this newspaper, the revolution was conceived as a productive process, which, when guided by moderation, was the only valuable tool to achieve freedom and quality. Revolution in this case did not equate with fear but rather implied an essential step toward imposing a social order based on justice.

El pacificador de Perú (*The Peacemaker of Peru*) 1821, a newspaper contemporary with *El censor de la revolución* and edited by the Creole patriots Bernardino Monteagudo and García del Río,[26] perceived the situation in Peru between 1811 and 1821 as a perennial

25. *El censor de la revolución*, no.1 (1820), 2–3.
26. The first two issues of *El pacificador de Perú* (April–September 1821) were published in April 1821 in Huaura, Perú. Issues number 3 through 11 were published in Barranca, and the last two issues (12 and 13), were published in Lima (Imprenta de J. A. López y Compañía). It has been reprinted in *La prensa en la Independencia de Perú*, Monteagudo, ed. The newspaper included a statement by the editor which was followed by letters from a number of Peruvian citizens describing the state of affairs in Lima, in which they expressed their fervent patriotism, and the need for Peru to be a free country. In the final issue, the newspaper reprinted a passage from the 'Message' delivered to Congress on December 3, 1821, by President James Monroe published in the *New-York Evening Post* (December 7, 1821). In it, Monroe commented on the South American independence movements. 'It is understood that the colonies in South America have had great success during the present year in the struggle for their independence. The new Government of Colombia has extended its territories and considerably augmented its strength, and at Buenos Ayres, where civil dissensions had for some time before prevailed, greater harmony and better order appear to have been established. Equal success has attended their efforts in the Provinces on the Pacific. It has long been manifest that it would be impossible for Spain to reduce these colonies by force, and equally so that no conditions short of their independence would be satisfactory to them. It may therefore be presumed, and it is earnestly hoped, that the Government of Spain, guided by enlightened and liberal councils, will find it to comport with its interests and due to its magnanimity to terminate this exhausting controversy on that basis. To promote this result by friendly counsel with the Government of Spain will be the object of the Government of the United States.' The editor of *El pacificador de Perú* commented that Peru was also looking forward to establishment of economic relationships with the United States once independence was achieved 13 (April 10, 1821):1–2.

state of revolution, full chaos, and uncertainty. The editors began all new issues of the newspaper with an epigraph taken from the United States Declaration of Independence: 'We must acquiesce in the necessity, which denounces our separation, and hold them, as we hold the rest of mankind—enemies in war—in peace, friends.'[27] The editors' purpose was to persuade Spain and Peruvians that the only way to pacify Peru and the rest of South America was for Spain 'To Recognize [Peru's] Independence.' Monteagudo and García stated their opinion that independence could bring economic benefits to both countries instead of total division. They saw commerce as being the potential 'great peacemaker between the two nations.'[28] Failure to recognize this would leave Peruvians, they agreed, with just one option: to continue the revolution. As the editors warned Spaniards: 'Damn a thousand times your stubbornness, as it will be the cause of your misfortunes and ours!'[29]

Continuation of the revolution would bring more horror and anxiety to both countries, and it was to this extent that the editors perceived their newspaper as an instrument to pacify both sides of the military struggle. Nevertheless, the editors warned, if Spain could not accept 'an honorable peace,' then 'let us all die in the fire if we cannot extinguish it before belonging to Spain.'[30] Although revolution was not a pacific vehicle for attaining justice, it nevertheless represented a justified means to reach equality and freedom. That end justified engaging in an 'eternal war against the Spanish, although as the editors also declared in that May issue, 'peace and Independence is the noble desire of all Americans.'[31]

---

27. *El pacificador de Perú*, no. 1 (April 10, 1821): 1.

28. Since the imposition of the Bourbon reforms, creoles were also adamant in wanting to establish free and direct commerce with other European countries as well as the United States. See E. Bradford Burns, *La revolución francesca y el mundo ibérico* (Madrid: Sociedad Estatal Quinto Centenario, 1989), introduction.

29. *El pacificador de Perú*, no.1 (April 10, 1821) 1: 2.

30. *El pacificador de Perú*, no.2 (April 20, 1821): 2.

31. *El pacificador de Perú*, no.6 (May 31, 1821): 1–2. For the editor this was more obvious when considering that, as of June 1821, almost all South America was free, including Nueva Granada (Venezuela, Colombia, and Ecuador), Buenos Aires, and Chile.

By 1823, Peruvian intellectuals had arrived at their own definition and manner of imagining their revolution. Their views of former and current revolutions such as the French, the American and the revolutions that were currently ongoing in Spanish America, enabled them to conclude that their own revolution was different. In an introductory article on May 28, 1823, *Gaceta del Gobierno del Perú (Gazette of the Government of Peru)* took a comprehensive approach to the issue of revolution. The editor began by stating that 'the history of revolutions, which have periodically changed the fate of people for ages, presents perhaps noble acts, but in the midst of the shadows and the horrors that cause the fermentation of private passions.'[32] This, however, had not been the case in Peru, where the editor hailed its 'saintly revolution which, without spilling one drop of blood, advances with majestic steps that, albeit slow, are safe.' He emphatically affirmed 'the moderation and sound judgment of the Capital of Peru will always serve as a model when it comes to the great crises of states.' It was the moderation of the creole patriots, their inclination to sacrifice, and the solidarity they felt among each other that would facilitate the expulsion of 'the last trace of Spanish despotism' from Peru.[33]

This belief that independence was the only vehicle to guarantee a successful future was anchored in what the American and French revolutions had achieved. In an anonymous article reflecting on the impact of Enlightenment philosophy on the ideological foundation of both revolutions, the author highlighted the crucial role

32. *Gaceta del Gobierno del Perú* (1821–25) was published in Lima by Imprenta del Gobierno and the Imprenta del Estado and also in Trujillo of Perú, where it was published as *Gaceta extraordinaria del gobierno del Perú* in the Imprenta Paredes. This newspaper included news about freedom of press, government edicts and royal decrees, anonymous articles criticizing Spain and advocating Peru's total independence, articles on Bolivar's visit to Peruvian territories, and news about the war between Spain and France among many other subjects. This newspaper was characterized by its global circulation of knowledge, reprinting articles from newspapers in England, France, Colombia, Haiti, Jamaica, Brazil, Portugal and the United States, such as Philadelphia and Baltimore. As with many newspapers of the time, the nature of its content was quite global, if, as Felicity Nussbaum has suggested, we view the term global as the 'movement of ideas across borders and over time.' Nussbaum, ed., *The Global Eighteenth Century* (Baltimore: The Johns Hopkins University Press, 2003), 1–19.

33. *Gaceta del Gobierno del Perú*, no. 43 (1823): 1.

that both revolutions had had in the fight for human rights, freedom, and quality. According to this contributor, Spanish America's fight against Spanish despotism was modeled and fostered by
the success of the French and North American revolutions. The
article stated that the North American Revolution had been
guided by 'noble principles,' which justified freedom from the
'hateful yoke' of oppressors. On the other hand, the French
Revolution had succeeded in guaranteeing the defense of human
rights for all citizens and the end of monarchical despotism. Both
revolutions lent themselves as models to follow in order that Peru
might attain similar success and end abuses perpetrated by 'the
tyrants of reason,' which had kept the country under a state of
'dejection and barbarism.' The revolution as seen here, was no
longer a sign of danger and fear, but rather an exemplum of positive changes in a society, and as such, an act to be emulated.[34]

Fear and the Productivity of a Political Idea

Newspapers played a vital role in the circulation of ideas and debates that generated the Spanish American wars of independence.
As Rebecca Earle observes: 'any thorough account of the move . . .
from colony to republic must consider the role of the press; during
this period.'[35] Newspapers turned into public patriotic spaces in
which political and social concerns were persistently debated or

34. *Gaceta del Gobierno del Perú*, no. 43 (1823): 195. The idea of the revolution as a positive conduit for liberty was quite evident on the eve of Peru's official independence, and
the year 1822 represented a key moment in the search for independence, In June 1822,
San Martin proclaimed Peru's independence. However, the interior remained under the
control of royalist forces. A fifty-one delegate congress took control of the government,
which later fell to a military coup naming José de Riva Agüero the first president of Peru.
Royalist troops forced Riva Agüero to escape to Callao, leaving the congress to appoint
Torre Tagle as the new president, whereupon Riva Agüero refused to relinquish his power
and allied himself with the royalist forces. Meanwhile Símón Bolívar was 'named military
dictator and commander of the armed forces' but was unable to rescue Lima from the
Spanish forces. Spain again had control of nearly all of Peru, except in the north, until December 1824, when Bolívar finally recaptured Lima and José de Sucre took control of the
highlands. On January 23, 1826, Peru obtained its official independence. See Peter Flin-
dell Klarén, *Peru: Society and Nationhood in the Andes* (New York: Oxford University Press,
2000).

35. Rebecca Earle, 'The Role of Print in the Spanish American Wars of Independence,' Jaksić, ed., *The Political Power of the Word*, 13.

exposed. These media outlets represented both a venue through which Spaniards and Creole Americans were able to articulate their own perceptions of how a revolution needed to be contained and be a blueprint for future change. However, Spanish authorities took full advantage by highlighting the horrendous and bloody nature of the French Revolution as was depicted in the *Mercurio peruano*. Through edicts, royal decrees, and news articles relating to the French Revolution that were reprinted in colonial Spanish American newspapers, Spanish authorities showed through their rhetoric of fear the anxiety that they felt towards the future—namely, losing control of their colonies.

In the case of the creoles after 1811, ignorance and lack of understanding were reasons that individuals would fear the revolution. For Creole Americans, fear, as Montesquieu had suggested in *The Spirit of the Laws* (1748), was associated with the principle of the despotic government—in this case Spanish—whose goals relied on silencing those who were perceived as a threat by imposing total obedience.[36] Ironically, as mentioned earlier, Peruvians in the nineteenth century came to conceive of monarchical government as equal to a despotic one—both guided by the same evil principles. In the Peruvian newspapers that supported the revolution, this word was associated with its original definition of 'radical change,' 'a sudden and violent change in government' and a 'change produced by time.' As with any change, it was approached with trepidation and anxiety due to its ever-changing nature. Revolution represented a social and political construct that aimed to mobilize the public to feel either fear or the strength to combat fear itself.

36. Montesquieu contended that all despotic government was motivated by fear. He also suggested that religion played a crucial role in this type of government that he opposed, preferring a monarchy, which he thought was motivated by honor, or the republican, organized on the principle of virtue. Montesquieu, Charles, *The Spirit of the Laws*, Anne M. Cohler, ed. (New York: Cambridge University Press, 1989), 32, 54, 70.

Written Constitutions
and Unenumerated Rights

ERIC SLAUTER

THE NINTH AMENDMENT to the Constitution of the United States, which declares that the 'enumeration in the Constitution, of certain rights, shall not be construed to deny or disparage others retained by the people,' raises an obvious problem for the practice of text-centered constitutional history. While scholars have traced the origins of most of the rights protected in the first ten amendments, sometimes devoting whole books to individual clauses, to date no one has written a similar study of the Ninth Amendment. It is easy to understand why. The enumerated rights of free speech or a free press present concrete objects for historical analysis, but because the nature and scope of the Ninth Amendment is itself subject to debate, it has not been especially clear what a prehistory of unenumerated rights would, should, or could examine.

Political and legal scholars, to be sure, have attended to the immediate context of the production of the Ninth Amendment and have tried to provide a sense of the content of its protections. Legislative histories focus especially on James Madison's proposals for amendments in June 1789 and on changes made to those proposals in Congress later that summer. Turning from the process by which the text was formulated to the question of what rights the Ninth Amendment was designed to protect, some legal commentators see rights not enumerated in the Constitution as

ERIC SLAUTER is an assistant professor of English at the University of Chicago.

enumerated somewhere else. To give content to the Ninth
Amendment these readers collate revolutionary declarations of
rights from individual states and look to the recommendations
some states made about amendments in the process of ratifying
the Constitution. Other legal interpreters contend that the Ninth
Amendment protects rights that are essentially unenumerable because they are infinite. In an attempt to explain what they see as a
pragmatic open-endedness behind the Ninth Amendment's protection of natural rights these interpreters point to pre-ratification
explanations by the supporters of the Constitution that characterized a Federal bill of rights as 'dangerous.' James Wilson and Alexander Hamilton, among others, argued that a partial enumeration
of rights would have the undesirable consequence of augmenting
Federal power in any area not specifically and textually reserved.
But despite the attention to political acts and political rhetoric,
legal approaches can seem insensitive to the politics of the Revolutionary period. After all, not all of the state declarations of rights
that provide evidence for 'positivists' were understood by contemporaries to have equal legitimacy; and the 'natural rights' school
seems to accept one side of a political argument as if it was a
widely held maxim—or indeed as if a strategic Federalist argument during ratification amounts to the same thing as the intention of the framers of the Ninth Amendment. [1]

In enumerating what had been left unenumerated legal scholars
have set aside a deeper history of the idea of unenumerated rights

1. For the basic outline of debates over the meaning of the Ninth Amendment, see the
articles by Raoul Berger, Charles L. Black, Jr., Thomas C. Grey, Sanford Levinson,
Thomas B. McAfee, Calvin R. Massey, and Suzanna Sherry collected in *The Rights Retained
by the People: The History and Meaning of the Ninth Amendment*, ed. Randy E. Barnett, 2 vols.
(Fairfax, Va.: George Mason University Press, 1989–93); and the exchange between Ro-
nald Dworkin and Richard A. Posner on the concept of unenumerated rights in *The Bill of
Rights in the Modern State*, eds. Geoffrey R. Stone, Richard A. Epstein, and Cass R. Sunstein
(Chicago: University of Chicago Press, 1992), 381–450. Gaspare J. Saladino's bibliographic
essay in *The Bill of Rights and the States*, eds. Patrick T. Conley and Joseph P. Kaminski
(Madison: Madison House, 1992), 461–514, is the best guide to scholarship before 1991.
For recent reflections, see Barnett, *Restoring the Lost Constitution: The Presumption of Liberty*
(Princeton: Princeton University Press, 2004); and Akhil Reed Amar, *America's Constitution:
A Biography* (New York: Random House, 2005), 327–29, 476–77.

and have largely ignored the cultural relation of writing to rights. In treating written constitutions cultural historians have emphasized textuality over (for want of a better term) atextuality. My purpose, then, is not to offer yet another history of the Ninth Amendment but to suggest some cultural strategies for thinking about the revolutionary relation of written constitutions and unenumerated rights.

A consideration of unenumerated rights in the late eighteenth century should begin by acknowledging the relatively recent expansion of enumerated rights. Between 1689 and 1789, discussions of rights in colonial British America and the early United States widened to include larger segments of the population and the kinds of rights claimed dramatically expanded. Rights were not 'invented' during this period. Historians of political thought make a convincing case that a modern language of rights was spoken in England by the close of the seventeenth century. But if the concept of rights was not novel, the rights themselves often were. A side-by-side comparison of declarations of rights made in the age of the American Revolution with similar documents produced in the English Revolution a century earlier confirms the relative novelty of some enumerated rights—from freedom of conscience, assembly, and speech to the right to consent to the quartering of troops in private houses during peacetime. Contemporaries sometimes tried to disguise the newness of certain rights by imagining ancient legal genealogies, though just as often they acknowledged that the rights they claimed had only been discovered and declared in their lifetimes; some took it further and observed that new experiences would inevitably lead to the discovery of other rights not yet known.[2]

2. On early modern ideas about rights, see J. G. A. Pocock, *The Ancient Constitution and the Feudal Law* (Cambridge: Cambridge University Press, 1957); Richard Tuck, *Natural Rights Theories: Their Origin and Development* (Cambridge: Cambridge University Press, 1979); Lois G. Schwoerer, *The Declaration of Rights, 1689* (Baltimore: The Johns Hopkins University Press, 1981); Michael Zuckert, *Natural Rights and the New Republicanism* (Princeton: Princeton University Press, 1994); Kirstie M. McClure, *Judging Rights: Lockean Politics and the Limits of Consent* (Ithaca: Cornell University Press, 1996); Quentin Skinner, *Liberty Before Liberalism* (Cambridge: Cambridge University Press, 1998); and David Armitage, *The Ideological Origins of the British Empire* (Cambridge: Cambridge University Press, 2000).

Histories of the rise of rights in colonial British America and the early United States tend to minimize the dramatic expansion of enumerated rights in the eighteenth century. Working backward from declarations of rights in early state constitutions and the United States Constitution, legal scholars and historians have explained how enumerated rights developed either out of a long history of English legal precedent or out of a much shorter history of internal political struggle and practice during the American Revolution.[3] Working forward from the seventeenth century, historians of political philosophy have narrated the evolution of ideas about rights in Europe and the transmission of those ideas to America.[4] The former approach is more structured around clauses and the latter around concepts, but practitioners of both approaches have found surprisingly little to say about the period between the English Declaration of Right of 1689 and the discussion of rights in the context of colonial American reactions to Parliament in the

3. For legal and political histories, see Edmund S. Morgan and Helen M. Morgan, *The Stamp Act Crisis: Prologue to Revolution* (Chapel Hill: University of North Carolina Press, 1953); Bernard Bailyn, *The Ideological Origins of the American Revolution* (Cambridge: Harvard University Press, 1967); Gordon S. Wood, *The Creation of the American Republic, 1776–1787* (Chapel Hill: University of North Carolina Press, 1969); Forrest McDonald, *Novus Ordo Seclorum: The Intellectual Origins of the Constitution* (Lawrence: University Press of Kansas, 1985); John Phillip Reid, *Constitutional History of the American Revolution*, 4 vols. (Madison: University of Wisconsin Press, 1986–1995), volume I: *The Authority of Rights*; Bernard Schwartz, *The Great Rights of Mankind: A History of the American Bill of Rights* (expanded ed.; Madison: Madison House, 1992); Jack N. Rakove, *Original Meanings: Politics and Ideas in the Making of the Constitution* (New York: Knopf, 1996); *The Bill of Rights: Government Proscribed*, eds. Ronald Hoffman and Peter J. Albert (Charlottesville: University Press of Virginia, 1997); Akhil Reed Amar, *The Bill of Rights: Creation and Reconstruction* (New Haven: Yale University Press, 1998); Leonard W. Levy, *Origins of the Bill of Rights* (New Haven: Yale University Press, 1999); and for a recent narrative of the framing of the Bill of Rights, see Richard Labunski, *James Madison and the Struggle for the Bill of Rights* (New York: Oxford University Press, 2006).

4. For philosophical approaches, see *The Virginia Statute of Religious Freedom: Its Evolution and Consequences in American History*, eds. Merrill D. Peterson and Robert C. Vaughn (Cambridge: Cambridge University Press, 1988); *A Culture of Rights: The Bill of Rights in Philosophy, Politics, and Law—1791 and 1991*, eds. Michael J. Lacey and Knud Haakonssen (Cambridge: Cambridge University Press, 1991); Richard A. Primus, *The American Language of Rights* (Cambridge: Cambridge University Press, 1999); and Murray Dry, *Civil Peace and the Quest for Truth: The First Amendment Freedoms in Political Philosophy and American Constitutionalism* (Lanham, Md.: Lexington Books, 2004).

mid 1760s.[5] Perhaps less surprisingly, these examinations have also shed little light on the relation between practices of writing or enumerating rights and concepts of rights themselves. Both approaches have obvious merit, but between attention to particular clauses and to general philosophic trends—that is, between the traditional provinces of legal and intellectual history—remains a largely unexplored cultural history of rights.

Cultural historians of early modern Europe are beginning to shape such a history for France and Britain by putting pressure on the naturalness of conceptions of rights in the eighteenth century. In doing so they have described a series of paradoxes. Rights declared to be self-evident in late eighteenth-century France, Lynn Hunt has argued, were declared precisely because they were not in fact self-evident or at least not that evident to many. For Hunt, the rise of the epistolary novel helped pre-Revolutionary French readers conceptualize human rights and gave meaning and content to later declarations. In the case of late-eighteenth-century England, as Dror Wahrman has provocatively suggested, claims of individual rights might have inaugurated rather than simply ratified a modern sense of self: at the very least Wahrman finds that such claims historically preceded if they did not bring about the concept of individualism upon which they would seem to rest. For both of these historians, paradoxes of rights tell us about larger cultural formations and about new conceptions of self and others.[6]

---

5. Even the largest documentary collections skip most of the eighteenth-century: see, for instance, *The Complete Bill of Rights: The Drafts, Debates, Sources, and Origins*, ed. Neil H. Cogan (New York: Oxford University Press, 1997) and *The Roots of the Bill of Rights: An Illustrated Source Book of American Freedom*, ed. Bernard Schwartz, 5 vols. (New York: Chelsea House, 1980), neither of which reprints material written between 1701 and 1760.

6. Lynn Hunt, 'The Paradoxical Origins of Human Rights,' in *Human Rights and Revolutions*, ed. Jeffrey N. Wasserstrom, Lynn Hunt, and Marilyn B. Young (Lanham, Md.: Rowman and Littlefield, 2000), 3–17; Hunt, *Inventing Human Rights: A History* (New York: W. W. Norton, 2007); Dror Wahrman, *The Making of the Modern Self: Culture and Identity in Eighteenth-Century England* (London: Yale University Press, 2004), 307–10. And for recent cultural analysis of women's rights in eighteenth-century America, see the essays by Sarah Knott and Rosemarie Zagarri in *Women, Gender, and Enlightenment*, ed. Sarah Knott and Barbara Taylor (New York: Palgrave Macmillan, 2005); and Mary Kelley, *Learning to Stand and Speak: Women, Education, and Public Life in America's Republic* (Chapel Hill: University of North Carolina Press, 2006).

CONSTITUCION

DE LOS ESTADOS UNIDOS.

LA Constitucion formada para los Estados Unidos de America por una Convencion de Diputados de los Estados de New-Hampshire, Massachusetts, Connecticut, New-York, New-Jersey, Pennsylvania, Delaware, Maryland, Virginia, North-Carolina, South-Carolina, y Georgia en una Sesion iniciada el 25 de Mayo y terminada el 17 de Septiembre de 1787.

NOS el Pueblo de los Estados Unidos en orden á formar una union la mas perfecta, establecer justicia, asegurar la tranquilidad domestica, proveer a la comun defensa, promover el bien general, y asegurar los derechos y prerogativas de la libertad para nosotros mismos y nuestra posteridad, ordenamos y establecemos la Constitucion de los Estados Unidos de America de la manera siguiente.

Fig. 1. The opening page of the earliest separate printing of the United States Constitution in the Spanish language. Dedicated to the lawyers of Caracas, it was intended for export in the cause of the Latin American independence movements. *Constitucion de los Estados Unidos de America.* Traducida del ingles al espanol por Don Jph. Manuel Villavicencio (Philadelphia: En la imprenta de Smith & M'Kenzie, 1810).

These findings provide benchmarks for considering the unique situation in colonial British America and the early United States, where the novel never achieved the prominence it attained in eighteenth-century Britain and France, where conceptions of liberal individualism were arguably delayed or eclipsed by expressed commitments to the corporate nature of the rights of mankind or the rights of the people, and where local institutions of colonialism and a system of slavery put a premium on ethnic and 'racial' difference at the same time that the reception of the European enlightenment helped crystallize ideas about universal humanity. Focused less on particular rights than on conceptions of rights, a cultural history of rights in early America might have a comparative advantage over purely political or legal histories insofar as it could illuminate the ways in which ordinary people made meaning of the rights declared in their name and contributed to the discovery (if not the declaration) of those rights.

Such a history would necessarily focus on the crucial question of how contemporaries in the late eighteenth century understood the relationship between textualized and non-textualized rights. Were declarations of rights merely the textual citation of pre-existing rights or were they the source of rights themselves? As David Armitage has argued, the Declaration of Independence was more noteworthy for its declaration of sovereignty than for its declaration of rights.[7] Thomas Jefferson and Congress devoted energy to the enumeration of wrongs, not rights; the famous list of rights in the second paragraph is patently non-exhaustive: 'among these' rights 'are Life, Liberty, and the Pursuit of Happiness,' Jefferson and Congress observed before moving toward defining with much more care the specific right of the people to alter governments. In the declarations of rights made shortly before and after the Declaration of Independence, different states enumerated rights differently. Though many of

7. David Armitage, *The Declaration of Independence: A Global History* (Cambridge, Mass.: Harvard University Press, 2007).

the same core rights appear on all of the newly drafted declarations of rights of the 1770s and early 1780s, a considerable residue of rights declared in some states but not in others remains. And it is clear that the very idea of enumeration meant different things to different states and different legislators. The Virginia Declaration of Rights of 1776, as well as the Pennsylvania Declaration which largely mimicked it, included sixteen sections; Maryland's Declaration, also drafted in 1776 and the longest of the period, ran to forty-two articles.

A cultural history of rights should take stock of the range of claims about natural rights made in the period and should move beyond the question of enumeration in state declarations. A census of the various suggestions about what exactly natural rights were in the Revolutionary period reveals some surprises. Consider, for instance, the natural rights described in a pamphlet published in Charleston, South Carolina, in 1783. The anonymous author of *Rudiments of Law and Government, Deduced from the Law of Nature* held that the 'Rights of Individuals from society by Natural Law, are Safety, Liberty, Kindness, and Due Portions of Common property, of Political Consequence, and of Social Emoluments.'[8] To be sure, while liberty, safety, and property were frequently mentioned in revolutionary declarations of rights, no state declared an individual right to kindness or, for that matter, a right to a portion of common property. This anonymous author obviously spoke for himself and, though he addressed lawmakers in South Carolina and elsewhere, he probably reached few readers. Nevertheless, the claims on behalf of such rights made by this author offer a suggestive preview of what might happen if analysts of the Ninth Amendment shifted attention away from legal enactments and declarations into a broader culture of rights or at the very least toward those period voices

8. *Rudiments of Law and Government, Deduced from the Law of Nature; Particularly addressed to the People of South-Carolina, But composed on Principles applicable to all Mankind* (Charleston: McIver, 1783), 15. The author seems to have had 'hospitality' in mind as the reciprocal duty (p. 18).

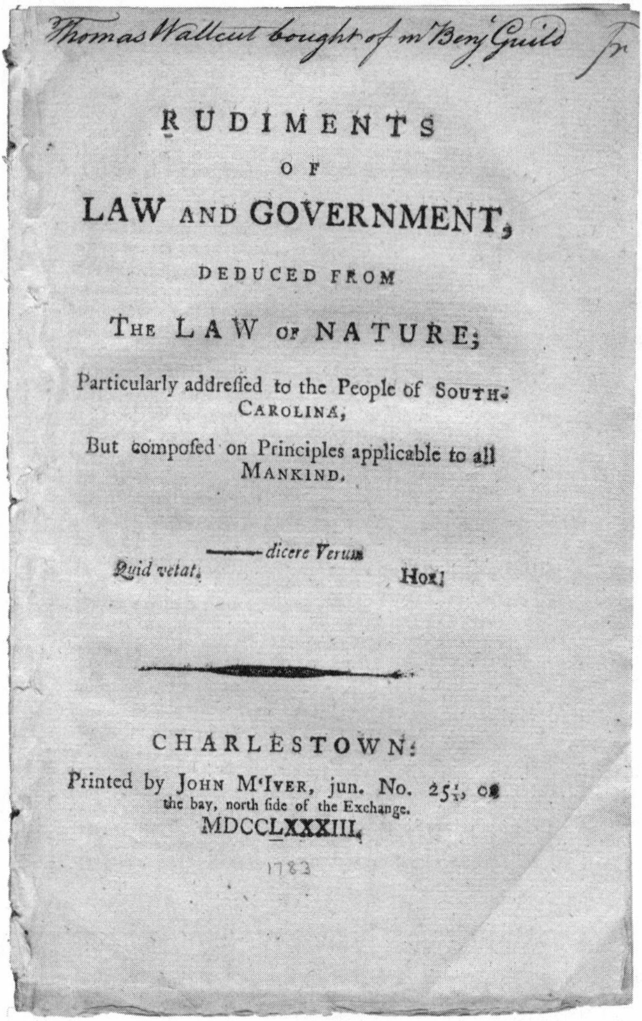

Thomas Wallcut bought of Mr Benj. Guild Jr

RUDIMENTS
OF
LAW AND GOVERNMENT,
DEDUCED FROM
THE LAW OF NATURE;
Particularly addressed to the People of SOUTH-CAROLINA;
But composed on Principles applicable to all MANKIND.

——dicere Verum
Quid vetat? Hor.

CHARLESTOWN:
Printed by JOHN M'IVER, jun. No. 25½, on the bay, north side of the Exchange.
MDCCLXXXIII.

1783

Fig. 2. The anonymous pamphlet, *Rudiments of law and government, deduced from the law of nature; : particularly addressed to the people of South-Carolina, but composed on principles applicable to all mankind*, was printed in Charleston, S. C. in 1783. The inscription, 'Thomas Wallcut bought of Mr. Benj. Guild,' indicates that this is one of the items retrieved from Wallcut's personal library by AAS Librarian Christopher Columbus Baldwin in 1834. Baldwin observed that he had to search through 'ancient trunks, bureaus, and chests, baskets, tea chests, and old drawers . . . and everything was covered with venerable dust. As I was under a slated roof and the thermometer at ninety-three, I had a pretty hot time of it. The value of the rarities I found, however, soon made me forget the heat and I never have never seen such happy moments.'

that argued for a broad range of rights requiring acknowledgement and protection.

Public debates about enumerating rights within the individual states provide another way to rethink the problem of unenumerated rights. Take the case of Pennsylvania. In May 1777, the physician Benjamin Rush, writing under the pseudonym 'Ludlow,' argued in a Philadelphia newspaper that the authors of the Pennsylvania Constitution of 1776 had failed to announce all the principles upon which the rights therein declared were based and, even worse, had made a crucial error by not restricting the legislature from altering the bill of rights. A number of writers came forward to answer various other charges of 'Ludlow,' but Thomas Paine was the only one to take up the question of rights. Writing under the familiar name of 'Common Sense,' Paine argued that an unalterable bill of rights was dangerous since new civil rights were emerging all the time. Given new situations, Paine wrote, 'it is impossible to say what improvements may be made.' But he strenuously objected to the idea that the bill of rights should enumerate all natural rights, 'for were all the great natural rights, or principles, as this writer calls them, to be admitted, it would be impossible that any government could be formed thereon, and instead of being a Bill of Rights fitted to a state of civil government, it would be a Bill of Rights fitted in a state of nature without any government at all.' 'It would be,' he joked, 'an Indian Bill of Rights.' Paine alluded to the widely held notion that native Americans stood as empirical examples (as political scientist Sankar Muthu has recently put it) 'of pure humans, that is, as human beings who inhabit a state of nature and who thus exhibit purely natural qualities, such as . . . an unmediated knowledge of natural laws and rights.'[9] Paine ignored descriptions of native American politics made by recent natural historians in order to make his point.

9. [Thomas Paine] 'Common Sense,' 'Candid and Critical Remarks on a Letter Signed Ludlow,' *Pennsylvania Journal*, June 4, 1777, reprinted in *Complete Writings of Thomas Paine*, ed. Philip S. Foner, 2 vols. (New York: Citadel Press, 1945), 2: 274; Sankar Muthu, *Enlightenment Against Empire* (Princeton: Princeton University Press, 2003), 7.

Governmental power derived from surrendered rights, hence overenumeration of rights risked the existence of government altogether. Though much more needs to be known about contemporary conceptions of native Americans as emblems of natural rights, the exchange between Rush and Paine highlights an important tension in period understandings of rights: Rush and Paine agreed that unenumerated rights were not protected rights, but Rush wished for a full and final enumeration of natural rights that could not be touched by successive legislatures and Paine held out the possibility of as yet unknown rights that would need the protection of precisely those legislatures.

The notion, advanced by both Rush and Paine in 1777, that rights enumerated on paper declarations were the only legitimate rights stood in stark contrast to pre-revolutionary claims that the rights of man derived from human nature and from God and were not to be, as Alexander Hamilton put it in 1775, 'rummaged for, among old parchments, or musty records.' But despite much verbal antipathy to the idea of documents as sources of rights, late colonial graphic artists routinely rendered portraits of prominent politicians and lawyers with copies of such documents. Bostonian Nathaniel Hurd's 1762 rendering of William Pitt, seated at a desk and surrounded by books, a quill, and a scroll inscribed 'Magna Carta et Libertas'—an image that suggested that Pitt had just composed the Magna Carta—was typical of a British graphic tradition. Late colonial lawyers and politicians appealed less and less to such documents, but graphic art remained static. A popular almanac image of John Dickinson, the author of a widely read series of essays by the 'Pennsylvania Farmer' in the late 1760s, portrayed Dickinson resting on a copy of Magna Carta, despite the fact that he had not mentioned the text. So too, the first official emblem for the Continental Congress in 1774 displayed a pillar of liberty perched atop Magna Carta, even though Congress repeatedly held that rights were pre-textual and God-given and that prior declarations on paper or parchment were not the source. It would have been easy for

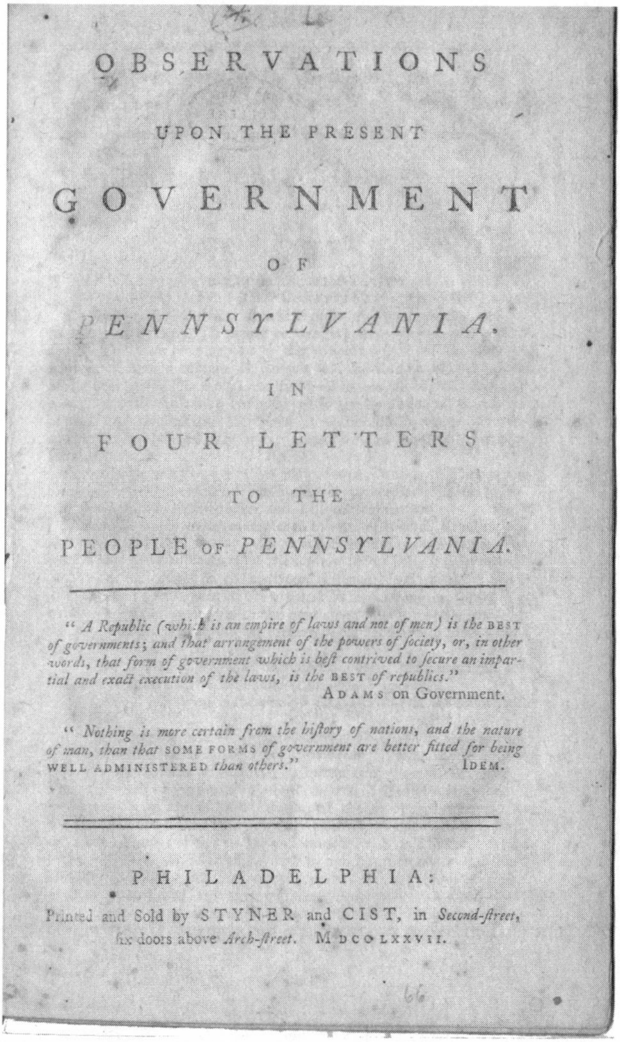

OBSERVATIONS

UPON THE PRESENT

GOVERNMENT

OF

PENNSYLVANIA,

IN

FOUR LETTERS

TO THE

PEOPLE OF PENNSYLVANIA.

"*A Republic (which is an empire of laws and not of men) is the* BEST *of governments; and that arrangement of the powers of society, or, in other words, that form of government which is best contrived to secure an impartial and exact execution of the laws, is the* BEST *of republics.*"
ADAMS on Government.

"*Nothing is more certain from the history of nations, and the nature of man, than that* SOME FORMS *of government are better fitted for being* WELL ADMINISTERED *than others.*"
IDEM.

PHILADELPHIA:

Printed and Sold by STYNER and CIST, in *Second-street*, six doors above *Arch-street.* MDCCLXXVII.

Fig. 3. In a series of newspaper articles signed 'Ludlow,' Benjamin Rush criticized the Pennsylvania Constitution for failing to make civil rights unalterable by the legislature and for an incomplete enumeration of natural rights. Thomas Paine responded that legislatures must be allowed to incorporate newly discovered civil rights and that a full enumeration of natural rights, which he termed 'an Indian Bill of Rights,' was suitable only for a state of nature. When Rush selected Paine's printers to reissue the articles as a pamphlet, opponents objected that he was deliberately trying to confuse readers [Benjamin Rush], *Observations upon the present government of Pennsylvania*. (Philadelphia: Styner and Cist, 1777).

most who saw these images to be confused, and to think that the paper documents were the true source of those rights. If we hope to understand the relationship between natural rights and positive rights, such images have much to tell us.[10] The division between verbal and visual representations suggests a larger tension about how political documents like constitutions and declarations of rights might be understood—indeed, the tension was at the heart of conversations about precisely what such texts were and what they documented.

The fact that constitutions were written documents was significant and novel, but it was not writing itself that made them meaningful or workable. It is a striking fact that *The Federalist*, often taken to be the best contemporary commentary on the meaning of the Constitution, rarely quotes the actual language of the text it defends. Though the series began in late October 1787, 'Publius' did not cite the text of the proposed Constitution until January 1788, after more than thirty essays had appeared. In part this stemmed from a strategic decision to treat the general concept of the union and the threats to its preservation before examining the proposed Constitution as the solution. In the end, just over a quarter of the eighty-five papers reproduced the language of the Constitution, but some citations are paraphrases or misquotations set within quotation marks rather than precise reproductions of constitutional language. Anti-Federalists frequently couched their objections to the Constitution by reference to the language of the text, and 'Publius' may have shied away from citation for that reason. But it is worth recalling James Madison's claims that 'parchment barriers,' 'mere declarations in the written constitution,' or 'a mere demarcation on parchment' served as insufficient safeguards for either the rights of citizens or the powers of

---

10. Alexander Hamilton, *The Farmer Refuted* (New York, 1775), in *The Papers of Alexander Hamilton*, ed. Harold C. Syrett and Jacob E. Cooke (New York: Columbia University Press, 1971–1987), 1: 122. For an extended discussion of the problem, see Eric Slauter, 'Being Alone in the Age of the Social Contract,' *William and Mary Quarterly*, 3d Ser., 62 (January 2005): 31–66.

particular branches of government.[11] The way to ensure such things was not through written constitutions per se but by drafting constitutions in a way that would allow parts of the government to check other parts and by finding protections for the rights of minorities through extra-textual means such as the scale of the republic. These were the topics Madison addressed in the papers that are now most read, *Federalist* 10 and 51, neither of which appealed to the actual language of the Constitution.

The printed Constitution emerged at a moment when political argumentation was undergoing a radical change in the nature and locus of authority, a fact that can be registered in the shifting ways authors cited texts. On the whole, in newspapers and in pamphlets, political writers tended to cite fewer and fewer authorities to make their points. The larger change can be seen in a dramatic, and admittedly extreme, comparison of the layout of typical pages in John Dickinson's *Letters from a Farmer in Pennsylvania to the Inhabitants of the British Colonies*, published in book form in 1768 after serialization in newspapers, and Thomas Paine's *Common Sense*, published first as a pamphlet in 1776. As arguments from precedent gave way to arguments from natural rights, citations declined dramatically. While the body of Dickinson's text often rested on half a page of citations in smaller type, Paine rarely cited other writers. One of Paine's few quotations was to the person he introduced as 'that wise observer on governments, Dragonetti.' Few of Paine's readers had probably heard of Giacinto Dragonetti's *Treatise of Virtues and Rewards*, an answer to Cesare Beccaria's *On Crimes and Punishments*; indeed, the reference raises questions about how political writings circulated in the late eighteenth-century Atlantic world. London booksellers in the

11. For Madison's remarks on 'parchment barriers' and governmental structure, see *The Federalist*, ed. Jacob E. Cooke (Middletown, Conn.: Wesleyan University Press, 1961), 333, 338, 343. For 'parchment barriers' with respect to rights, see Madison to Jefferson, October 17, 1788, in *The Papers of James Madison*, eds. William T. Hutchinson, William M. E. Rachel, Robert Rutland et al., 17 vols. (Chicago: University of Chicago Press; Charlottesville: University Press of Virginia, 1962–91), 11: 298.

late 1760s and into the middle of the 1770s worked to stock the bookshelves of colonial radicals; and colonial booksellers stocked such books and occasionally reprinted shorter ones. But while a Charleston printer in 1777 and a Philadelphia printer in 1778 reprinted Beccaria's essay, Dragonetti's book was not a popular text. It does not seem to have been serialized in newspapers or other periodicals, and existed in a single, dual-language edition printed in London in 1769. Modern search engines for digital texts suggest that Paine was the only writer citing this text in print in the period. How did he find it? Asking such questions allows us to move away from influence studies that center on citations to 'liberal' or republican texts and towards an appreciation not simply of the sources of political thought but the way in which sources were marshaled and, in some cases, even circulated.

Paying more attention to the market for political writing in the period and to the empirical realities of printing can help us assess period claims for the significance of written constitutions. For all of our rough sense of the availability of certain texts on revolutionary bookshelves, we know little about the real market for political literature or, for that matter, the marketing of political literature. How should we interpret the fact that *Rudiments of Law and Government*, the anonymously authored fifty-six-page pamphlet that stipulated a right to kindness and due portions of common property, sold for a dollar in Charleston in August 1783, for half-a-dollar in September, and for two shillings and four pence in December?[12] The declining price suggests both a lack of demand and the possibility of appeal to different audiences over a short span of time. Does it matter that Benjamin Rush, after publishing his critique of the Pennsylvania Constitution's failure to fully enumerate natural rights in a Philadelphia newspaper, reprinted his 'Ludlow' letters in a pamphlet? The fact that Rush repackaged his newspaper articles as a new essay and had selected

12. On the declining price of *Rudiments*, see *South Carolina Weekly Gazette*, August 16, 1783, and December 12, 1783; and *South Carolina Journal*, September 2–9, 1783. A dollar was the equivalent of six shillings.

the same printers and booksellers who distributed Paine's *American Crisis* angered an opponent named 'Whitlocke,' who grumbled that readers were buying them under a '*double* mistake.' The notion that a reader might mistake one of the opponents of 'Common Sense' for 'Common Sense' himself was a problem. The physical marketplace of ideas, with its pseudonymous authors and with printers who played both sides of an issue, was a confusing place.[13]

The printed constitution was part of a larger movement for new standards of transparency in government, but some of these standards tested the limits of empirical possibility. Defenders of Pennsylvania's unicameral Constitution of 1776 believed that the public could function as an effective second legislative branch with oversight of the first. Section 15 of the Pennsylvania Constitution stipulated that all bills of a public nature would be printed before they were approved and that the preambles would be written specifically to help readers understand what the laws were designed to do. Critics of that Constitution, like Rush as 'Ludlow,' complained that this provision offered no real check on legislative overreaching, since citizens depended on the good will of the legislature to print unenacted legislation. Rush pointed out that the legislature had failed to comply with this provision in early 1777. But beyond the issue of compliance it was not clear just how public oversight by means of print would work: How exactly were laws to be circulated? How long did the public have to read them? Would citizens express consent or disapproval by voting or by rioting? The theory of print as a check against government was clearly in advance of technologies to make that theory practicable.

The real world of price and printers raises a more central question about the availability of printed constitutions. Trish Loughran's recent reassessment of Paine's claims for sales of *Common Sense* should perhaps make us suspicious of the cherished

---

13. For Rush's pamphlet, which identified John Adams as the author of *Thoughts on Government* by way of an epigraph, see *Observations upon the Present Government of Pennsylvania* (Philadelphia: Styner and Cist, 1777); and see 'Whitlocke,' 'Letter III. To Ludlow,' *Dunlap's Pennsylvania Packet*, June 10, 1777.

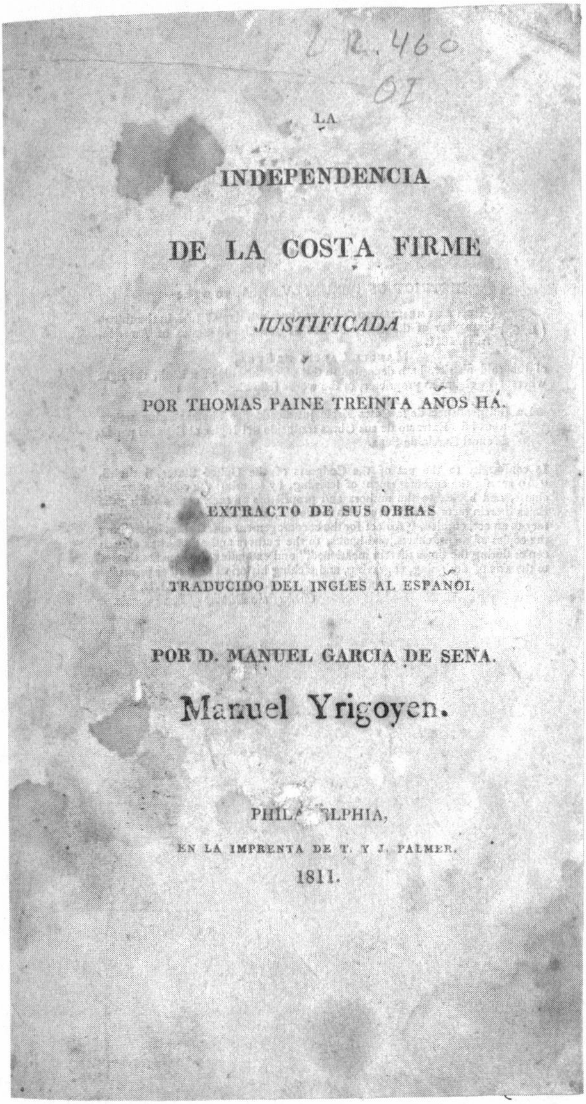

LA

INDEPENDENCIA

DE LA COSTA FIRME

JUSTIFICADA

POR THOMAS PAINE TREINTA AÑOS HÁ.

EXTRACTO DE SUS OBRAS

TRADUCIDO DEL INGLES AL ESPAÑOL

POR D. MANUEL GARCIA DE SENA.

Manuel Yrigoyen.

PHILADELPHIA,
EN LA IMPRENTA DE T. Y J. PALMER.
1811.

Fig. 4. Produced in Philadelphia for export to Buenos Aires, Manuel García de Sena's Spanish translation of Paine's *Common Sense*, the Declaration of Independence, and the Constitution of the United States influenced discussions about federalism during the framing of the 1811 Constitution of Venezuela and was later included on a list of books forbidden by the Inquisition of New Spain. *La independencia de la Costa Firme justificada por Thomas Paine treinta años há extracto de sus obras, traducido del inglés al español por D. Manuel Garcia de Sena* (Philadelphia: T. & J. Palmer, 1811).

claim in *Rights of Man* that almost every family in Pennsylvania had a copy of a constitution, and that legislators and ordinary citizens could pull them from their pockets at will. For all of the special supplements in newspapers and the printings in almanacs, small-scale copies of the Constitution of the United States or of the individual states were simply not as plentiful as Paine would have it. Pennsylvania never issued a copy of the Constitution that was truly pocket-sized. But with five editions of its Constitution printed between 1776 and 1786, Pennsylvania was atypical: most states did not have so many; and some state constitutions seem never to have been printed separately in the period.[14]

Available or not, the printed constitution was and is often celebrated as the great political innovation of the age. During the bicentennial of the Constitution a number of scholars placed the revolutionary-era constitutions in the context of larger transformations in the history of printing, but by far the most subtle and suggestive analysis came from Michael Warner, who delivered a lecture at the American Antiquarian Society in April 1987 that was subsequently printed in these pages as 'Textuality and Legitimacy in the Printed Constitution.' Warner's brilliant essay, later republished in his *Letters of the Republic: Publication and the Public Sphere in Eighteenth Century America*, offers one of the most compelling explanations not just for the writing of constitutions but for how such texts were understood and valued by contemporaries. American revolutionaries confronted a peculiar problem: how to give law legitimacy? Written constitutions literalized popular sovereignty; and the process of diffusion through print allowed constitutions to break off from the specific individuals who framed them and to become or seem to become, by a sleight of hand that forestalled a legitimation crisis, expressions of the

14. Trish Loughran, 'Disseminating *Common Sense*: Thomas Paine and the Problem of the Early National Bestseller,' *American Literature* 78 (March 2006): 1–28. For Paine's remarks on the ubiquity of the Pennsylvania Constitution, see *The Rights of Man, Part 2* (1792), in *Complete Works*, ed. Foner, 1: 378. The smallest surviving copy of the Pennsylvania Constitution, issued by John Dunlap in 1777 (Evans 15512), was a duodecimo pamphlet; most were octavo-sized.

people themselves. The mechanism that made the Constitution meaningful to its immediate contemporaries, Warner argued, would have made judicial appeals to the intentions of particular framers illegitimate, a contention he raised against the hermeneutics of original intention endorsed by then Attorney General Edwin Meese. When Gordon S. Wood came to review Warner's book he observed that 'many revolutionaries actually thought that written texts . . . would eliminate judicial and magisterial interpretation.' What they needed, Wood quipped, was 'some postmodern literary critics to tell them how naïve they were in believing that texts could be determinate and stable.' Despite the dig, Warner and Wood were on very similar interpretive ground—indeed, eight of Warner's twenty-six footnotes approvingly cited Wood's scholarship or acknowledged citations of primary sources reproduced from citations in Wood's *Creation of the American Republic, 1776–1787.* From different perspectives, Wood's review and Warner's work both described the written constitution as a tool designed to limit particular kinds of interpretation; both reflected the public debate over original intent.[15]

But we inhabit a different moment, one that compels us to think about written constitutions in different ways. Since the celebrations of the bicentennial of the Constitution of the United States, sixty-nine countries–from the nations of post-Communist Central and Eastern Europe, to South Africa, to Afganistan and Iraq–have drafted constitutions. Over the past decade and a half, as constitutional consultants have traveled a circuit from law schools in the United States to the former 'Eastern Bloc' and to Kabul and

15. Michael Warner, 'Textuality and Legitimacy in the Printed Constitution,' *Proceedings of the American Antiquarian Society* 97 (April 1987): 59–84; Warner, *Letters of the Republic: Publication and the Public Sphere in Eighteenth-Century America* (Cambridge: Harvard University Press, 1990), 97–117; Gordon S. Wood, 'The Liberation of Print,' review of *The Letters of the Republic*, by Michael Warner, *New Republic*, November 12, 1990, p. 42. For other treatments of print and constitutionalism during the bicentennial, see Patrick H. Hutton, 'The Print Revolution of the Eighteenth Century and the Drafting of Written Constitutions,' *Vermont History* 56 (Summer 1988): 154–65; and Walter F. Pratt, Jr., 'Oral and Written Cultures: North Carolina and the Constitution, 1787-1791,' in *The South's Role in the Creation of the Bill of Rights*, ed. Robert J. Haws (Jackson: University Press of Mississippi, 1991), 77–99.

Baghdad, it has perhaps become difficult to think of modern written constitutions as fundamental expressions of a particular people. It has also become harder to distinguish between culturally conditioned constitutional practices and putatively culture-free constitutional norms. The major cultural question about written constitutions of our moment is not about hermeneutics or intentionality, but about whether constitutions travel well.

It is an Enlightenment question. One of the great constitutional debates American Revolutionaries engaged in was about which came first, culture or politics? Some were cultural determinists: they held that manners, morals, customs, and tastes were the foundations upon which governments were erected. Others were political determinists: they affirmed that manners, morals, and tastes were really the product of political form and could be molded accordingly.[16] Though revolutionaries disagreed whether constitutions were best thought of as expressions of a people or as a way of reforming a people, most would have agreed with John Adams, who described the last quarter of the eighteenth century and the first part of the nineteenth century as 'the age of revolutions and constitutions.'[17] Adams gave a name to the period in a letter on the prospect of revolutionizing South America written in March 1815; Adams thought the prospect was doubtful. In a more sanguine mode that same month the architect of the Capitol, William Thornton, published in Washington his *Outlines of a Constitution for United North & South Columbia*. Thornton fantasized that all of the revolutions of the age might give way to a single constitution, a 'general plan of a grand government' for the hemisphere.

Between 1776 and 1826, the new states of the Americas drafted almost sixty constitutions, twenty of them in Latin America.[18] In

16. I discuss this debate in *The State as a Work of Art: The Cultural Origins of the Constitution* (forthcoming).

17. John Adams to James Lloyd, March 29, 1815, in *The Works of John Adams*, ed. Charles Francis Adams, 10 vols. (Boston: Little, Brown, and Co., 1850–56), 10: 149.

18. For a list of Latin American constitutions, see Keith S. Rosenn, 'The Success of Constitutionalism in the United States and its Failure in Latin America: An Explanation,' *University of Miami Inter-American Law Review* 22: 1 (1990–1991): 1–37.

1811, Manuel García de Sena, a native of Venezuela, translated Paine's *Common Sense*, the Declaration of Independence, and the Constitution into Spanish and had these works published in Philadelphia. A decade later, also in Philadelphia, Vincente Roca-fuerte published a similar anthology of constitutional documents from the United States. But while some Latin Americans dreamed of exporting the language and concepts of United States constitutionalism to Latin America, Simón Bolívar objected to the very idea that one nation's constitution could serve as a model for any other's; and he did so in the name of the Enlightenment's major constitutional thinker. Does not Montesquieu state, he asked, 'that laws should be suited to the people for whom they are made; that it would be a major coincidence if those of one nation could be adapted to another; that laws must . . . be in keeping with . . . the religion of the inhabitants, their inclinations, resources, number, commerce, habits, and customs?' 'This is the code we must consult,' Bolívar exclaimed, 'not the code of Washington!'[19] Many of the newly independent states of the Americas did look to the United States Constitution for inspiration and even for particular language. It was an age of revolutionary and constitutional mimesis, but Bolívar's remark is a powerful reminder that Enlightenment and revolution meant textually enshrining local customs and rights as often as it meant transcending them in favor of another nation's self-evident truths.

19. On the circulation of constitutions, see Robert J. Kolesar, 'North American Constitutionalism and Spanish America,' in *American Constitutionalism Abroad*, ed. George A. Billias (New York: Greenwood, 1990), 41-63; and Bernard Bailyn, 'Atlantic Dimensions,' in *To Begin the World Anew* (New York: Knopf, 2003), 131-49. For Manuel García de Sena's translations and the Inquisition of New Spain, see Pedro Grases's introduction to the second edition of *La independencia de la Costa Firme justificada por Thomas Paine treinta años ha* (Caracas: Imprenta López de Buenas Aires, 1949) and Harry Bernstein's review of this volume in *The Hispanic American Historical Review* 31 (1951): 127-28. Simón Bolívar, 'Address Delivered at the Second National Congress of Venezuela in Angostura' (February 15, 1819), cited in Miguel Schor, 'Constitutionalism Through the Looking Glass of Latin America,' *Texas International Law Journal* 41 (Winter 2006): 16-17.

Print Culture and the Haitian Revolution: The Written and the Spoken Word

DAVID GEGGUS

THE FIFTEEN-YEAR STRUGGLE that ended slavery and racial discrimination in French Saint Domingue and climaxed, in 1804, with the creation of independent Haiti was arguably the only one of four Atlantic revolutions of the period 1776 to 1824 that fully embodied the ideals of liberty, equality, and independence. Haiti's revolution, however, seems perhaps the furthest removed of the four conflicts from the print culture of the Enlightenment and from the liberal democratic ideology that it helped to develop. The emblematic event of the revolution was a slave uprising, not a declaration of independence or a constitution. The country's first head of state, like most of his subjects, was neither literate nor able to speak a European language.[1] Haiti's presses published few works during the first decade of independence, and five of its six constitutions of the period 1801–1816 were explicitly dictatorial.[2] Liberty in the Haitian

---

1. Born in Saint Domingue, Jean-Jacques Dessalines spoke only Haitian creole, which is technically not an Indo-European language, although most of its vocabulary derives from French.

2. The exception, the constitution of 1806, ended up being ignored by president Alexandre Pétion, who chose to rule without the Senate.

DAVID GEGGUS is professor of history, University of Florida.

Revolution came to be construed in the profound, but narrow, sense of freedom from slavery rather than as political rights.

Such a view of the Haitian Revolution, as the odd one out among liberal revolutions, is not inaccurate, but it is skewed by the tendency of recent scholarship to ignore the early stages of Saint Domingue's transformation—that part of the revolution that was largely internal to the colony's white population. The struggle for different degrees of political autonomy and economic liberalism 1789 to 1793 produced a substantial print archive but it has attracted remarkably few historians.

Although Saint Domingue had a weekly newspaper from 1764 onward, the revolution initiated a torrent of journalism that created thirty or more new periodicals between 1789 and 1803.[3] The best known but still barely studied segment of this revolutionary journalism is, curiously, that of the printers and polemicists who fled the colony to Philadelphia in the mid-1790s. There, radicals and conservatives continued their battles for several years in a new, refugee press.[4] It was also in the United States that the first histories of the revolution were published in 1794 and 1795.[5] Their authors were, again, refugee colonists and they ranged from the radical (Chotard *aîné*) to the ultra-conservative (Mahy de Cormeré).[6] The next two major histories published were also products of the refugee diaspora but appeared in

3. The claim of 'fifty or so' in Marie-Antoinette Menier, Gabriel Debien, 'Journaux de Saint-Domingue,' *Revue d'Histoire des Colonies* 127–28 (1949): 424–75, seems to result from counting slight changes of title.

4. Justin E. Cartera, *Bref Coup d'oeil sur les origines de la presse hatienne (1764–1850)*, (Port-au-Prince: Deschamps, 1986), 8; see Clarence S. Brigham, 'Cabon's History of Haiti Journalism,' *Proceedings of the American Antiquarian Society* 49 (1939): 121–205; Jean-Charles Benzaken, 'De Montauban au Cap Français: l'itinéraire du journaliste Gatereau pendant la Révolution française,' 126e Congrès national des sociétés historiques et scientifiques (Toulouse, 2001), thème 2, Structures politiques; introduction by Chris Bongie to Jean-Baptiste Picquenard, *Zoflora ou la bonne négresse: Anecdote coloniale* (Paris: L'Harmattan, 2006).

5. When the revolution was barely a year old, there appeared in the colonial press a prospectus for a spectacularly premature three-volume history, entitled *Relation historique de la Révolution de Saint-Domingue*. See *Affiches Américaines* (Cap-Français), September 15, 1790. It was never published.

6. Guillaume-François Mahy de Cormeré, *Histoire de la Révolution de la Partie Française de St. Domingue* (Baltimore, 1794); Chotard aîné, *Précis de la Révolution de Saint-Domingue, depuis la fin de 1789, jusqu'au 18 juin 1794* (Philadelphia: Parent, 1795).

France: the *Histoire des désastres de Saint-Domingue* and *Réflexions sur la colonie de Saint-Domingue*. Hardly any historian of the Haitian Revolution has read even one of these substantial works and—to give an idea how neglected this material is—the latter two books, both anonymously authored, have been bizarrely misidentified for the past one hundred and fifty years in the world's major bibliographies and library catalogues, which attribute them to two quite improbable figures (the botanist Descourtilz and the administrator Barbé-Marbois). They were clearly written, however, by one and the same person, an obscure Dominguan coffee planter.[7]

But to return to the colonial press: one consequence of the scholarly neglect of the revolutionary newspapers is a general ignorance of the parliamentary debates that they reported in Saint Domingue's two colonial assemblies. Each of these assemblies produced a stillborn constitution–in 1790 and 1792. This is key material for assessing the political ideas and intellectual affiliations of Saint Domingue's white revolution, its backward linkages to the Enlightenment, and also its forward connection to Toussaint Louverture's much better known constitution of 1801.

Prominent among the radical printer-journalists, was one Jean Baillio, who worked for different colonial assemblies and radical clubs and published a newspaper and several pamphlets in Saint Domingue and France. Although he initially opposed racial integration and slave emancipation, he was one of the few white Frenchmen to adopt Haitian citizenship after independence. In 1810, however, he moved to Venezuela, where he set up (as Juan Baillío) that country's second printing press. He published Venezuela's first constitution and, later, after returning from Haiti with Simón Bolívar, the first slave emancipation laws.[8]

---

7. He appears to have been a member of the Rotureau family of Limbé parish.
8. Paul Verna, 'Tras las huellas de Juan Baillío, el impresor de la Independencia,' *Boletín Histórico* (Caracas) 10 (1966): 5–32; Verna, *Bolívar y los emigrados patriotas* (Caracas: INCE, 1983), 87–88.

These initial comments are intended to suggest two points. First, Saint Domingue's white settler revolution, sandwiched geographically and chronologically between those of North and South America, had a strong Atlantic dimension. Secondly, before that revolution can be adequately situated in that context, historians need to pay much more attention to its newspapers and parliamentary debates, its participant histories and constitutions.

But what of the *real* Haitian Revolution? What role did print culture play in the black revolution that quickly overshadowed, then obliterated, that of Saint Domingue's whites?

The free people of color, who made up an economically and demographically important middle sector in Saint Domingue society, were at least half as likely as white colonists to be able to sign their name.[9] They produced no journalists or historians during the revolution, but they authored many pamphlets and other political texts, including the declaration of independence.[10] The vast majority of slaves, in contrast, more than half of whom were Africans, was neither literate nor spoke a written language.[11] A few insurgents were described as carrying amulets that contained Arabic phrases written on folded paper, but Muslims formed a very small proportion of the Africans in Saint Domingue.[12]

9. John D. Garrigus, *Before Haiti: Race and Citizenship in French Saint-Domingue* (New York: Palgrave Macmillan, 2006), 125. The claim that most free men of color could read, although most slaves could not, seems considerably exaggerated ([Jean-Félix] Carteau, *Soirées bermudiennes ou entretiens sur les événemens qui ont opéré la ruine de la partie française de l'île Saint-Domingue* [Bordeaux: Pellier-Lawalle, 1802], 76). Several studies show that, of those who used the services of a notary—an atypically wealthy subgroup—only about half could sign their name.

10. The *Mémoires pour servir à l'histoire d'Haïti* (1804; Port-au-Prince: Editions des Antilles, 1991), a brief, polemical account of the campaign of 1802–3 by the declaration's author, Louis Félix Boisrond-Tonnerre, is the only text close to being a history.

11. Jean Fouchard's pioneering *Les marrons du syllabaire* (Port-au-Prince: Deschamps, 1953) is not very successful in its challenge to this viewpoint. With the exception of Hausa, written in an Arabic-derived script, there seems to be no hard evidence that West Africa produced indigenous scripts before 1800.

12. Correspondence March/April 1792, F3/97, Centre des Archives d'Outre-mer, Aix-en-Provence (hereafter CAOM); [Charles] Malenfant, *Des colonies et particulièrement de celle de Saint-Domingue* (Paris: Audibert, 1814), 212. On the slave population's ethnic composition, see D. Geggus, 'Sugar and Coffee Cultivation in Saint Domingue and the Shaping of the Slave Labor Force,' in *Cultivation and Culture: Labor and the Shaping of Slave Life in the Americas*, ed. Ira Berlin, and Philip Morgan (Charlottesville: University Press of Virginia, 1993), 73–98.

The lingua franca of the slave population and—one may guess, of the free nonwhite population—was *créole*. As Haitian creole could not be termed a written language until the mid-twentieth century, it is notable that in 1793 and 1802 government officials attempting to run the colony printed a series of proclamations in creole that were intended to be read out to the black population. They mostly concerned the regulation of plantation labor, before and after the ending of slavery, and included the act of emancipation.[13]

Curiously, although these proclamations are linguistically almost unique, more may have been printed in creole during the revolution than was written longhand. In the surviving manuscripts of the period creole was generally used just for brief excerpts of reported speech.[14] When rebel slave leaders corresponded with one another—and a good deal of their correspondence has survived—it was always in French. Such letters were probably dictated in creole but were invariably written down, by a free colored or white secretary, in some approximation of standard French.

This near-absence of creole from the written and printed record impoverishes our knowledge of the Haitian Revolution. Before the declaration of independence was read out on January 1, 1804, we know that Jean-Jacques Dessalines made a speech, but we don't know much about what he said. Contemporaries of Toussaint Louverture described him as a gifted orator in creole, and in the Fon language of his ancestors, but we have no way of sensing those abilities except in his French letters, which were almost all collaborations between him and his white secretaries.

13. Two are reproduced in Jean Bernabé, 'Les proclamations en créole de Sonthonax et Bonaparte: graphie, histoire et glottopolitique,' in *De la Révolution française aux révolutions créoles et nègres*, ed. Michel Martin and Alain Yacou (Paris: Editions Caribéennes, 1989), 135–50.

14. However, a rare petition in creole by ex-slaves is included in *Arrêtés des différentes communes de la colonie de St. Domingue, adressées à l'Agent particulier du Directoire au Général en chef et à l'Administration municipale du Cap* (N.p., 1799), 19. It is cited by Malick Ghachem in 'The Colonial Vendée,' unpublished paper, John Carter Brown Library Conference, June 2004.

Spoken in unwritten languages, much of the voice of the black revolution is as irrecoverable as the talking drum messages that accompanied the outbreak of the slave uprising.

Nevertheless, both printed and written texts played a significant part in the slave revolution, but it is worth remembering that whether producing texts or reacting to them, preliterate Creole speakers had to rely on literate Francophone intermediaries. For the latter reason, it is difficult to accord too much importance to supposedly inspirational texts. In the fall of 1789, administrators in Saint Domingue complained of the circulation of antislavery books in the colony and feared that free people of color were sharing their contents with slaves. Similar complaints came from Martinique and Jamaica at the same time however.[15] And news of the nascent abolitionism in England and France, as of the French Revolution, circulated independently of its texts. Slaves spoke with new arrivals from Europe and overheard the heated discussions of angry colonists.

A similar case is presented by the abbé Grégoire's incendiary pamphlet *Lettre aux citoyens de couleur*, which predicted an end to slavery and arrived in Saint Domingue the month before the August 1791 uprising.[16] It was widely discussed by colonists and, when the revolt broke out, was blamed for causing the insurgents' mistaken belief that a royal emancipation decree was being covered up by the planters.[17] Grégoire's pamphlet doubtless helped encourage such rumors, but these had a wide variety of sources (in recent political and legislative events) and had been circulating for years. Moreover, a prominent subset of these rumors—that slaves had been granted three free days per week—

15. David Geggus, 'Slavery, War, and Revolution in the Greater Caribbean, 1789–1815,' in *A Turbulent Time: The French Revolution and the Greater Caribbean*, ed. D. B. Gaspar and D. P. Geggus (Bloomington: Indiana University Press, 1997), 36, n.39.

16. Henri-Baptiste Grégoire, *Lettre aux citoyens de couleur et nègres libres de Saint-Domingue* (Paris: Imp. du Patriote François, 1791). His *Mémoire en faveur des gens de couleur ou sang-mêlés de St.-Domingue, et des autres isles françaises de l'Amérique* (Paris: Belin, 1789) was rather more inflammatory.

17. F3/196, f. 527, 859, CAOM; *Supplément au mémoire de M. de Blanchelande* (n.p., n.d.), 8; WO 1/58, f. 1–11, Public Record Office, London.

has proved difficult to connect with any publication, although it spread across the Caribbean and survived for decades.[18]

Finally, there is an oft-told story about the black freedman Toussaint Louverture. Toussaint, who may have secretly been the mastermind behind the slave uprising, supposedly had read, long before, in Raynal's *Histoire des deux mondes*, Diderot's passage that rhetorically called for a black Spartacus to arise in the Caribbean. This story originated in what might be called a press interview that Toussaint gave at the height of his power. It is perhaps a propaganda piece, intended to shape the black leader's image for the French public. Yet the story is also quite plausible, given the ubiquity of Raynal's book, especially as the account has Toussaint hearing about the passage several times before seeking out a copy to read.[19] It seems unlikely, however, that this experience was a major influence in shaping the black leader's destiny.

Another story told in all histories of the Haitian Revolution concerns a secret meeting at which the slave revolt was planned. Supposedly reading aloud from newspapers, a light-skinned young man announced that the king had accorded three free days per week to the slaves.[20] The alleged presence of the printed text (glossed implausibly in many accounts as a 'forged gazette') is an important clue that at least this manifestation of the emancipation-decree rumor was not simply a matter of confusion but involved deliberate manipulation by the slaves' leaders. False rumors of various sorts had flourished since the start of the revolution, favored by slow transatlantic communications, illiteracy, and wishful thinking. False rumors of new decrees were in fact becoming something of a trend at that point,

18. Geggus, 'Slavery, War, and Revolution in the Greater Caribbean, 1789–1815,' 7–11 n. 37, n.47, and n. 48.

19. *Le Moniteur* (Paris) (1799): 585 bis. Jean-Félix Carteau (*Soirees bermudiennes,* 76) claimed in 1802 he had seen the works of Raynal and Hilliard d'Auberteuil in the hands of some blacks who had secretly bought them from sailors, especially abolitionist Bordeaux sea captains.

20. The original source is 'Extraits des détails authentiques apportés par les 6 Crs. du Cap,' F3/197, CAOM.

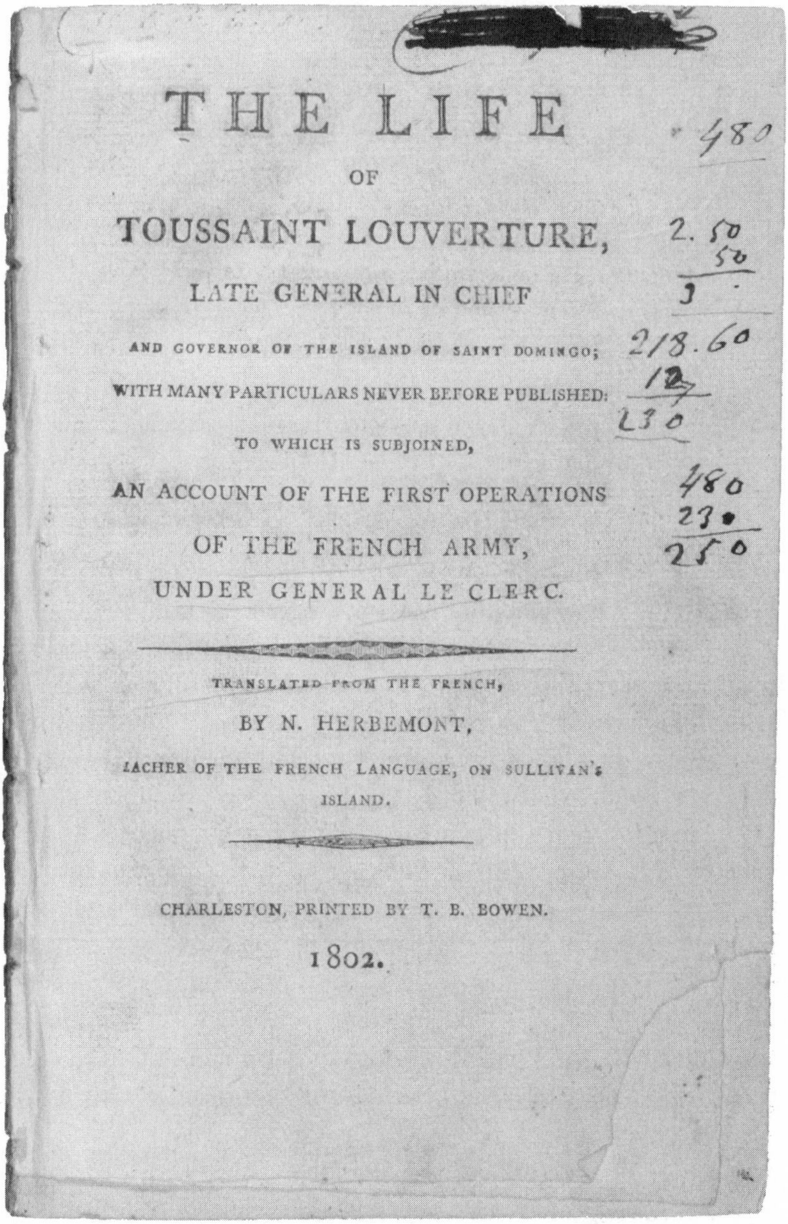

THE LIFE

OF

TOUSSAINT LOUVERTURE,

LATE GENERAL IN CHIEF

AND GOVERNOR OF THE ISLAND OF SAINT DOMINGO;

WITH MANY PARTICULARS NEVER BEFORE PUBLISHED:

TO WHICH IS SUBJOINED,

AN ACCOUNT OF THE FIRST OPERATIONS

OF THE FRENCH ARMY,

UNDER GENERAL LE CLERC.

TRANSLATED FROM THE FRENCH,

BY N. HERBEMONT,

TEACHER OF THE FRENCH LANGUAGE, ON SULLIVAN'S ISLAND.

CHARLESTON, PRINTED BY T. B. BOWEN.

1802.

Fig. 1. Dubroca's *La Vie de Toussaint-Louverture* was hastily translated into English by N. Herbemont, and published as *The Life of Toussaint Louverture, late General in Chief and Governor of the Island of Saint Domingo with Many Particulars Never Before Published* (Charleston [S. C.]: T. B. Bowen, 1802).

though mainly among the white community, where they had fueled violent altercations between radicals and conservatives and between troops and their officers.[21]

It is not clear if forged documents were used to support any of these rumors, but one striking case of a false document used in the slave uprising is the so-called royalist commission of Toussaint Louverture. This was a handwritten warrant seemingly signed by a miscellany of white royalists, which authorized Toussaint to organize a slave uprising on behalf of the counterrevolution. To judge from a Spanish translation, which survives in Spain, this document was a naïve and clumsy fraud. Whether it was really used by Toussaint, or was part of a false claim made about him by some of his collaborators, remains a mystery.[22] Yet there is good reason to believe that Toussaint had earlier propagated the rumor of a counterrevolutionary plot so as to divide his white opponents. The best documentary evidence for this royalist conspiracy, a captivity narrative published by a white radical named Gros, largely rests on its account of a supposed meeting that was not witnessed by Gros but merely described to him by Toussaint shortly before Gros's release.[23]

In the recollections of one black insurgent, recorded decades later by a Haitian historian, Toussaint's royalist commission was a sort of passport that had allowed him to circulate freely.[24] Passports certainly were used in the rebel camps after the uprising broke out; one that survives bears a cryptic acronym and the

21. The Port-au-Prince Regiment mutinied in March partly because of a rumored 'decree of December 17' that supposedly retracted the National Assembly's support for its colonel. In June/July, talk about a decree that made officers and soldiers equals created uproar at Môle Saint Nicolas.

22. David Geggus, 'Toussaint Louverture: avant et après le soulèvement de 1791,' in *Mémoire de révolution d'esclaves à Saint-Domingue*, ed. Franklin Midi (Montreal: CIDHICA, 2006), 113–29; a second, expanded edition is forthcoming.

23. David Geggus, 'Toussant Louverture and the Haitian Revolution,' forthcoming in *Profiles of Revolutionaries on Both Sides of the Atlantic: 1750–1850*, ed. R. William Weisberger (New York: Columbia University Press, 2007), note 19.

24. Beaubrun Ardouin, *Études sur l'histoire d'Haïti* (1853–60; Port-au-Prince: Dalencour, 1958), 1:51.

25. See above, note 20.

phrases 'The iron rod is broken. Long live the king!'[25] These safe-conduct passes, which doubtless grew out of the pass-system used by Saint Domingue slaveowners, seem to reflect a fetishization of the written word and 'ritualistic use of bureaucratic mannerisms,' such as later found in twentieth-century African protest movements and the passports of modern Haiti's secret societies.[26]

Several of the themes just touched upon—falsified documents, rumor and written sources, the use of free colored scribes by illiterate slave leaders—are central to the key issue of uncovering the intentions of the black insurgents. For the first year of the slave uprising, historians working in the archives confront a diverse range of reports of what different groups of insurgents supposedly claimed to want. Some called for freedom, land, and the expulsion of the whites; others for only modest reforms, such as extra free days per week. Some mentioned the Rights of Man; others advocated restoring the king to his throne. While we might expect aspirations to have varied in a movement of many thousands, and to have been adjusted according to changing circumstances, it is troubling that it was usually white radical observers who depicted the slave insurrection as a tool of the counterrevolution and conservatives who saw in it the influence of radical ideology.

Representations of the black revolution are thus not only distorted by the usual ethnic and class biases of white observers, but filtered through the bitter conflicts of French Revolutionary politics. Documents generated by the slave rebels themselves are thus of great importance, but they, too, regrettably are not entirely free of these problems. There are three main examples to consider.

Two are proclamations, ostensibly by the slave leadership that their white recipients quickly had printed. They are in fact the

26. Wyatt MacGaffey, John M. Janzen, *An Anthology of Kongo Religion: Primary Texts from Lower Zaïre* (Lawrence: University of Kansas Press, 1974), 13 (quotation), 136; Jean Kerboull, *Vaudou et pratiques magiques* (Paris: Belfond, 1977), photograph of modern passports between pages 32 and 33.

only formal demands for a complete end to slavery that were made during the slave revolution. The first, which dates from the first month of the uprising, is often cited. It is a powerful text that summons the whites to pick up their jewelry and leave Saint Domingue to the slaves, whose sweat and blood have earned them title to the land. Because of the anonymous text's stylish prose, it has generally been assumed that the author was a white prisoner of the insurgents and probably the radical cleric Jacques Delahaye. The writer was in fact, another captive, an obscure French butcher named Claude Boisbrun. The text, though, was dictated to him by the free colored secretary of the sadistic slave leader Jeannot.[27] Long depicted as a unidimensional monster, Jeannot's military and political importance have gone unrecognized. Since he was also behind the 'Médecin-Général' letters traditionally attributed to Toussaint Louverture, this document provides another reason for learning more about his secretary, who seems to have been the free black Jean-Baptiste Godard.[28]

The second of the insurgents' proclamations dates from July 1792. It was signed by the two main slave leaders, Jean-François and Georges Biassou, but exists only in printed versions. These were made by a radical sympathizer of the slaves in Paris, as well as by the document's supposed recipient, Colonel Cambefort, who headed the military campaign against the insurgents.[29] Whereas the first proclamation was mildly royalist in coloring, the second one is imbued with radical ideology. The language of the text has a suspiciously inauthentic look. Its combination of sophisticated vocabulary and rhetoric with simplistic errors of

27. See Delaval to Assemblée du Sud, September 29, 1791, 1ETA34, Archives départementales de la Loire-Inférieure, Nantes; deposition of Claude Boisbrun, F3/197, CAOM. The proclamation, written September 24, has long been misdated because of a transcription error.

28. See Geggus, 'Toussaint Louverture and the Haitian Revolution,' note 13.

29. [Joseph-Paul-Augustin de] Cambefort, *Quatrième partie du Mémoire justificatif* (Paris, 1793), 4–11. The proclamation has a third signatory, 'Belair'—not Charles Belair, as sometimes thought, but Gabriel Aimé Bellair, an officer of Biassou. The sympathizer was Claude Milscent, who published the piece in his newspaper *Le Créole Patriote*, February 9, 1793.

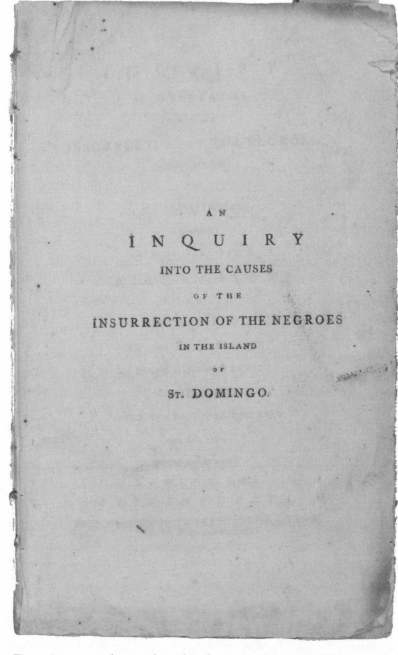

AN

INQUIRY

INTO THE CAUSES

OF THE

INSURRECTION OF THE NEGROES

IN THE ISLAND

OF

ST. DOMINGO.

Fig. 2. A report and a speech read to the National Assembly, February 29, 1792, was published in Philadelphia later that year. *An Inquiry into the Causes of the Insurrection of the Negroes in the Island of St. Domingo* (London; reprint Philadelphia: Joseph Crukshank, 1792).

spelling and grammar makes it unlike any other surviving text from this milieu. It was probably a fraud, concocted by the royalist de Cambefort. He was then the target of increasingly frequent charges of counterrevolutionary influence on the slave revolt. The letter was thus a means of striking back at the radicals.

This cuts in half the documentary evidence of formal demands for abolishing slavery made by the insurgents, and it means that none came from the main leaders, Jean-François and Georges Biassou, who executed their rival Jeannot and are perhaps best known for the abortive peace negotiations they undertook in mid-December 1791. Facing the imminent arrival of troops from France, they offered to help force their followers back to work on the plantations in return for an improvement in working conditions and the freeing of just fifty slave leaders. The correspondence associated with these negotiations constitutes the third case of documentation generated by the slave rebels. This material raises a thicket of issues, but the two points I would like to highlight concern its authorship and the difference between the original manuscripts and the versions printed by the colonists.[30]

The versions reported by the colonists have numerous inaccuracies but the most egregious distortion is the inclusion in the written overtures of a demand for freeing just fifty people.[31] This demand was made, but orally and in secret. The colonists evidently put it in the newspaper to increase friction between the creole slave leaders and their mainly African followers. In this they succeeded explaining why the negotiations were broken off.

As for the authorship of these documents, they have a curiously hybrid, 'them and us' character. They were not just written by

---

30. The precise dating of the process remains problematic. Clearly erroneous is the placing of the overtures in October in John Thornton, *Africa and Africans in the Formation of the Atlantic World, 1400–1680* (Cambridge: Cambridge Univesrity Press, 1992), 333–34.

31. *Moniteur Colonial* (Cap Français) 35, December 19, 1791; Augustin Brulley and Pierre-François Page, *Courte réponse . . . au Précis de justification de Paul-Augustin de Cambefort* (Paris, 1793); J.A. Marie Albert, *Des véritables causes qui ont amené la ruine de la colonie de Saint-Domingue* (Paris: Dentu, 1815), 21–26. Most of the originals are in Dxxv/1/4, Archives Nationales, Paris.

free men of color on behalf of the slave generals, but by the free coloreds in the rebel camp, who were discreetly negotiating for themselves as well as for the slave leadership. The government had just offered amnesty to free men of color, but not to slaves, and free coloreds elsewhere in the colony had just won acceptance of their demand for political rights. This is what the most sophisticated passages in the overtures allude to and that has most impressed historians because of the precise references to recent legislation. Addressing the concerns of the free men in the rebel camp, they do not really support the contention of certain historians that the slave leaders demanded 'full political rights.'[32]

We are a long way from the language of rights in these documents signed by Jean-François and Georges Biassou, which represent the insurgents as misguided victims of manipulation and their own royalist zeal. Demands for a limited reform of slavery, as Laurent Dubois observes, were not prominent in these overtures, and they took form only as the negotiations progressed, doubtless in response to pressure from the rank-and-file insurgents.[33] The slave leaders wanted not citizenship, but amnesty for their followers and freedom for themselves and their families to keep their booty and settle elsewhere. They had already put forward these demands in late November, when they were ignored, and Jean-François, with Toussaint, would repeat them the following summer.[34] They achieved their aim several years later, when Jean-François settled in Spain and Biassou in Florida. By then the French had abolished slavery, and the black revolution had come under the leadership of the freedman Toussaint Louverture.

32. Robin Blackburn, *The Overthrow of Colonial Slavery* (London: Verso, 1988), 194 (quotation); C.L.R. *The Black Jacobins: Toussaint L'Ouverture and the San Domingo Revolution* (1938; 3rd ed., London: Alison and Busby, 1980), 105–6.

33. Laurent Dubois, *Avengers of the New World: The Story of the Haitian Revolution* (Cambridge: Harvard University Press), 128.

34. Both of these approaches have been overlooked in the historical literature. See document 258, Dxxv/46/439, Archives Nationales; D. Geggus, 'Toussaint Louverture et l'abolition de l'esclavage à Saint-Domingue,' in *Les abolitions dans les Amériques*, ed. Liliane Chauleau (Fort de France: Société des Amis des Archives, 2001), 109–16.

If the print archive of the white revolution is large but little studied, that of the slave revolution of 1791–93 is small, superficially more familiar, but insufficiently problematized. Moreover, the written record gives voice solely to the slaves' leaders; to divine the aspirations of their followers we have only a few reports of their spoken words and their actions.

The closing stages of the Haitian Revolution have also given rise to a number of historical questions that involve issues of oral and written transmission. One concerns Napoleon Bonaparte's decision to attempt to restore slavery in Saint Domingue in 1802. Some historians think that decision was not taken until several months after an expeditionary force was sent to reassert metropolitan control and that the troops expected only to oust blacks from positions of power but not reenslave them. Others believe the decision was taken (secretly) long before, despite many government pronouncements to the contrary, and that at least the French commander, Leclerc, and perhaps his fellow officers, were aware of the policy they were meant to carry out.[35] As Bonaparte's written instructions to Leclerc clearly support the former position, proponents of the latter thesis argue that the government's true intentions must have been transmitted orally.[36] Since the instructions were secret, however, and already contained plenty of inflammatory material, it is not evident why such concealment should have been necessary. Leclerc's correspondence with Bonaparte offers no conclusive proof but, although ambiguous, on balance is suggestive of a prior oral understanding.[37]

35. D. Geggus, 'French Imperialism and the Louisiana Purchase,' in *The Louisiana Purchase and Its Peoples: Perspectives from the New Orleans Conference*, ed. Paul Hoffman (Lafayette: University of Louisiana, 2004), 30; Thomas Ott, *The Haitian Revolution* (Knoxville: University of Tennessee Press, 1973), 184–85.

36. The instructions are printed in Gustav Roloff, *Die Kolonialpolitik Napoleons I* (Munich: Oldenbourg, 1899), 244–54.

37. See Paul Roussier, ed., *Lettres du Général Leclerc, commandant en chef de l'armée de Saint-Domingue en 1802* (Paris: Société de l'Histoire de Colonies Françaises, 1937) 202, 206, 208. For the editor's (contrary) opinion, see p. 33.

HISTORY
OF THE
REVOLUTIONS OF HAYTI.

BY M. SAINT AMAND,
Advocate, former Member of the Constitutional
Assembly of Hayti.

Preface.

Translated expressly for The Pine and Palm.

The History of the Revolutions in Hayti will be published in four volumes. The first, which I offer to the public, includes the period from 1789 to 1792: consists of the white colonists among themselves: revolutionary committees: provincial and colonial assemblies: insurrections of men of color, and of the blacks.

It is currently understood by Frenchmen that St. Domingo, or Hayti, once belonged to France; but with the exception of a few men of learning, general ignorance prevails as to the causes which induced the loss, to France, of that fine country, the richest and oldest of her trans-marine possessions. We shall confine ourselves, particularly in this first volume, to an investigation and statement as to what were the cause and who the authors of the ruin of that colony. The three other volumes will be published successively during the course of the year 1860. They will comprise:

Volume II.—The period from 1792 to 1800; French, civil commissions, and the wars of Independence.

Volume III.—The period from 1800 to 1818; Dessalines, emperor; Christophe, king; Pétion, president.

Volume IV.—The period from 1818 to 1859; J. P. Boyer, president; Revolution of 1843; Hérard Rivière, Pierrot, and Riché, presidents in succession; their downfall, or their death; revolutions; Faustin Soulouque, president and emperor; Revolution of 1859; his downfall.

I have borrowed the statement of nearly all the incidents narrated in this first volume from the official report made to the National Convention of France, by Deputy Garran de Coulon. That rare work is the completest and most impartial of the contemporary accounts of those times of anarchy and confusion.

I have preferred, upon examination, to draw from that source rather than refer to oral traditions nearly always erroneous, even when neither fabricated nor distorted by partisan passion, or hate. The excellent work of my fellow-countryman and friend, Mr. B. Ardouin—Studies on the History of Hayti—has been of great service to me. It is a remarkable work of assured success.

J. SAINT AMAND.

History.

We know that in the midst of the archipelago of the Antilles, between Cuba, or Havana, Porto Rico and Jamaica, rises a large island discovered by Christopher Columbus, towards the end of the fifteenth century; that this daring navigator and his companions called it Hispaniola in memory of their country; and that, in the course of time, custom bestowed upon the island the name of its capital—St. Domingo, or Santo Domingo.

The territory of the island was divided into two colonies, one of which belonged to France and the other to Spain; and they were commonly distinguished by the double appellation — the French part and the Spanish part of St. Domingo. At the present time the island belongs neither to France nor to Spain; its actual possessors, negroes and mulattoes, have restored to its original title, that which the Indians, its first inhabitants, gave to it—Hayti. Reunited in 1823 under the same laws, these two parts formed one State, the Republic of Hayti, under the presidency of Gen. Boyer. But in 1843, in the midst of the disorder arising out of the revolution which deposed that ruler, a new separation was violently effected; the old French part remained the Republic of Hayti, and the old Spanish portion formed a second commonwealth—the Republic of Dominica.

No natural division separates the French and Spanish parts; the separation is defined by the two seats of government, the difference of the nationalities, and the rivalry of the former masters. But should not the common origin of its possessors, of itself, be at this time, a sufficient motive for obliterating this division, at variance with the geographical configuration of the island, and which is as impolitic as it is injurious to the prosperity of the two young Republics?

This anomalous division is but a sad legacy of that abominable rule whose last traces the Haytians should apply themselves to efface. Their independence has surely nothing more to fear either from France or Spain; these two powers have solemnly recognised it; but not far from the shores of their island dwell covetous and invading neighbors, whose corrupting genius is more to be feared, perhaps, than the power of their arms. These dangerous neighbors have substituted annexation for conquest; this new method though less violent, is not less absorbing than conquest—and these neighbors are slaveholders. Civil strife has ever been the cause of the greatest misfortunes and of the ruin of nations. It is in union and harmony that the weak find the strength necessary to resist their enemies.

If the French colonists had not been disunited by civil dissensions, France, probably, would not have lost her finest colony; if the men of color and the blacks had not formed a union they would not have achieved liberty and independence. The events which we are about to narrate afford proof of these truisms. Let Haytians then profit by the teachings which flow from them; where will they find better? it is their history.

II.

In 1789 the French part of St. Domingo was the richest and the most flourishing of all th) colonies of France; it was the Queen of the Antilles. Its territory embracing a surface of about 6,000 square miles* was divided into three provinces, that of the North, that of the Centre, or the West, and that of the South.

The province of the North containing 1440 square miles had for its capital the city of the Cape. It was the smallest and the richest of the three provinces; it comprised twenty-six parishes, distributed into three seneschalates.

That of the Centre, or the West, 2,418 square miles in extent, having Port-au-Prince for its capital, comprised six parishes, divided into four seneschalates.

And that of the South, of 2,100 square miles, capital the city of Cayes, contains only eleven parishes, arranged in three seneschalates. Three seneschalates had their seats in the North: at Fort Dauphin, at Cape Francis, and at Port-de-Paix. In the West: at Port-au-Prince, at St. Mark, at Petit Goâve and at Jeremie. And in the South: at the Cayes, at St. Louis, and at Jacmel.

These three provinces constitute about two-fifths of the island; the remainder comprises the Spanish part, 9,600 square miles. Many small islands surround the island of Hayti and are dependent on it such as la Fortue, the most important, la Gonâve, la Béate, those of la Saône, St. Catharine, Alta Vela, a Vaches, and the Caymites.

Hayti, in the language of its Aborigines, means mountainous land; and in reality it is traversed in every direction by mountain ranges, the chief of which are Cibao, Selle, Bahoruco and Hotte. Nearly all these mountains are covered with a magnificent vegetation, and between them lie valleys and plains of extraordinary fertility.

The Suna, the Grand-Yague, the Artibonite, the Neybe, and the Ozama, are as many rivers whose fructifying waters perpetually contribute to a fertility to which the soil of Europe affords no comparison.

In order to form some idea of the prosperity of the French part of St. Domingo at the period of its possession by France, we must consult the official returns published at the beginning of the year 1789, by Mr. Barbé de Marbois, at that time intendant of revenues in the Colony. It will be found that the

* The Spanish part contains 9,600 square miles.

Fig. 3. A page from a bound volume of newspaper clippings about Haiti compiled by the Reverend John Weiss and in the collections of the American Antiquarian Society. Included are accounts of Jean Amand Lacaste's *History of the Revolutions of Hayti* and other texts.

Another issue concerns the naming of Haiti, and why a population of African descent should choose an Amerindian place name that had fallen out of use three centuries earlier. Some romantic nationalists have related the choice to the supposed survival of an Amerindian population, or at least an Amerindian cultural influence, in Saint Domingue into the late colonial period. All the evidence suggests, however, that the Taino place name was preserved in scholarly and travel literature and that it was first suggested as a replacement for 'Saint Domingue' by a French writer in 1788. It may have been popularized among the colony's free people of color in 1800, when many of their leaders were exiled to France, where they could have encountered it in *Zoflora*, one of the first novels written about the Haitian Revolution. Free colored officers made up a large proportion of the thirty-seven men who signed the declaration of independence, in which the new country was first named on January 1, 1804.[38]

Leslie Manigat has recently shown that that document was in fact the country's second declaration of independence.[39] An earlier text, dated November 29, 1803, and declared a fake by the country's first historian Thomas Madiou, turns out to have been genuine, although inconsequential. The January 1 document, penned by Paris-educated Louis Félix Boisrond-Tonnerre, is well known for its unorthodox French usage, in which the writer apparently expressed his disdain for the colonizer's language. It is well known, too, for openly inciting vengeance for past wrongs against the several thousand French who remained in the former colony. Since the declaration was a prelude to the massacres of February–April 1804 that systematically eliminated almost all of that population, it is surprising so many French chose to remain after it had been read out on the main square in Gonaïves on the

38. See D. Geggus, *Haitian Revolutionary Studies* (Bloomington: Indiana University Press, 1983), ch. 13.

39. Leslie Manigat, 'Une brève analyse-commentaire critique d'un document historique,' *Revue de la Société haïtienne d'histoire et de géographie*, 221 (2005):44–56.

first day of independence. Probably very few whites were present on that occasion to hear its call for revenge,[40] and its publication was presumably delayed until the massacres were completed.

40. One was Pierre Nicolas Mallet, the document's only white signatory, who was an early victim of the massacres. Gonaïves seems to have been a center of black power after the massacre there of some one hundred and fifty colonists in April 1794.

The Abbé Grégoire and the Atlantic Republic of Letters

ALYSSA GOLDSTEIN SEPINWALL

I N 1806 THE FRENCH revolutionary and priest Henri Grégoire wrote to his American friends Ruth and Joel Barlow, who had formerly lived in Paris, of his eternal friendship for them: 'Friendship traverses the seas and we are often in spirit in Washington City. Oh, if you only knew how many times and with what tender emotion we speak of you and Mr. Barlow! Why are you so far away? Will the heavens allow us to see you again?'[1]

Little did he guess that within a few years, a poem would tear his friendship with the Barlows apart. In 1807 Barlow published his opus *The Columbiad*, and Grégoire was stunned by its contents. The poem's republicanism did not offend Grégoire, one of the earliest French revolutionaries to support eliminating the monarchy. Nor did its abolitionist message, since opposition to slavery had long united the two men. Nor was Grégoire bothered in the least by the poem's vision of an America on the rise, ready to overtake Europe. On the contrary, by the early nineteenth century, Grégoire was dismayed by the fate of republicanism in Europe and pinned many of his hopes for the future of humanity on the New World. One passage in the poem, however—in which

---

1. Grégoire to Ruth Barlow, August 17, 1806, Barlow Papers, bMS AM 1448, Houghton Library, Harvard University, fol. 605. Cited by permission of the Houghton Library, Harvard University.

ALYSSA GOLDSTEIN SEPINWALL is associate professor of history, California State University–San Marcos.

Barlow attacked the Catholic Church—sparked a rift that would never heal.

Atlantic friendships were particularly important for Grégoire in the early nineteenth century because of his disillusionment with a France returned to monarchy. A Catholic priest and active Jacobin, Grégoire had been elated by the progress of the French Revolution; he saw its ideals of liberty, equality, and fraternity as identical to those of the Gospels. Radical dechristianization ultimately disillusioned him, however—and the ascent of Napoleon and the return of the Bourbons would further cement his frustration with his homeland. Unlike the majority of other former revolutionaries, who abandoned their republican hopes, Grégoire passionately retained his. He hoped, however, for the emergence of a more moderate, and religiously and racially plural, republicanism, which could blossom in the New World and then be reimported to Europe.

To Grégoire, the Americas represented a world of uncorrupted possibilities. He particularly admired the United States, which had sparked the modern republican trend, and Haiti, where people of African descent had overthrown slavery. He also supported would-be republicans in Latin America. He knew, however, that a new republic was a shaky proposition; many revolutions had crumbled, turning back to monarchy or toward military dictators. For Grégoire, Americans' ability to avoid these pitfalls would be crucial to the future of republicanism worldwide. As a veteran of the French Revolution's failure, Grégoire felt he had valuable lessons to impart. From the late 1790s until his death in 1831, he corresponded with a varied set of New World residents, from North American and Haitian statesmen to Mexican priests. He also established personal relationships with New World republicans who visited him in Paris.

Grégoire was thus an important focal point in an Atlantic republican republic of letters, even without leaving Europe. This network blossomed in the early nineteenth century, as republicans around the Atlantic eagerly sought relationships with one another. Nevertheless, the Atlantic republic of letters was fragile and sometimes contentious. In practical terms, transoceanic correspondence was threatened by the Napoleonic Wars, and letter-writers could go years without knowing whether a correspondent was irate over something they had written, or whether letters were simply not getting through. More importantly, views of republicanism around the Atlantic were not always the same, and Grégoire would discover that New World republicans were not always as eager to correspond with him as he was with them. His disagreements with them often centered on two topics: slavery and religion. His dealings with Thomas Jefferson—and his disagreement with Joel Barlow over the *Columbiad*—would be emblematic of his admiration for and frustration with American republicans. Similarly, the rise and fall of his relations with Haitian leaders reveal the tensions inherent in Atlantic relationships in which each party had separate needs and interests.

Grégoire monitored republican movements in Latin America with a great deal of interest. He had personal relationships with figures in Mexico, Colombia, Guatemala, and Brazil, and was excited about the progress of Latin American colonies toward independence. As an 1823 review he wrote in the *Revue encyclopédique* indicates, Grégoire very much supported the efforts of Simon Bolívar to break free of Spain and create an independent Gran Colombia. As he argued passionately in the review, Spain should have 'recognized the independence of its American colonies, which have an imprescriptible right to this independence, having reached, so to speak, their political puberty.' He argued that those in Europe must not ignore others half a world away: 'all peoples must, more than ever, recognize that solidarity requires them to make a sweet exchange of affection with each other, to extend fraternal helping hands to one another.'[2]

2. [Grégoire], 'Notice critique sur l'ouvrage: La Bibliotheca columbiana,' *Revue encyclopédique* 18 (avril 1823): 107–8. For additional discussion of and references on Grégoire's interest in Latin America and the Americas in general, see Alyssa Goldstein Sepinwall, *The Abbé Grégoire and the French Revolution: The Making of Modern Universalism* (Berkeley: University of California Press, 2005), esp. ch. 7 from which some of the material in this essay is drawn (permission granted by the Regents of the University of California/University of California Press).

Grégoire also kept an eye on the status of Catholicism in Latin America, monitoring writings in Mexico for example, to see if conservative or Gallican (republican-leaning) Catholics would predominate. He was particularly worried about the 'masses of obscene and impious books' being sent to Mexico by other Frenchmen, which 'can only corrupt minds and hearts.' In addition, he tried to remain up-to-date on the status of indigenous peoples in Spanish America. He blasted Spain for not letting Amerindians 'develop their natural talents' and denounced Spanish missionaries for not permitting the ordination of indigenous priests. [3]

Most importantly, Grégoire monitored the progress of the abolitionist movement in Latin America and the Caribbean and hoped that countries in these regions would soon 'occupy themselves seriously with freeing the slaves.' He tracked the attempts of the newly established republic of Colombia to abolish slavery and approved of them heartily as a way of heading off violence: 'the measures taken by the republic of Colombia are very wise. Justice and prudence dictated them. May Heaven grant that the same will happen elsewhere, in order to avoid the deplorable catastrophes which, sooner or later, will arise from prolonging the tyranny against Africans.'[4]

Grégoire's interest in Latin America was reciprocated, and he had a steady stream of visitors. For example, when Fray Servando Teresa de Mier, a central figure in the Mexican independence movement, escaped Spanish imprisonment in 1801, he fled to France, where Grégoire welcomed him and became his 'French mentor.' Other founders of Mexico invoked Grégoire's work as they sought to reconcile the competing claims of church and state.[5]

3. [Grégoire], 'Notice critique sur l'ouvrage: La Bibliotheca columbiana,' 108; and Grégoire to [Trognon], September 30, 1825, Bibliothèque Abbé-Grégoire, Blois, France, ms. 870.

4. Grégoire to Verplanck, May 17, 1823, New-York Historical Society, Gulian Verplanck Papers, Box #4, Folder G, fol. 69, p. 2; see also Grégoire to Thomas Clarkson, May 13, 1823, Clarkson Papers, CN 103, Henry Huntington Library.

5. D. A. Brading, *The First America: The Spanish Monarchy, Creole Patriots, and the Liberal State, 1492–1867* (New York: Cambridge University Press, 1991), 585–90; and letters

Grégoire's writings could spark controversy, though, among Latin American writers. His *Apologie de Barthélemy de Las-Casas*— on the famous sixteenth-century defender of Amerindians—was one of his most divisive works. Las Casas had been tarnished by accusations that he had sparked the launch of the African slave trade by urging that African labor replace that of Amerindians. Grégoire vigorously contested this charge, insisting that the Spanish priest was one of the few Catholic heroes of the antislavery movement. Many Latin American intellectuals shared Grégoire's admiration of Las Casas and were sympathetic to the abbé's effort to rehabilitate him. Others, however, took offense at Grégoire's impugning of certain Spanish historians while trying to defend Las Casas, who, they argued, had indeed supported African slavery. Several pamphlets appeared in Spanish criticizing or defending Grégoire's *Apologie*.[6] News of his activities and writings also appeared frequently in Latin American newspapers.[7]

Grégoire's interest in the United States was even greater. He corresponded eagerly with Americans to find out more about their republic and to offer his advice. As a founding member of France's *Institut national*, he hoped to revive the Old Regime tradition of correspondence between intellectuals and institutions in different countries. One of his most sustained relationships was

---

between Servando and Grégoire, in Bibliothèque de l'Arsenal ('Ars.') Ms. 6339, fol. 26-33, and *Escritos inéditos de fray Servando Teresa de Mier*, eds. J. M. Miquel i Vergés and Hugo Díaz-Thomé (México: El Colegio de México–Centro de estudios históricos, 1944), 507-12.

6. See *Coleccion de las Obras del venerable obispo de Chiapa, don Bartolomé de Las Casas, Defensor de la libertad de los Americanos. . .*, ed. Juan Antonio Llorente (Paris: En casa de Rosa, 1822); and Bernard Plongeron, 'Apologie de Barthélémy de Las Casas, Evêque de Chiapas, par le Citoyen Grégoire,' in *Grégoire et la cause des noirs (1789–1831), combats et projets*, ed. Yves Benot and Marcel Dorigny (Paris: Société française d'histoire d'outremer/APECE, 2000), 37-50. Recent research has revealed that Grégoire's efforts were somewhat misguided, as Las Casas did support the enslavement of Africans early in his life and only renounced it later. See Laurie Barbara Gunst, 'Bartolomé de las Casas and the Question of Negro Slavery in the Early Spanish Indies' (Ph.D. diss., Harvard University, 1982); and Henry Raup Wagner and Helen Rand Parish, *The Life and Writings of Bartolomé de Las Casas* (Albuquerque: University of New Mexico Press, 1967), 246, and passim.

7. This fact was reported to me during the conference by Mariselle Meléndez and Elise Bartosik-Velez. These newspapers included the *El censor de la revolución*, *El pacificador del Perú*, and the *Gaceta del gobierno del Perú*.

with the American Philosophical Society (APS) in Philadelphia, the preeminent American intellectual institution. Grégoire was gravely concerned that Americans avoid a repeat of the Terror, and the books he sent reflect his beliefs about how republican governments could remain stable, such as by enforcing meritocracy and remaining vigilant against would-be monarchists.[8]

Grégoire was particularly interested in religious diversity in the New World; despite being a Catholic priest, he had been famed during the French Revolution for his defense of persecuted religious minorities like Jews. In addition to sending the APS and other American intellectuals some of his writings on Jews, he sought information from Americans about the integration of different religious and racial groups in their republic.[9]

Even as he hoped that the United States would be tolerant of people of all religions, Grégoire nevertheless saw Catholicism as the one true faith, and he hoped for universal conversion. His interest in Jews in the United States thus related to this goal. He corresponded with Hannah Adams and other American Christians who desired to convert the Jews, sharing information on the progress of this project in their respective countries. He also wanted to make sure Amerindians would be brought into the American polity and the church. He even tried to proselytize American Protestants, telling Adams of his hope that she and others would soon return to the Catholic Church.[10]

---

8. Information about Grégoire's gifts comes from the American Philosophical Society's Association File Card Catalog in its Philadelphia library and the *Transactions of the American Philosophical Society*.

9. *Observations nouvelles sur les juifs . . . d'Allemagne* (Pam. v. 43, no. 11, APS) and *Observations nouvelles sur les juifs . . . d'Amsterdam* (Pam. v. 43, no. 12, APS, donated on February 5, 1808; and 'Articles recommandés à la bienveillance de Mr. Michaux . . . [From Mon. Le Sénateur Grégoire . . . to his friend B. Vaughan],' APS, Benjamin Vaughan Papers, B V46p.

10. Hannah Adams, *The History of the Jews from the Destruction of Jerusalem to the Nineteenth Century*, 2 vols. (Boston: John Eliot, 1812), 2: 152; Grégoire, 'Articles recommandés à la bienveillance de Mr. Michaux,' Bibliothèque de la Société de Port-Royal, Collection Grégoire, Rév. 147/20; and Grégoire to Adams, January 19, 1811, Thomas and Hannah Adams Papers (Mss. 665), unnumbered fols., New England Historic Genealogical Society (NEHGS). See also Grégoire's discussions of American Protestants in *Histoire des sectes religieuses* (1st. ed.; Paris: Potey, 1810), lxxiii–lxxiv, and passim.

Because of his religious convictions, Grégoire looked to American Catholics as natural allies. He was particularly keen to correspond with John Carroll, the archbishop of Baltimore and leader of the Catholic Church in America. Carroll, after all, was a bishop living in a republic and had been known in the 1780s as an enlightened republican Catholic who wanted the American church to be independent of Rome. Like other Americans who became more conservative following the French Revolution, however, Carroll by the late 1790s had become a Federalist and a more traditional supporter of the Pope. To the older Carroll, Grégoire's support for the French Revolution was suspect; Carroll's few letters to the French priest expressed his firm disapproval of the latter's ideas. Grégoire thus found himself unable to build a solid relationship with the leading American Catholic.[11]

Grégoire's inability to connect with American Catholics compounded two other frustrations he encountered in dealing with the United States. First, he felt that American ideals held great promise but were not always implemented. For instance, he prized the American policy of separating church and state, but was disturbed to learn that a Jew serving as American consul in Tunis had his position revoked by President James Monroe because of his religion.[12]

More importantly, Grégoire was disgusted by the American accommodation with slavery. He considered it a scandal that the young republic not only had not abolished, but had in fact enshrined, slavery into its constitution through the three-fifths compromise. He therefore tried to convince American leaders of

11. See Jacques M. Gres-Gayer, 'Four Letters from Henri Grégoire to John Carroll, 1809–1814,' *Catholic Historical Review* 79 (1993): 681–703 (originals in the Archdiocese of Baltimore Archives); and Jay P. Dolan, *The American Catholic Experience: A History from Colonial Times to the Present* (Notre Dame: University of Notre Dame Press, 1992), 101–24. Carroll did, however, praise Grégoire's criticism of Barlow's *Columbiad*.

12. Grégoire, *Discours sur la liberté des cultes* (n. p.: 1794), 7; Richard H. Popkin, 'An Aspect of the Problem of Religious Freedom in the French and American Revolutions,' *Freedom. Proceedings of the American Catholic Philosophical Association* 50 (1976): 146–61; Grégoire, *De la liberté de conscience et de culte à Haïti* (Paris: Baudouin Frères, 1824), 16; and R. Popkin, 'Mordecai Noah, The Abbé Grégoire and the Paris Sanhedrin,' *Modern Judaism* 2 (1982): 132.

the brutality of slavery, sending antislavery works to the APS and corresponding with American abolitionist societies.[13]

Grégoire's most important effort to influence American opinion on this subject was his 1808 book *De la littérature des nègres*. Grégoire had been incensed by Thomas Jefferson's comments in *Notes on the State of Virginia*, that blacks were naturally incapable of the same intellectual achievements as whites. Though Grégoire praised the Virginian in the preface for his work against the slave trade, later in the work he attacked Jefferson's view that blacks were by nature intellectually inferior. Grégoire countered the idea of separate origins of the races with the argument that all human beings belonged to a single species. Only historical events—particularly the brutality of slavery, he insisted—had degraded blacks: 'What sentiments of dignity, of self-respect, can possibly exist in beings treated like beasts. . .? What can become of individuals degraded below the level of brutes. . .?'[14]

In his text, Grégoire rebuked Jefferson by name numerous times. Arguing that whites who claimed superiority were guided by self-interest, he noted, 'It is maddening to find the same prejudice in a man whose name is ordinarily pronounced among us only with . . . a well-deserved respect: Jefferson.' After giving many details of the talents of people of African descent, Grégoire added in exasperation, 'These details make clear . . . what one must think when . . . Jefferson tells us that they have never erected a civilized society.' 'The more imposing and respectable the authority of Jefferson,' he declared, 'the more essential it is to combat his judgment.'[15]

Grégoire's abolitionist efforts attracted much positive attention in the United States. The New-York Historical Society offered

13. Pennsylvania Abolition Society Papers, Committee of Correspondence letter book, 1794–1809, 71–73, 78–80, 83–85, 87–89, AmS 081, Historical Society of Pennsylvania; and Grégoire to Verplanck, May 17, 1823.

14. Grégoire, *De la littérature des nègres* (Paris: Maradan, 1808), 14, 44–45, 35.

15. Grégoire, *De la littérature des nègres* 36, 150, 255–56, 260.

him honorary membership, praising him as 'the friend of the oppressed.'[16] The Library Company of Philadelphia purchased a number of his writings in French,[17] and several of his works were translated into English.[18] American travelers to Europe were also anxious to meet the famous French republican priest. These included the Reverend William Ellery Channing, a leading American Unitarian and abolitionist, and future Harvard professor George Ticknor.[19]

Other Americans viewed the notorious Frenchman with suspicion, however. After the passing of the 1798 Alien and Sedition Acts and then the XYZ Affair, it was risky for an immigrant to be identified with French radicals. In 1798 Benjamin Vaughan, an English-born republican living in Maine, narrowly escaped prosecution under the Alien and Sedition Acts when a confiscated letter was published revealing his close friendship with French revolutionaries such as Grégoire. It even proved dangerous to spend time with the abbé in Paris, as Ticknor discovered when the French police began to harass and follow him on account of his visiting Grégoire and other republicans.[20]

16. Gulian C. Verplanck, *An Anniversary Discourse, Delivered Before the New-York Historical Society, December 7, 1818* (New York: James Eastburn & Co., 1818), 15.

17. The Library Company owned Grégoire's *Lettre aux philantropes sur les malheurs, les droits et les réclamations des gens de couleur de Saint-Domingue* . . . (Paris: Belin, 1790), and a 1791 English translation of Grégoire's 1789 *Essai sur la régénération physique, morale et politique des juifs [An essay on the physical, moral, and political reformation of the Jews* (London: Forster, 1791)] by the time it printed its 1807 catalogue. It is not known when its two French copies of *De la littérature* were purchased.

18. *Critical Observations on the Poem of Mr. Joel Barlow, 'The Columbiad'* (Washington City: Printed by Roger Chew Weightman, 1809); *An Enquiry Concerning the Intellectual and Moral Faculties, and Literature of Negroes* . . . , D. B. Warden, trans. (Brooklyn: Printed by Thomas Kirk, 1810); and *Report on the Means of Compleating and Distributing the National Library* . . . (Philadelphia: Market Street, 1794).

19. Channing to Vaughan, May 13, 1822, Benjamin Vaughan Papers, B V46p, APS; and [George Ticknor], *Life, Letters, and Journals*, 2 vols. (Boston: J.R. Osgood, 1876), 1: 130.

20. [John Hurford Stone], *Copies of Original Letters Recently Written by Persons in Paris to Dr. Priestley in America* . . . (Philadelphia: James Humphreys, 1798), 19; and Ticknor, *Life, Letters, and Journals*, 1: 142–43. On Grégoire and Vaughan, see Craig C. Murray, *Benjamin Vaughan (1751–1835): The Life of an Anglo-American Intellectual* (New York: Arno Press, 1982), 276–77, 343, 362 n35, 388, 417, and passim; and *Mémoires de l'abbé Grégoire*, ed. J. M. Leniaud and preface by J. N. Jeanneney (Paris: Éditions de Santé, 1989), 66–67.

'The final resignation of prejudices.' This engraving by Goulding appeared in Joel Barlow, *The Columbiad: A Poem* (Philadelphia: C. Conrad and Co., 1807), 380.

Moreover, to Grégoire's consternation, the republican network often seemed fragile. By 1805, he was regularly complaining to Barlow that the Pennsylvania Abolition Society was ignoring him and that he had not heard anything from them in two years.[21] A few years later, he was distraught when he did not hear from Hannah Adams for fifteen months, despite sending her several letters and several of his writings.[22]

Jefferson, meanwhile, seemed unpersuaded about Grégoire's arguments on the unity of the human species. In a well-known letter to the French prelate, Jefferson politely thanked him for *De la littérature des nègres*, and swore that he had been impressed by it. He pledged that his mind was still open on the subject of blacks' natural intelligence: 'no person living wishes more sincerely than I do, to see a complete refutation of the doubts I have myself entertained and expressed on the grade of understanding allowed to them [blacks] by nature.' Furthermore, he insisted, his doubts about their abilities had nothing to do with their rights. In a lesser-known letter to their mutual friend Barlow, written later that year, however, Jefferson showed a different face. He depicted Grégoire as simple-minded, and commented that he had given the Frenchman a 'soft answer.' Jefferson accused Grégoire of naïveté and implied that whatever those chronicled in *De la littérature* had achieved, it was only because they had some white blood.[23]

---

21. Grégoire to Joel Barlow, December 21, 1805, June 3, 1806, and September 1, 1806, and to Ruth Barlow, August 17, 1806, fol. 603–6, Barlow Papers, Houghton Library. It is not known why the Pennsylvania Abolition Society (PAS) stopped writing to Grégoire, although it possibly related to the Haitian Revolution in 1804; most Americans, including members of the PAS, were horrified by Haitian violence and fearful of its potentially contagious effects on American slaves. See Richard S. Newman, *The Transformation of American Abolitionism: Fighting Slavery in the Early Republic* (Chapel Hill: University of North Carolina Press, 2002), 26; and Sepinwall, 'La révolution haïtienne et les États-Unis: Étude historiographique,' *1802: Rétablissement de l'esclavage dans les colonies françaises: Aux origines de Haïti*, ed. Y. Benot and M. Dorigny (Paris: Maisonneuve et Larose, 2003), 387–401.

22. Grégoire to Adams, December 4, 1811, Adams Papers, NEHGS.

23. Jefferson to Grégoire, February 25, 1809; and Jefferson to Barlow, October 8, 1809, in Paul L. Ford, ed., *Writings of Thomas Jefferson*, 10 vols. (New York: Putnam, 1892–99), 9: 246, 261.

Fractures could develop even in Grégoire's relationships with more committed New World abolitionists. His friendship with Barlow reveals the explosive potential of theological differences in the Atlantic republican world. Their relationship had begun when the American poet arrived in Paris with other foreign republicans and had deepened when Barlow accompanied Grégoire on an official voyage to the Savoy region.[24] In the late 1790s, Grégoire, his 'adopted mother' Mme. Dubois, and the Barlows had a common circle of friends and spent vacations in the same spa town.

When the Barlows returned to the United States after Napoleon came to power, Grégoire and Mme. Dubois were crushed. 'No matter what physical distance the seas place between you and us,' he assured them in 1805, 'our inviolable attachment . . . will accompany you across the Atlantic.' 'Our friends, along with Mme. Dubois and I, will never forget you. Our friendship would be as strong in fifty years as today if we remained on this earth.' Grégoire's relationship with Barlow was built not only on personal compatibility, but also on common political attachments, such as to republicanism and abolitionism. Because of their long history, Grégoire had long awaited the *Columbiad*, hoping it could fuel antislavery sentiment in the United States.[25]

The friendship would ultimately shatter, however, over religious matters. When Barlow's *Columbiad* finally appeared in France, Grégoire was shocked to discover sentiments in it that he felt were anti-Christian. He was particularly shocked by an engraving that depicted the stamping out of prejudice by showing an image of the crushed remnants of a cross and crown, and by the closing passage of the poem. It included the lines,

> 'Beneath the footstool all destructive things,
> The mask of priesthood and the mace of kings,

24. *Mémoires de l'abbé Grégoire*, 95.

25. Grégoire to Joel and Ruth Barlow, December 21, 1805; Grégoire to J. Barlow, June 3, 1806; and Grégoire to J. Barlow, Oct. 26 [1807], Barlow Papers, fols. 602–4, Houghton Library.

Lie trampled in the dust; for here at last
Fraud, folly, error all their emblems cast. . . .
Swords, sceptres, mitres, crowns and globes and stars
Codes of false fame and stimulants to wars
Sink in the settling mass; since guile began,
These are the agents of the woes of man.'[26]

In March 1809, Grégoire published an open letter to his friend, entitled *Observations critiques sur le poème de M. Joël Barlow* . . . . He began these *Observations* gently, noting that there were many aspects of the work which had pleased him, such as its illustrating advances in American print technology.[27] Grégoire quickly moved, however, to a bitter condemnation of the poem's religious content. He focused his anger on 'certain verses and an engraving which bears the following inscription: *Final destruction of prejudices.* . . . Prejudices! No one more than I, perhaps, wishes for their destruction. But to what are you referring with this ambiguous term? . . . The symbols of the Catholic ministry and . . . the cross of Jesus-Christ! What?! Is that what you call *prejudices*?'[28] Barlow tried to mend fences by sending Grégoire a letter in which he argued that his friend had misinterpreted the poem. 'I am pained to tears,' he wrote, 'and my heart bleeds, to learn . . . that my poem wounded your religious principles. . . . Nothing was further from my heart. . . .'[29]

26. Barlow, *The Columbiad* (London: Richard Phillips, 1809), 340 (Book 10, lines 599–610), http://moa.umdl.umich.edu/cgi/sgml/moa-idx?notisid=APT9199, accessed June 2006.

27. Grégoire, *Observations critiques sur le poème de M. Joël Barlow, The Colombiad* (Paris: Maradan, 1809), 3; translated into English as *Critical Observations on the Poem of Mr. Joël Barlow, The Columbiad.*

28. Grégoire, *Observations critiques*, 4. In fact, the poem was received less enthusiastically than Grégoire imagined. See James Woodress, *A Yankee's Odyssey: The Life of Joel Barlow* (Philadelphia: J. B. Lippincott Company, 1958), esp. 266–71; and John Bidwell, 'The Publication of Joel Barlow's The Columbiad,' *Proceedings of the American Antiquarian Society* 93 (1984): 337–80.

29. Barlow to Grégoire, March 15, 1809, in Archives nationales, Paris, 510 AP 2, dossier "A-B."

Once Grégoire's letter began to be reprinted widely in American newspapers, though, Barlow worried that the critique was damaging his public standing. Indeed, one scholar has argued that, although Barlow was a deist, he feared that his political views would be ignored if his full opposition to Christianity was made public. He therefore published a separate open response to Grégoire in September 1809. He swore there that the infamous engraving was inserted into his book without his permission. Moreover, he claimed, his poem was hardly deist, but reflected 'the genuine principles . . . of the christian system, as inculcated in the gospels. . . .' He insisted that any religious differences between him and his friend were only on the surface.[30] Despite proclaiming their fundamental agreement, however, Barlow suggested several key differences between him and Grégoire. Chief among them was that Grégoire, he felt, confused the core values of Christianity and its outward symbols, viewing an attack on the physical emblems of the Catholic Church as an assault on the Gospels themselves.[31]

Barlow was particularly concerned about his reputation and the damage caused by the controversy because Grégoire's letter was circulated more widely than his own response. As one friend wrote Barlow from Vermont: 'The Bishop's letter has been read and applauded thro[ughout] this part of the country. Yours has not been published in the papers . . . .'[32]

Grégoire was in fact dismayed when he learned that newspapers were portraying his friend as an atheist, which he knew him not to be. In a personal letter responding to Barlow's open

30. Barlow, *Letter to Henry Gregoire . . . in Reply to His Letter on The Columbiad* (Washington: Roger Chew Weightman, 1809), 4–8.

31. Barlow, *Letter to Henry Gregoire*, 6, 9–10.

32. Stephen Jacob to Barlow, Windsor, Vermont, December 7, 1809; see also William Little to Barlow, Boston, October 12, 1809; Henry Dearborn to Barlow, Boston, January 22, 1810; Jonathan Law to Barlow, Hartford, October 14, 1809; and T. Law to Barlow, Philadelphia, October 16, 1809, respectively M995, M1001, M970, M998 and M999, Pequot Papers, Beinecke Rare Book and Manuscript Library; and *Correspondence, Critical and Literary, on the Subject of The Columbiad, an American Epic Poem of Joel Barlow, Esq.* (Ballston Spa, N.Y.: Brown and Miller, 1810), 2.

one, he continued to call the American 'my dear friend' and acknowledged the latter's regret about the notorious engraving: 'I am more persuaded than ever that you did not intend the least offense to your Catholic brother.' He did not, however, retreat from his attack on the poem's religious content. Pointedly, he countered Barlow's critique of Catholicism with one of Protestantism: Grégoire called the latter dangerous precisely because it 'authoriz[es] each individual to interpret the Bible as he pleases.'[33]

Because of their past closeness, Grégoire and Barlow made great efforts to work through this disagreement; new evidence shows that they were still on speaking terms in late 1811.[34] Yet the *Columbiad* had opened a deep rift between them, and their friendship was never again the same. As deeply as they shared a commitment to republicanism and antislavery, Grégoire and Barlow could not agree on theological matters. Grégoire saw the ideal republic as Catholic, while his American friend found Catholic iconography and 'idol-worship' to be inimical to free thought.

The controversy had a chilling effect in the short term on Grégoire's American relationships. Though some Federalists praised his critique of Barlow, he shared little in common otherwise with these men, who tended towards staunch anti-Jacobinism. Though Republicans' views of the French Revolution were more positive, Grégoire's *Observations* ended up distancing him from many of them. Men like Jefferson commiserated with Barlow, and said the abbé 'did not deserve' Barlow's apologetic response.[35] The controversy thus isolated the French priest from his most natural American allies.

Religion and slavery therefore divided Grégoire from many North Americans. Most American republicans did not see the abolition of slavery as essential to their republic; while French republicans had decreed the abolition of slavery only two years after proclaiming a republic, it took more than seventy years for

33. Grégoire to Barlow, [1810], M 981, Pequot Papers, Beinecke Library.
34. See Grégoire to H. Adams, December 4, 1811, in Adams Papers, NEHGS.
35. Jefferson to Barlow, October 8, 1809, in *Writings of Thomas Jefferson*, 9: 261.

the American republic to outlaw slavery.[36] Most Americans also did not share his religious beliefs, while those closest to him in matters of faith, like Bishop Carroll, viewed his Jacobinism with suspicion.

One might have expected Grégoire to have more in common with Latin American republicans, since the majority of them were Catholics and many of them were Gallican sympathizers. Nevertheless, even as religion and politics united him with Latin American republicans, attitudes toward slavery often did not.

The Colonial Laboratory in Haiti

The white republics of the United States and Latin America were not the only hopes for republicanism in the New World, however. The Haitian republic seemed to Grégoire the most promising site in the New World for perfecting the Revolution's legacy. Unlike peoples he viewed as 'civilized,' the Haitians represented for him a *tabula rasa*. Moreover, with its political leaders of African descent, Haiti offered living proof of Grégoire's contention that people of color had great potential if they were free. Starved for information about Haiti, Grégoire corresponded with the men and women who composed its elite. He had correspondents in both the black monarchy in the North (led by Henri Christophe [1767–1820]) and the mixed-race-led republic of the South (headed by Alexandre Pétion [1770–1818] and then Jean-Pierre Boyer [1776–1850]).

The North was particularly eager to win Grégoire's allegiance. Christophe's foreign minister, the Comte de Limonade, told the abbé in 1814 that the King loved *De la littérature des nègres* and had ordered fifty copies. He called Grégoire Haiti's only European friend and called him 'a new *Las Casas*': 'You are the only European who has had the courage to say the truth without fear of attracting hate. . . . The happiest day for my sovereign would

---

36. After Napoleon's reimposition of slavery in France in 1802, slavery would be permanently abolished by the Second French Republic in 1848.

be the day which he could see you and press you to his heart.'[37]
De Limonade hoped Grégoire could 'raise his voice' in favor of
Christophe's monarchy, but Grégoire refused even to enter into a
correspondence with its leaders; disgusted with the return of
monarchy to France, he hardly wanted Haiti to cap its revolution
with the same.

Grégoire was delighted, however, to correspond with Boyer
and other republicans in the South. He had long been a magnet
for mixed-race Haitians arriving in Paris and a subject for their
praise. Grégoire's portrait was purchased for Boyer's presidential
palace, Haitian leaders lavished him with expensive gifts such as
coffee, and Boyer reportedly invited him to be the bishop of
Haiti. Grégoire was delighted to assist these southern republicans, whom he saw as progressive even though modern historians
have noted that their 'republic' was largely an oligarchy and not
necessarily better for ex-slaves than the northern monarchy. In
his correspondence and published works, Grégoire emphasized
his admiration for Haitians' hard-won independence and his profound identification with them.

Yet strains also appeared in Grégoire's relationships with Haitian leaders. At the risk of angering President Boyer, Grégoire
could not restrain himself from offering advice on moral matters.
Portraying himself as an older and wiser man, he appealed to
Boyer not to divorce morality from politics. He insisted that 'Religion, august and holy religion . . . is the fundamental rock of all
society' and that Haitian civil strife resulted from neglecting it.
Grégoire called Boyer's attention to issues which concerned him
that included religious intolerance, insulting treatment of the
masses, and extramarital relationships (particularly daring because Boyer himself was living with someone to whom he was not
married). Saddened by reports of discrimination by people of

37. Comte de Limonade to Grégoire, June 10, 1814, Ars. Ms. 6339, fols. 44 -47. For an
expanded discussion of Grégoire's interactions with Haitian leaders, see Sepinwall, *The
Abbé Grégoire and the French Revolution*, ch. 8.

mixed race against blacks and against whites, Grégoire also urged Boyer to prevent the 'eruption of hate between the colors.'[38] Finally, he insisted on Haitian women's assuming their 'natural' civilizing roles. If they neglected to do so, he suggested, Haiti could never recover from the debilitating effects of colonialism.[39]

While Haitians generally cheered Grégoire's interest in them, he would eventually discover that his pupils had minds of their own. When Boyer began to receive overtures from previously hostile European governments in the mid-1820s, some Haitian leaders were quick to distance themselves from Grégoire, reportedly referring to him as a lemon whose juice had been squeezed. When representatives of Charles X came calling in Port-au-Prince, Boyer quickly removed the portrait of Grégoire that hung in the presidential palace. A toast to Grégoire at a state dinner welcoming the French was suppressed from the official government newspaper.[40]

Grégoire would eventually write a bitter *Epître aux Haïtiens*, which the Haitian government was charitable enough to print and distribute in 1827. He claimed that he had tried to guide them on the right moral path; likening himself to the prophet Samuel, he noted that he may not always have told them what they wanted to hear. But even as he removed himself from direct involvement in Haitian affairs, he promised he would always remember them in his prayers. 'I have ardent wishes for your spiritual happiness and your temporal prosperity,' he noted. 'But I regret not being able to raise my hopes to the level of my desires .... Haitians, *adieu!*'[41]

Grégoire would continue to monitor developments in the Americas and receive visitors from the Western hemisphere until his death in 1831. He learned, however, that Atlantic networking could

38. Grégoire to Boyer, June 22, 1821, Ars. Ms. 15049/194.
39. See Sepinwall, *The Abbé Grégoire and the French Revolution*, 190–93.
40. See Ruth Necheles, *The Abbé Grégoire 1787–1831. The Odyssey of an Egalitarian* (Westport, Conn.: Greenwood, 1971), 243.
41. Grégoire, *Epître aux Haïtiens* (Port-au-Prince: L'Imprimerie du Gouvernement, 1827), 14, 15.

have frustrations as well as joys. Some of these were practical, yet the problems of the Atlantic republic of letters were deeper. Even as members thirsted for contact with like-minded thinkers abroad, they often found that their versions of republicanism had irreconcilable differences. Grégoire's experiences are a useful reminder that even as we seek Atlantic commonalities in our study of the past, we must also remember the differences that could make enemies even of the closest of friends.

Writing Back to Empire: Juan Pablo Viscardo y Guzmán's 'Letter to the Spanish Americans'

KAREN STOLLEY

JUAN PABLO VISCARDO Y GUZMAN's 'Letter to the Spanish Americans' (1791) begins with this stirring invocation to his 'brothers and countrymen':

> Our near approach to the fourth century since the establishment of our ancestors in the New World, is an occurrence too remarkable, not seriously to interest our attention. The discovery of so great a portion of the earth is, and ever will be, to mankind, the most memorable event in their annals; but to us who are its inhabitants, and to our descendants, it is an object of greatest importance. The New World is our country; its history is ours; and it is in the latter, that duty and interest oblige us to examine our present situation with its causes, in order to determine us, after mature deliberation, to espouse with courage, the part dictated by the most indispensable of duties towards ourselves and our successors.[1]

Viscardo here alludes to several key themes that will be developed throughout the letter: a sense of history (more than three hundred years of New World history link Spanish Americans to the

---

1. Juan Pablo Viscardo y Guzmán, *Letter to the Spanish Americans: A Facsimile of the Second English edition (London, 1810)*, introduction by D. A. Brading (Providence, R.I.: The John Carter Brown Library, 2002), 62–63. All quotations are taken from this facsimile edition.

KAREN STOLLEY is associate professor of Spanish, Emory University.

ancestors who preceded them and the successors who will follow); a sense of enlightened self-interest and duty that compels
Spanish Americans to mature examination and deliberation of
their present circumstances; and a sense of ownership and investment in the New World (we are struck by the repeated use of the
collective possessive pronouns—our, ours, us, ourselves).

Viscardo's exhortation to his Spanish American brethren is
carefully constructed through what we might call a rhetoric of
immediacy and urgency that serves not only as a call to arms but
also attempts to erase any trace of geographic and linguistic distance between the writer and his readers. Scholars have argued
that Viscardo is an ideological precursor of Spanish American
independence, and his letter has been enshrined as a text written
by a Spanish American for Spanish Americans about Spanish
America. At the same time, it is worth noting that Viscardo's
writings are a prime example of the way in which key texts of the
late eighteenth and early nineteenth century were written, revised, translated, and disseminated in a complex context of
cross-cultural interpretation and influence that the American
Antiquarian Society's book history conference, 'Liberty/Ega-
litlé/Independencia: Print Culture, Enlightenment, and Revolution in the Americas, 1776–1826,' was organized to address.
The trajectory of Viscardo and his letter—from Peru to Italy to
England to France and back to the Americas—reminds us that,
as Elizabeth Dillon has suggested, creole (or *criollo*) cosmopolitanism is as much part of the story of American independence as
creole nationalism.

Juan Pablo Viscardo y Guzmán was born in Arequipa, Peru, in
1748 to a family of modestly wealthy *criollo*s, descendents of a
Spaniard who had settled there in the early seventeenth century.
His grandfather had served as lieutenant to a local *corregidor*, and
the family (like many other *criollo* families) was related by marriage to Indian *kurakas*. Viscardo and his younger brother, who
had both professed minor Jesuit orders, were forced into exile in

Italy after the 1767 expulsion of Jesuits from all Spanish territories. For years Spain held out to exiled Jesuits the possibility of returning to their homelands in exchange for the renunciation of their vows. But Viscardo's frequent entreaties to be able to return to Peru were rejected by Spanish authorities, and he grew increasingly disillusioned and bitter.[2]

He subsequently sought to affirm his Peruvian roots by developing connections with like-minded Europeans who were interested in the cause of Spanish American emancipation. After meeting John Udney, English consul in Livorno, Viscardo wrote him in 1781 to send news of the Tupac Amaru rebellion in the Andean highlands.[3] Viscardo's tone is that of a concerned and 'in the know' observer: 'Very much concerned to inform you completely about the situation and disorder in Peru, I take the liberty of adding to the news I have already communicated to you additional information I've garnered since returning from that city. Most is taken from a letter from America that I was able to read a short time ago, after careful investigation that I did in order to know its content which was hidden with much mystery.'[4] Viscardo goes to great lengths here to erase the distance that separates him from the actual events, and he bolsters his own involvement by referring to his investigations of unspecified mysteries. Viscardo quotes at length from the letter, stressing that Tupac

2. Carlos Deustua Pimentel, *Juan Pablo Viscardo y Guzmán* (Lima: Editorial Brasa, 1994), 11–13. There is, however, no mention of Viscardo in Jorge Cañizares-Esguerra, *How to Write the History of the New World. Historiographies, Epistemologies, and Identities in the Eighteenth-Century Atlantic World* (Stanford, Calif: Stanford University Press, 2001).

3. As Pagden has explained, this was a revolt sparked by Bourbon reforms that aimed to abolish the post of *corregidor* and do away with all taxes and customs dues—a convenient conflation of *criollo* interests and indigenous ones. See Anthony Pagden, 'Old Constitutions and Ancient Indian Empires: Juan Pablo Viscardo and the Languages of Revolution in Spanish America,' *Spanish Imperialism and the Political Imagination* (New Haven: Yale University Press, 1990, 127. David S. Shields's discussion of secret correspondence and verbal rumors in early filibusterism (included in this volume) offers insight into Viscardo's remarks to Udney.

4. Juan Pablo Viscardo y Guzmán, *Obras completas* (Lima: Banco de Crédito del Perú, 1988), 5.

Amaru had studied in San Martín, one of the premier Jesuit colleges of the region, and that he enjoyed the support of both the indigenous population and Spanish Peruvians: 'They say that he has exhorted the citizens [of Lima] to recognize him spontaneously without obliging him to resort to force of arms, as he would rather that not one drop of blood be spilt. . . . '[5]

Here and in later communications with Udney, Viscardo makes repeated efforts to convince the British consul and his compatriots to intervene on behalf of Spanish American independence. Among Viscardo's many proposals was a British expedition to seize the Peruvian port of Coquimbo, a land attack by a force of six thousand soldiers on Arequipa, and—probably his most celebrated scheme—an attack on the Spanish empire in the River Plate region. Viscardo and his brother eventually moved to London with their travel expenses paid by Udney's superior in the office of the Secretary of State who had been impressed by either the daring or the lunacy of Viscardo's various schemes. This was part of a larger strategy (suggested by Francisco de Miranda to British Prime Minister William Pitt) of recruiting exiled Jesuits both as a source of information about Spanish America and as a means of influencing public opinion.[6] Of course, these disaffected Jesuits had plenty of baggage (despite the fact that they were prohibited by the expulsion edict from carrying much with them into exile). One official from the British Foreign Office reported that Viscardo 'is a very strange and mistrustful man, albeit sincere and honest and appears to be very spoilt and careful of himself.'[7]

---

5. Viscardo, *Obras completas*, 5.

6. Francisco de Miranda (1750–1816) had left Venezuela in the 1770s to devote himself to revolutionary causes in North America and France. Later, with financial support from British government and in collaboration with James Mills, he tried unsuccessfully to spark revolutionary movements in Spanish America, arguing (like King) that Britain must come to the aid of the Spanish American independence efforts in order to counteract the pernicious influence of the French. See Karen Racine, *Francisco de Miranda, a Transatlantic Life in the Age of Revolution* (Wilmington, Del.: Scholarly Resources, 2003); François-Xavier Guerra, *Modernidad e independencias. Ensayos sobre las revoluciones hispánicas* (México: Editorial MAPFRE, 1992)

7. D. A. Brading, intro. to Viscardo, *Letter to the Spanish Americans* (2002), 10.

Viscardo lived in London from June 1782 to March 1784, during which time he continued to press his case. But the opportunity for British intervention in Spanish America was lost: Tupac Amaru was eventually defeated, and the 1783 Peace of Versailles ended the war between Spain and England on terms that left the British little disposed to meddle in Spanish affairs. After two years a discouraged Viscardo found himself once again in Italy; however, he returned to London sometime in late 1790 or early 1791 and would remain there until his death in 1798. During those years he wrote continually on the issue of Spanish American politics, and even as he lay dying he received a visit by Rufus King, the American minister in London. King's agenda was that he was that he too was lobbying for Anglo-American intervention in Spanish America (in large part to forestall French meddling). In King's own words: 'if it is not assisted by England, its work will be done by France, who will introduce her detestable principles, divide it into small Republics, put bad men at their head, and by these means facilitate her meditated Enterprises against us.'[8]

The intersection of interests that come together around the deathbed of this odd and passionate Peruvian Jesuit is fascinating (though the triangulation of Spanish, French, and British interests in Europe and the Americas leads to many such scenarios, reminding us that the history of the Americas in the eighteenth and early nineteenth centuries cannot be understood separately from the history of Europe, nor can a single national story be told without linking it to those of other nations and peoples). Before he died, Viscardo entrusted his 'parcel of papers' to King, with 'a request that [he] would have it published for his credit and the happiness of mankind.'[9] King soon after shared the papers with Miranda, the international revolutionary figure and acquaintance of Viscardo's (despite the Peruvian's deathbed fulminations about Miranda's possible treachery to him and to the revolutionary

8. Rufus King, quoted by Brading, intro., 3.
9. Brading, intro., 3.

cause). Of all the Viscardo papers that King shared with him, Miranda chose to publish only the 'Letter,' no doubt because its brevity, focus, and exalted tone served his purposes at the time. In an introductory note to the first English edition, Miranda explained: 'The following interesting Letter, from an American Spaniard to his countrymen, is translated from a French copy printed conformable with the manuscript, written by the author himself, who died in London in the month of February 1798. The Translator begs, at this highly interesting moment, to present to the British nation this valuable little tract; which came to his hands only a short time since, and which does equal honor to the writer, as an enlightened patriot, politician, and Christian.'[10] Miranda functioned as agent/editor/translator for Viscardo, disseminating the 'Letter to the Spanish Americans' in a number of forms and venues. The rest of Viscardo's papers ended up back with Rufus King and were donated to the library of the New-York Historical Society, where they languished in complete obscurity until they were 'discovered' by Merle E. Simmons 184 years later (a discovery to which I'll return later).

Miranda began by publishing the 'Lettre aux espagnols américains' as a forty-one-page pamphlet in French in 1799, shortly after Viscardo's death. Until Merle E. Simmons' discovery of the cache of Viscardo papers in the New York Historical Society, it was commonly assumed that Viscardo had originally composed all his works in French, as there were no extant manuscripts in Spanish.[11] This is a surprising assumption, perhaps, but

10. 'Lettre aux espagnols américains' 1799 Francisco de Miranda, 'Review of "Lettre aux Espagnois-Américains, par Viscardo," extracted from the Edinburgh review for Jan. 1809,' *South American emancipation: Documents, historical and explanatory, shewing the designs which have been in progress, and the exertions made by General Miranda, for the attainment of that object during the last twenty-five years*, ed. J. M. Antepara (London, 1810), 96.

11. Merle E. Simmons, 'The Papers of Juan Pablo Viscardo y Guzmán in the Library of the New York Historical Society,' *Studies in Eighteenth-Century Spanish Literature and Romanticism in Honor of John Clarkson Dowling*, Douglas and Linda Jane Barnette, ed. (Newark, Del: Juan de la Cuesta, 1985), 1–15. Burton Van Name Edwards, 'Bibliographical Note,' *Letter to the Spanish Americans* (2002), 89. Merle E. Simmons, *Los escritos de Juan Pablo Viscardo y Guzmán. Precursor de la Independencia Hispanoamericana* (Caracas: Universidad Católica Andrés Bello, 1983).

before we attribute it to excessive Francophilia, we should re-member that exiled Jesuits like Viscardo moved easily and by ne-cessity among several languages—Spanish, French, Latin, Ital-ian—and had in some cases mastered indigenous languages as well. The original Spanish manuscript of the 'Letter to the Span-ish Americans' is missing, but comparative study of various ver-sions of the French text, as well as correspondence between Vis-cardo and James Bland Burges, the undersecretary of state in the British Foreign Office in the early 1790s, permitted Simmons to conclude that the letter had originally been redacted in Spanish and later translated by Viscardo himself into French.[12]

Translation, then, is an important part of the story of Viscardo's letter, as well as an often-overlooked aspect of the circulation of enlightened thought and revolutionary ideas in the Atlantic world. Silvio Zavala, in his classic work on how America figures in eighteenth-century French thinking and cultural production, stresses the importance of French translations of Spanish colonial histories, both in terms of the information disseminated through those translations and the role played by the prefatory comments of editors and translators, who provided a context for the presen-tation of the Spanish colonial project to French-speaking read-ers.[13] Other changes were incorporated into the texts themselves. For example, Miranda's 1799 publication of Viscardo's 'Letter' was a revised version of the French-language text Viscardo had

12. Edwards, 'Bibliographical Note,' 89–91. Edwards also suggests that the 1799 French translation was most likely printed in London by the same press that printed the 1801 Spanish translation (despite the false imprint of Philadelphia as the place of publica-tion, a common strategy at the time).

13. Silvio Zavala, *América en el espíritu francés del siglo XVIII* (1949; reprint, México: El Colegio Nacional, 1998), 221ss. Zavala cites Oviedo's *Historia natural y general de las Indias*, Cortés letters to Charles V, Las Casas's *Brevísima relación* (of course) and, moving to the eighteenth century, accounts by Jorge Juan and Antonio de Ulloa. These and other obser-vations on Spanish conquest and colonial administration, natural history, the nature of the indigenous and *criollo* population were also translated into other languages such as En-glish, Dutch, and German, permitting a lively debate that spanned several continents and several languages and that continued into the nineteenth century. For an exhaustive ac-count of these debates, see Antonello Gerbi, *The Dispute of the New World: The History of a Polemic, 1750–1900*, trans. Jeremy Moyle (1955; reprint, Pittsburgh: University of Pitts-burgh Press, 1973).

given to King. The revisions included the addition of a passage from the Dominican friar Bartolomé de Las Casas (legendary defender of America's indigenous population) and a list of exiled Jesuits living in Italy.[14] While the changes did not alter the fundamental thrust of the document, Miranda clearly hoped to strengthen the letter's denunciatory effect by invoking the infamous Black Legend and by enumerating the victims of the Spanish expulsion of the Jesuits (among whom, of course, could be counted the author of the letter). Miranda added references to key moments in Spanish American history that resonated with larger themes Viscardo develops, as can be seen in the opening words quoted earlier in this essay. In many instances the circulation of translated documents served, like reprints of newspaper articles, to circumvent Spanish efforts at censorship and must be taken into account in any discussion of emerging print culture.

Miranda also oversaw the letter's translation into Spanish in 1801 and into English in 1808, when it was published along with a brief treatise by a 'William Burke' (probably James Mill) on British policy in South America.[15] This publication was an important element in the collaboration efforts of Miranda and Mill in an effort to persuade the British to intervene in South America — efforts that were to prove futile, as we have seen. When Miranda set sail for Venezuela in 1806 to initiate what would be a failed revolutionary expedition there, he made certain that the '*Leandre*' had a small printing press on board so that he would be able to print copies of a 'Carta a los españoles americanos' for distribution upon landing. Unfortunately, the inhabitants of the Venezuelan coast settlement of Coro, where Miranda came ashore, were for the most part illiterate slaves who were not in a position to fully appreciate Viscardo's fiery prose and even less to read it as

14. The second English edition omitted these additions and is thus more faithful to the Viscardo original than Miranda's version.

15. For a fascinating account of Miranda's relationship with Mill, see Mario Rodríguez, 'Mario Rodríguez, '*William Burke' and Francisco de Miranda. The Word and the Deed in Spanish America's Emancipation* (Lanham, Md.: University Press of America, 1994).

a call to arms.[16] Nevertheless, Viscardo's 'Letter to the Spanish Americans' was read and copied and circulated among its intended audience, who responded to its passionate recapitulation of *criollo* complaints that had been voiced for over a century.

Before I turn to those complaints, I'd like to discuss briefly the critical reception of Viscardo's writing—an interesting story reflecting a number of historical and academic sub-fields. One such sub-field is the history of the Jesuits in the Americas and their 1767 expulsion. Miguel Batllori has studied the Hispano-Italian culture of Jesuit exiles in one important book and tellingly retains Viscardo's Jesuit honorific in the title of yet another: *El Abate Viscardo. Historia y mito de la intervención de los jesuitas en la independencia de Hispanoamérica*. A second sub-field is the canon of Peruvian national history to which Rubén Vargas Ugarte and a host of more recent commentators have contributed.[17] These scholars tend to promote Viscardo as a precursor or promoter of Americanist revolutionary thought, giving him ideological pride of place along with Miranda and Bolívar—perhaps in part to compensate for the belated achievement of Peruvian independence. Finally we have broader considerations of the background for, and evolution of, Spanish American independence movements in the Americas and in Europe by scholars such as Brading.

Here, as I have already mentioned, Merle E. Simmons has played a key role. In a 1985 article and a subsequent book-length study he explains with understandable satisfaction how he located the missing Viscardo papers, for which historians had searched for decades, in Box 81 of the Rufus King Collection in the New-York

16. It was here in Coro that the infiltration of revolutionary ideas from Haiti had led in 1797 to an unsuccessful conspiracy of mulattos and black slaves. See D. A. Brading, *The First America The Spanish Monarchy, Creole Patriots, and the Liberal State, 1492–1867* (Cambridge: Cambridge University Press, 1991), 604.

17. See Javier de Belaunde Ruiz de Somocurcio, *Juan Pablo Viscardo y Guzmán: Ideólogo y promotor de la independencia hispanoamericana* (Lima: Fondo Editorial del Congreso del Perú, 2002); Deustua Pimentel, *Juan Pablo Viscardo y Guzmán*; Luis Valera, *Juan Pablo Viscardo y Guzmán (1748–1798): El hombre y su tiempo*, 3 vols. (Lima: Fondo Editorial del Congreso del Perú. 1999); and Gustavo Vergara Arias, *Juan Pablo Viscardo y Guzmán. Primer precursor Ideológico de la Emancipación Hispanoamericana* (Lima: La Universidad Nacional Mayor de San Marcos, 1963).

Historical Society. Like most Peruvian scholars, Simmons empha-
sizes the letter's importance, citing the Mexican Carlos Pereyra,
who declared that Viscardo 'wrote a document that could be called
the 'Declaration of Independence of Spanish America'.[18] A latter-
day Miranda, Simmons functions not only as editor and translator
of the 400 manuscript pages found in the King collection, but also
as a polemical agent who argues for a central role for Viscardo in
the history of Spanish American independence: 'No other ma-
nipulator of the pen approximates him whether for antiquity as a
conspirator, for the abundance of his writings, or for the richness
and variety of his ideas.'[19]

At least one reviewer of the Simmons publication, Timothy
Anna, felt that these claims were overstated, even hyperbolic,
given that few people seem to have read Viscardo's writings at
the time, and even Miranda seems not to have been overly persuaded by them (despite his willingness to pass them out to the
unwitting citizens of Coro). Anna argues that Viscardo's faith in
Britain was misplaced, and he objects to his characterization of
three centuries of colonial rule as 'ingratitude, injustice, slavery,
and desolation.'[20] Perhaps more significantly, he questions,
'Does writing down ideas in manuscripts that, unfortunately,
end up not being read again for nearly two centuries make one a
major figure in the history of ideas?'[21] Anna is right, I suppose,
to call into question nationalist histories' obsession with the
'great man' or the founding father, or to point out that Thomas
Paine (with whom Viscardo y Guzman has frequently been
compared) had a clear revolutionary impact that the Peruvian

---

18. Merle E. Simmons, *Los escritos de Juan Pablo Viscardo y Guzmán: Precursor de la Independencia Hispanoamericana* (Caracas: Universidad Católica Andrés Bello, 1983), 5 (my
translation)

19. Simmons, *Los escritos de Juan Pablo Viscardo y Guzmán*, 141–42.

20. Here we might respond that Viscardo is writing within the Las Casian tradition of
hyperbolic enumeration. Indeed, Anna refers indirectly to the influence of Las Casas
when he asks, 'How are we to respond to a polemicist whose primary points added new
passion and misinformation to the Black Legend of Spain in America for a British cabinet
that already believed the worst allegations?' Timothy E Anna, 'Review of Merle E. Simmons, "Los escritos de Juan Pablo Viscardo y Guzman: Precursor de la independencia hispanoamericana,"' *Hispanic American Historical Review* 65 (1985): 563.

21. Anna, 'Review of Simmons, *Los escritos de Juan Pablo Viscardo*,' 564.

never had.[22] However, in order to appreciate fully Viscardo's importance in the history of Spanish American emancipation, it may be helpful to think about print culture as only one element in the complex process of the production and reception of revolutionary ideas.

I will now turn to a discussion of the salient issues that Viscardo raises in the 'Letter' as he resorts to a number of different strategies to awaken the revolutionary spirit of his fellow Spanish Americans. First, and not surprisingly, Viscardo appeals to a providentialist interpretation of the 1492 'discovery,' but giving it a new twist:

> It would be a blasphemy to imagine, that the Supreme Benefactor of man has permitted the discovery of the New World, merely that a small number of imbecile knaves might / always be at liberty to desolate it; and that they should incessantly have the odious pleasure of stripping millions of men, who have given them no cause of complaint, of essential rights received from his divine hand to imagine that his eternal wisdom wished to deprive the remainder of mankind of the immense advantages which, in the order of nature, so great an event ought to procure for them, and to condemn them to wish with a groan, that the New World had remained for ever unknown.'[23]

Divine intervention in the discovery of America here represents not a blank check but rather a debt to be repaid through good governance and the procurement of essential rights for its inhabitants. To that end Viscardo proposes a second discovery: 'Let us throw open a second time America to all our brother inhabitants of this globe, from whence ingratitude, injustice, and the most senseless avarice have exiled us; the recompense will not be less to us than to them.'[24]

---

22. Another reviewer of the Simmons publication concludes: 'The picture of Viscardo which emerges from the pages of these documents seems far more reminiscent of the prototypical "ambivalent revolutionary" of Peru described elsewhere by John Lynch and Timothy Anna rather than the hostile and bitter paranoiac sketched by Father Miguel Batllori among others.' Leon G. Campbell, 'Review of Merle E. Simmons, *Los escritos de Juan Pablo Viscardo y Guzman. Precursor de la independencia hispanoamericana,*' *The Americas* 42 (1985): 272.

23. Viscardo, *Letter to the Spanish Americans* 82–83.

24. Viscardo, *Letter to the Spanish Americans*, 83.

He also invokes the traditional concept of Spanish honor by challenging his compatriots to match the revolutionary efforts of the Anglo-Americans:

> The valour with which the English colonies of America have fought for the liberty, which they gloriously enjoy, covers our indolence with shame; we have yielded to them the palm with which they have been the first to crown the New World by their sovereign independence. Add the eagerness of the Courts of Spain and France to assist the cause / of the English Americans; it accuses us of insensibility; let at least the feelings of honour be roused—by outrages which have endured for three hundred years.[25]

Lurking behind much of Viscardo's inflammatory rhetoric, I would argue, is an ever-present sense of outrage stemming from his exile as a Jesuit. In fact, he frequently uses 'exile' as a metaphor to express a general sense of alienation and estrangement among all *criollos* arising from Spanish abuses in the New World. Moreover, Viscardo makes several specific references to the Jesuit expulsions, both in the body of the letter and in a series of footnotes. Here is one such reference: 'The supreme economical power, and the motives reserved in the royal bosom (expressions which cannot fail to astonish posterity) discovery at last the vanity of all the reveries of mankind about the eternal principles of justice, on the rights and duties of nature and of society, have suddenly displayed their irresistible force on more than *five thousand* Spanish citizens.'[26]

Charles III, in the 1767 expulsion edict, had prohibited the exiled Jesuits from writing about the circumstances of the expulsion itself. In response, they recreated Spanish America in their writings as both the earthly paradise from which they have been expelled and a utopian future, ever more sharply differentiated

---

25. Viscardo, *Letter to the Spanish Americans*, 83–84.
26. The reference to 'motives reserved in the royal bosom' paraphrases Charles III's expulsion edict. Viscardo, *Letter to the Spanish Americans*, 75; see also 71. Viscardo also writes: 'The expulsion and the ruin of the Jesuits had, according to every appearance, no other motives than the report of their riches. . . . ' (78).

from a European past. For these Jesuits, as we see in Viscardo's letter, *patria* must be a rhetorical construction. According to Miguel Batllori, the New World historiography they produced, tinged by nostalgia and ambivalently positioned between Europe and America, served as a foundation for an emerging sense of *criollo* identity.[27]

Viscardo, exiled and peripatetic, suffered from a condition that is marked by pathos and possibility. In the 'Letter,' he speaks to Spanish Americans in general about all of Spanish America, but with frequent recourse to firsthand knowledge and nostalgia for his native Peru. For this reason, Viscardo's use of history in the letter is often couched in genealogical terms. We see this as he explains the relationship between Spanish Americans and Spain: 'Nature has separated us from Spain by immense seas; a son who should find himself at a similar distance from his father would without doubt be a fool, if in the conduct / of his least concerns, he always waited for the decision of the father. The son is set free by natural right: and out of a numerous people, who do not depend for any thing on another people, of whom they have no need, to be subjected to them like the vilest slaves?'[28] But Viscardo also looked to genealogy and family relations in quoting extensively from the *Comentarios reales*, using El Inca Garcilaso's defense of 'those who were born in this country, of Indian mothers and Spanish fathers' against false accusations of treachery and rebellion.[29] Here Viscardo was able to forge a link between sixteenth-century Spanish abuses and the recent uprisings of Tupac Amaru in Peru. In appropriating and allying himself with

27. Miguel Batllori, *El Abate Viscardo: Historia y mito de la intervención de los jesuítas en la independencia de Hispanoamérica* (Caracas: Instituto Panamericano de Geografía e Historia, 1953), 578.

28. Viscardo, *Letter to the Spanish Americans*, 81–82.

29. Miranda would have been especially interested in Viscardo's references to the Inca past, as his proposal to reestablish the Inca Empire under the protection of British proconsul laid out in the fragment, 'Projet de constitution pour les colonies hispano-américaines,' is a bizarre mix of medieval governance and Inca imperial practice. See Campbell, 'Review of Merle E. Simmons,' 272; Pagden, 'Old Constitutions and Ancient Indian Empires,' 131.

an indigenous past, Viscardo was performing a sleight of hand used by other eighteenth-century writers such as Clavigero in his ancient *History of Mexico*.[30]

Commerce is another unifying theme in the 'Letter.' Viscardo complains bitterly about the penury to which *criollos* are reduced as a result of Spanish mismanagement. He quotes Juan and Ulloa on the scarcity of wine that had the effect of limiting the occasions on which Mass could be celebrated—a wonderful example of the convergence of revolutionary and traditional zeal.[31] America's potential for commercial riches was presented as an opportunity for defraying the costs of the revolutionary projects Viscardo is proposing, and also as the glue that will unite an independent America with the larger world: 'We should then alone frequent the ports of Spain, and become masters of her commerce, of her riches and of her destiny.'[32] This is a theme of enlightened political economists that we find elsewhere in Viscardo's writings such as his essay 'Peace and the Happiness of the Next Century,' written just before his death.[33]

Viscardo's challenge is to help his readers imagine and embrace new political identities as familiar and legitimate. To do this he appeals to Spanish medieval tradition justifying popular resistance to an unjust king: 'After the memorable epoch of the arbitrary power and injustice of the last Gothic kings, which brought on the ruin of their empire and of the Spanish nation, our ancestors, in reestablishing the kingdom and its government, thought

30. Abbé Francesco Saverie Clavigero, *The History of Mexico*, 3 vols. (Philadelphia: Thomas Dobson, 1804).Pagden observes that 'Independence for Viscardo was to be an act of restoration, a restoration of the political values of Castile, a restoration of the culture of the ancient Indian world, and in many cases, a restoration of the Garcilassan project for a multiracial community.' Pagden, 'Old Constitutions and Ancient Indian Empires, 129.

31. Viscardo, *Letter to the Spanish Americans*, 66; see Brading, *The First America*, 536.

32. Viscardo, *Letter to the Spanish Americans*, 80.

33. Onuf explains with reference to Jefferson: 'The notion of reciprocal benefits in mutually beneficial exchange was particularly attractive to colonists who chafed under a mercantilist regime that they believed enriched the metropolitan core at the expense of the provincial periphery.' Peter S. Onuf, "'Empire for Liberty': Center and Peripheries in Postcolonial America,' *Negotiated Empires: Centers and Peripheries in the Americas, 1500–1820*, Christine Daniels and Michael V. Kennedy, eds. (New York and London: Routledge, 2002), 309. See also Pagden, 'Old Constitutions and Ancient Indian Empires, 117; Deustua Pimentel, *Juan Pablo Viscardo y Guzmán*, 6–7.

only of guarding against the absolute power to which our kings have always aspired.[34] By privileging medieval constitutionalism, Viscardo is able to trace a continuum from the old to the new and propose revolution not as disorder but rather as a kind of restoration of order.[35]

Moving beyond his immediate audience of Spanish American *criollos*, Viscardo concludes by envisioning a new 'reign of reason, of justice, and of humanity. . .' open to all—even the 'wise and virtuous' Spaniards who will join a host of others:

> What an agreeable and affecting spectacle will the fertile shores of America present, covered with men from all nations exchanging the productions of their country against ours! How many from among them, flying oppression or misery, will come to enrich us by their industry and their knowledge, and to repair our exhausted population? Thus would America unite the extremities of the earth; and her inhabitants, united by a common interest, would form one GREAT FAMILY OF BROTHERS.[36]

This is a curious call that combines echoes of Garcilasan universalism and an anticipation of nineteenth-century calls by Sarmiento and Alberdi for European immigration to revitalize and colonize the pampas—reminding us once again of the vital link played by late eighteenth and early nineteenth-century writers in the evolution of a discourse of Spanish American identity.

In conclusion, I'd like to return to the title of this essay, 'Writing Back to Empire.' I use the phrase 'writing back' in both contestatory and chronological terms, and 'empire' to refer to a number of historical moments. Viscardo wrote back to the British Empire in hopes that it will support him and his fellow 'Spanish

---

34. Viscardo, *Letter to the Spanish Americans*, 73.

35. Brading,. *The First America*, 539; Onuf argues that Jeffersonian Republicans do something similar by incorporating enlightened thinking on behalf of an antique imperial vision: 'As reform-minded proponents of an idealized world order, made fully and finally compatible with natural rights, free exchange, the progressive diffusion of civilization, and the rights of self-government within and among confederated states, Jeffersonian-Republican imperialists looked backward.' (Onuf, 'Empire for Liberty,' 303.)

36. Viscardo, *Letter to the Spanish Americans*, 85.

Americans' in their quest for independence from Spain. He wrote back to the Spanish Empire, denouncing its colonial history as one of 'ingratitude, injustice, slavery, and desolation.'[37] But he also writes back to the Inca Empire in search of legitimizing models for the future he envisioned for an independent Spanish America. In doing so, he gave voice to *criollo* aspirations that would continue to resonate until political independence was finally achieved.

Other Works Consulted

Bacorzo, Jorge Gustavo Xavier. *Los hermanos Viscardo y Guzmán: pensamiento y acción americanistas*. Pról. Merle E. Simmons. Lima: Universidad Ricardo Palma, 2000.

Cussen, Antonio. *Bello and Bolívar. Poetry and Politics in the Spanish American Revolution*. Cambridge and New York: Cambridge University Press, 1992.

Outram, Dorinda. *The Enlightenment*. Cambridge and New York: Cambridge University Press, 1995.

Shields, David. *Oracles of Empire: Poetry, Politics, and Commerce in British America, 1690–1750*. Chicago: University of Chicago Press, 1990.

Viscardo. *Carta dirigida a los españoles americanos*. Intro. David Brading. México: Fondo de Cultura Económica, 2004.

37. Viscardo, *Letter to the Spanish Americans*, 63.

Caribbean Revolution and Print Publics: Leonora Sansay and 'The Secret History of the Haitian Revolution'

ELIZABETH MADDOCK DILLON

I N A NOW OFTEN-QUOTED PHRASE, the historian Michel-Rolph Trouillot has described the Haitian Revolution as 'unthinkable.' In his book, *Silencing the Past: Power and the Production of History*, Trouillot writes: 'The Haitian Revolution did challenge the ontological and political assumptions of the most radical writers of the Enlightenment. The events that shook up Saint Domingue from 1791 to 1804 constituted a sequence for which not even the extreme political left in France or in England had a conceptual frame of reference. They were "unthinkable" facts in the framework of Western thought.'[1]

The question of the unthinkable is different from what is secret, what is private, or what is hidden. The unthinkable is not that which does not appear but that which cannot be comprehended, even when it does appear. The unthinkable, one might say, is what is hidden in plain sight. As Trouillot indicates, the

---

1. Michel-Rolph Trouillot, *Silencing the Past: Power and the Production of History* (Boston: Beacon Press, 1995), 82.

ELIZABETH MADDOCK DILLON is associate professor of English and American Studies, Yale University.

Haitian Revolution has not, historically, been included in accounts of the so-called 'Age of Revolutions' and this is so for two reasons: first, because a culturally dominant ontology presupposed that there were degrees of humanity indexed by race; and second, because the colonial system relied upon this increasingly racialized ontology to effect its day-to-day workings. Such a system understood slaves to be collectively content if not individually so, as well as fundamentally dependent and incapable of political self-determination. In the face of such an ontology, empirical evidence to the contrary, such as that provided by the Haitian Revolution, simply failed to register on the screen of Western history.

In contrast to this account of an unthinkable history of revolution, theoretical work on print culture and revolution rests upon the presumption of the transparent nature of historical evidence and political argument as it appears in print. To print is to make public and thus make known; to read is to 'see' both visually and conceptually. The association of print with liberty has generated a body of work exploring the historical intersection of publicity and political freedom. In its most well-known, though certainly not uncontested formulation, Jürgen Habermas has described publicity or the public sphere as constitutive of liberal political formations dating to the eighteenth century.[2] The model of the print public sphere that we have associated with the rise of liberal republicanism and democratic nationalism presupposes that information circulates according to a principle of critical rationality and that this principle binds publics together into larger political communities. Habermas's formulation—whether we want to understand it as a historically descriptive model or a normative one—owes its enduring appeal to the clarity of self-evidence. Once people are free to express their ideas, so the theory goes, ideas will compete with one another on the basis of their logic

2. Jürgen Habermas, *The Structural Transformation of the Public Sphere*, trans. Thomas Burger (Cambridge, Mass.: MIT Press 1989).

and rationality rather than on the basis of the prestige or power of their speakers: the impersonality of print, or, alternatively, the rules of public sphere engagement, ideally guarantee the triumph of reason and its Enlightenment corollary, justice. But another historical corollary of Enlightenment has cast a shadow on the sunshine of the rational public sphere, and this corollary is that of colonialism and the geopolitics of race, including race slavery and the genocide of indigenous peoples in the Americas. Is modernity, then—as associated with the Enlightenment, with rational critical debate, publicity, print, and universalism—a project that was simply incomplete in its eighteenth-century Atlantic formulations? Or, alternatively, does modernity have a constitutive underside to it—an underside of violence and oppression that gives the lie to a theory of the print public sphere as a source of reason and political liberation?

A number of intriguing answers to this question have been proposed, among the most prominent of which is that of Paul Gilroy who has articulated a model of diasporic African-Atlantic culture that he identifies as a 'counter-culture of modernity.' He identifies the roots of this culture as largely distinct from, if not antithetical to, norms of communicative reason as well as print publicity. For Gilroy, privileged instances of this counter-culture are music and memory as characterized by an aesthetic of indirection and of resistance that is 'not reducible to the cognitive.' Gilroy explains that 'the extreme patterns of communication defined by the institution of plantation slavery dictate that we recognize the anti-discursive and extra-linguistic ramifications of power at work in shaping communicative acts.'[3] In other words, given the ways in which slaves within an Atlantic plantation culture were forbidden from using a Habermasian toolkit of rational communication, an alternative, counter-culture of expression developed, characterized above all by its resistance to the form and content

---

3. Paul Gilroy, *The Black Atlantic: Modernity and Double Consciousness* (Cambridge, Mass.: Harvard University Press, 1993), 57.

of Western Enlightenment and rationality. The rules of rational communication, one might say, were precisely what needed to be evaded so that interchange could take place among slaves while avoiding (increased) violence at the hands of white masters.

Such a formulation about the nature of an alternative communication system would seem to be something of an answer to Trouillot's question concerning the silence of the slave revolt in Haiti. Gilroy gives an account of a response to the fact that the rationality of the Enlightenment contains and constrains its 'other' to irrationality, such that the logic and even the reality of slave revolt became unassimilable to public histories of enlightenment revolution. And yet it seems clear, as well, that Gilroy captures a problem of production in his account of alternative communication more so than he accounts for matters of reception or reading. If, as I will argue below, accounts of the Haitian Revolution are hidden in plain sight, this means not that such accounts were never written, never printed, or never circulated, but that somehow that circulation did not compel an audience to make sense of it, did not compel an audience of readers to integrate the Haitian Revolution into an understanding of the Age of Revolutions, or into histories of, say, the Louisiana Purchase and United States Manifest Destiny, but instead enabled the Haitian Revolution to remain within a shroud of non-publicity—a shroud of isolation from world history and a shroud of silence.

In this essay, then, I explore not the lack of production of information or printed materials about the Haitian revolution, but their lack of reception among a reading public. The problem of reception is not, however, unrelated to Gilroy's claims concerning the counter-culture of Atlantic modernity. Given that Gilroy proposes that a counter-culture was created in antithesis to the discursive norms of Enlightenment rationality, recovering or reading the traces of this counter-culture (or of the many counter-cultures of the Atlantic) will require techniques of reading and reception other than those with which we are most familiar.[4] In what follows, I consider a question of reading and reception that arises in relation to a single printed text, namely, a novel written by an American woman named Leonora Sansay that was published in 1808, titled *Secret History, or the Horrors of St. Domingo*. I turn to this novel for a number of reasons: first, the oxymoronic tension within the very term, 'secret history' seems particularly germane to the question of how publicity does or does not operate with respect to revolution; second, as a literary scholar I am interested in the genre of the novel and the theoretical questions raised by considering works of literature in relation to the politics of liberty and revolution in Atlantic print culture.

With respect to the literary form of the novel, even more so than with respect to the political pamphlet, philosophical treatise, or even the newspaper, it seems crucial to ask whether print generates its audience and therefore its reception procedurally or by way of argument. Does the activity of reading serve to shape political communities or, alternatively, does the content of print have a persuasive effect upon a reader and thus an effect in creating political communities? A Habermasian account would indicate that the content of the argument is what matters about print, but Benedict Anderson's influential account of the novel and its relation to the formation of the imagined community of

4. A number of scholars have begun to engage in precisely this work—that is, scholarship that proposes new modes of reading Atlantic culture. Sibylle Fischer, in *Modernity Disavowed: Haiti and the Cultures of Slavery in the Age of Revolution* (Durham: Duke University Press, 2004), for instance, analyzes materials as diverse as wall paintings and political, religious, and historical paintings from the nineteenth century in relation to the Haitian Revolution; Joanna Brooks in *American Lazarus: Religion and the Rise of African-American and Native American Literatures* (New York: Oxford University Press, 2003), excavates a rich culture of early printed work by Native Americans and African Americans in relation to a specific institutions such as the church and freemason societies; performance studies scholars including Joseph Roach (in *Cities of the Dead: Circum-Atlantic Performance* [New York: Columbia University Press, 1996]) and Jill Lane (*Blackface Cuba, 1840–1945* [Philadelphia: University of Pennsylvania Press, 2005]), have generated important new accounts of circum-Atlantic and hemispheric culture in their work; and Fred Moten (*In the Break: The Aesthetics of the Black Radical Tradition* [Minneapolis: University of Minnesota Press, 2003]) has proposed an analytics of diasporic and African-American music that stands to revise our understanding of the archive of modernity. Much of this work exists at the intersection of print culture with performance, visual arts, and music.

SECRET HISTORY;

OR,

THE HORRORS OF ST. DOMINGO,

IN

A SERIES OF LETTERS,

WRITTEN BY A LADY AT CAPE FRANCOIS.

[Mrs. Leonora Sansay]

TO

COLONEL BURR,

LATE VICE-PRESIDENT OF THE UNITED STATES,

PRINCIPALLY DURING THE COMMAND OF

GENERAL ROCHAMBEAU.

PHILADELPHIA:

PUBLISHED BY BRADFORD & INSKEEP.

R. CARR, PRINTER.

. . . .

1808.

[Leonora Sansay], *Secret History or, The Horrors of St. Domingo, in a Series of Letters, Written by a Lady at Cape François, to Colonel Burr, Late Vice-President of the United States, Principally During the Command of General Rochambeau* (Philadelphia: Bradford and Inskeep, 1808).

the nation suggests that the procedure of reading may be as significant as the content of what is read. According to Anderson, the novel and the nation serve as analogues insofar as both operate within an 'empty, homogenous' time—a time in which a variety of persons (citizens of a nation, characters in a novel) pursue their own lives yet understand themselves to stand in relation to others whom they don't know—other individuals who occupy a narrative/national 'meanwhile.' Further, Anderson specifically provides a model of creole nationhood that is generated in relation to the print forms of the newspaper and the novel; his examples in *Imagined Communities* include Mexico, Peru, and the Philippines. Consider, for instance, his account of the colonial newspaper, which, like the novel, procedurally links disparately located individuals in a shared imaginary space:

> What were the characteristics of the first American newspapers, North or South? They began essentially as appendages of the market. Early gazettes contained ... commercial news (when ships would arrive and depart, what prices were current for what commodities in what ports), as well as colonial political appointments, marriages of the wealthy, and so forth. In other words, what brought together, on the same page, *this* marriage with *that* ship, *this* price with *that* bishop, was the very structure of the colonial administration and market-system itself. In this way, the newspaper of Caracas quite naturally, and even apolitically, created an imagined community among a specific assemblage of fellow-readers, to whom *these* ships, brides, bishops and prices belonged. In time, of course, it was only to be expected that political elements would enter in.[5]

Only in the last sentence of this passage do we find an oblique reference to revolution: Anderson argues that because people understand themselves to occupy the homogenous time and space of the nation insofar as they read newspapers and novels

---

5. Benedict Anderson, *Imagined Communities: Reflections on the Origin and Spread of Nationalism*, 2nd ed., (London: Verso Editions/NLB, 1991), 62.

that they understand to be addressed to people like themselves, so too do they develop a sense of community that would 'of course' generate a new political formation. For Anderson, print generates a readership that generates revolution.

In contrast to Habermas's account of the relation between print and revolution, Anderson indicates that an imaginative engagement in a collectivity (a new public) results in the new political form of the nation. But to what extent does temporal homogeneity in the novel or the newspaper generate a homogenous community of readers? And is the political form that results from this community logically a nation? In a useful critique of Anderson, Ed White has argued that the United States was not conceived in its earliest form as an imagined nation, in the terms Anderson suggests, but rather was at its origin an imagined empire—an empire constituted as a series of nations rather than as a single nation. White further suggests that a sense of unified nationhood was late to arrive in the United States; only under the presidency of Andrew Jackson did a stronger sense of unity begin to script United States culture, despite the advent of the United States nation as a political entity some fifty years earlier.[6] Following White's analysis, I would suggest that the framework of United States nationalism that has pervaded the study of the early American novel has contributed to making Sansay's novel about the Haitian Revolution illegible, just as the Enlightenment rubric of the 'Age of Revolutions' has rendered the Haitian Revolution invisible. Read in light of an alternative geopolitical imaginary, however, Sansay's novel has much to say about both the nature of early America and the significance of revolution in Haiti.

Both at the time of its printing and in the nearly two hundred years that have elapsed since then, Sansay's novel about the Haitian Revolution has not generated a wide readership. Unlike novels such as Susanna Rowson's *Charlotte Temple*, or Hannah Webster

6. Ed White, 'Early American Nations as Imagined Communities,' *American Quarterly* 56 (2004): 49–81.

Foster's *Coquette*, which went through multiple editions and found large readerships in the United States, Sansay's novel was published in one 1808 edition by Bradford and Inskeep in Philadelphia. It has not, since then, found a wide scholarly audience either; indeed it has long been out of print, although a new scholarly edition edited by Michael Drexler is forthcoming.[7] Further, the novel is not included in accounts of the early American novel; most notably it does not appear in Cathy Davidson's fairly exhaustive account of the early American novel, despite the fact that it was written by an American author and published in Philadelphia.[8] Yet in what follows, I argue that Sansay's novel has been hidden in plain sight. Her novel provides a secret history not of creole nationalism, but of a creole cosmopolitanism that has been overwritten by accounts of print and the novel as generative of and legible in relation to national publics. The dominant national imaginary of the United States ultimately took the form of a racially white identification; as a result, the creole cosmopolitan origins of the United States that were abundantly evident when the American Revolution was placed next to the Haitian Revolution have been effectively erased. Sansay's novel, however, brings the shared creole politics of the early United States and the Haitian Revolution into view.

Sansay's epistolary novel recounts the journeys of two sisters, Mary and Clara, who travel to Saint Domingue in 1802 with Clara's French husband, St. Louis, in order to reclaim property he abandoned there at the outset of revolutionary violence in the 1790s. When the novel opens, the main city of Saint Domingue, Le Cap Français, is controlled by the French General Charles Victor Emmanuel Leclerc, who had been sent by Napoleon to reassert French colonial control over the island. Sansay thus depicts a historical moment at which the French sought to reinstall

7. Leonora Sansay, *Secret History; or the Horrors of St. Domingo and Laura*, ed. Michael J. Drexler (Peterborough, Ont.: Broadview Press, 2007). Further citations are from this edition.

8. Cathy Davidson, *Revolution and the Word: The Rise of the Novel in America* (1986; reprint New York: Oxford University Press, 2004).

a colonial regime of race slavery, and thus to turn back the clock on a decade of turmoil during which blacks had successfully fought to abolish slavery and had consolidated political leadership in the figure of Toussaint Louverture. When Leclerc's expedition arrived with massive numbers of troops, Toussaint was serving as governor of the island in the name of the French Republic. Toussaint was thus by no means an official enemy of the French state, yet Napoleon was clearly worried by the degree of power exercised by the black leader, and gave Leclerc orders to depose immediately all black generals from positions of power and thus to reestablish a racial hierarchy on the island that coincided with the ontological claims of colonial race slavery. Napoleon imagined that it would not be difficult to take over the island and indeed, proposed that Leclerc's expedition would proceed to Louisiana after establishing control of Saint Domingue. Yet Napoleon was proven quite wrong: while Leclerc managed to capture Toussaint and remove him from the island, Leclerc's troops died by the thousands, devastated by war and disease. News of the reinstitution of slavery by the French in nearby Guadeloupe galvanized black forces on the island under the leadership of Jean-Jacques Dessalines. Leclerc himself died of yellow fever in 1802 and was replaced by General Donatien Marie Joseph de Rochambeau, a man who quickly became notorious for the atrocities he committed against black revolutionaries. Ultimately, however, Rochambeau's forces were routed by Dessalines and Haiti was established as the first independent black republic in the west under Dessalines's leadership in 1804.

In its main outlines, Sansay's novel is strikingly autobiographical and thus true to the historical events of the final years of the Haitian Revolution. Sansay was herself married to a French planter, Louis Sansay, and she traveled with him to Saint Domingue in 1802, where she observed the death throes of French colonial rule that she describes in the novel. In the novel, the primary correspondent, Mary, writes to her close friend, Aaron Burr, then vice president of the United States, about her travels with her sister Clara to Saint Domingue, their flight from the island during the overthrow of French rule, and their travels among a refugee community of women in the Caribbean in the wake of the revolution. Sansay was, herself, a close friend and perhaps a lover of Aaron Burr's and the novel thus duplicates her own experience in this regard as well, albeit with one important distinction—namely, the novel bifurcates Sansay's persona into the character of two sisters, thereby enabling Sansay to recount the intrigues of Clara's love life through the eyes of a more distant observer, Mary. The tale recounted in the novel is bifurcated as well. On the one hand, the novel tells the story of the final years of the Haitian Revolution, during which the slave regime of French colonials was overthrown by the only successful slave revolt in the modern West. And on the other hand, the novel trains its attentions on the 'domestic' account of Clara's troubled relation with her tyrannical husband, St. Louis, and the affairs of the heart of elite colonials and creoles in Saint Domingue.

In its opening pages the novel strives to evoke the fantasy of coloniality that Napoleon and his military emissaries sought to recreate. Mary writes, for instance, that she would like to see the black revolutionary forces defeated in order to enjoy a life of white colonial luxury: 'I wish [the black revolutionaries] were reduced to order that I might see the so much vaunted habitations where I should repose beneath the shade of orange groves; walk on carpets of rose leaves and frenchipone; be fanned to sleep by silent slaves, or have my feet tickled into extacy by the soft hand of a female attendant' (58). Yet Mary is repeatedly forced to acknowledge that this ideal is not possible: 'the moment of enjoying these pleasures,' she writes, 'is, I fear, far distant'(58). More intriguing than the fact that colonialism and white privilege are fatally under attack in the novel, however, is the critique of colonial nostalgia that Sansay presents through the development of her white characters. While Mary initially seeks to find the pleasures of colonial luxury, Sansay also posits that Mary eventually abandons her pursuit of them because she becomes suspicious of them—

that is, as the novel progresses, the fantasy begins to fade, not because it is unachievable (although it is ultimately that), but because it becomes undesirable.

Interestingly, however, the luster of colonial fantasy is dispelled within the novel as much in relation to a developing critique of the gender politics of colonialism as in relation to racial politics. The primary figure around whom the allure of luxury is constellated in the novel is Mary's sister, Clara. Unhappy in her marriage, only the diversions of society and the staging of her beauty before wealthy admirers draws her out of her lassitude in Saint Domingue. Ballroom scenes thus become theatrical centerpieces within the early pages of the novel. Mary writes:

> The ball announced by the admiral exceeded all expectations and we are still all extacy. Boats, covered with carpets, conveyed the company from the shore to the vessel, which was anchored about half a mile from the land, and on entering the ball room a fairy palace presented itself to the view. . . . Never had I beheld [Clara] so interesting. A robe of white crape shewed to advantage the contours of her elegant person. Her arms and bosom were bare; her black hair, fastened on the top with a brilliant comb, was ornamented by a rose which seemed to have been thrown there by accident. (59)

In both her regal glamour and her island ennui, Clara is represented as analogous to another figure whom Mary meets upon arrival in Saint Domingue, namely, Pauline Leclerc, the beautiful wife of General Leclerc and the sister of Napoleon. Madame Leclerc spends her days languishing upon a sofa in a darkened room, entertained by an intrigue with one General Boyer, whom she bewitches with her 'blue eyes . . . flaxen hair . . . [and] voluptuous mouth' (52). However, the aura of conquest in which both Clara and Madame Leclerc seem to bathe is soon dispersed by the revelation that the women are themselves forms of property embedded within the colonial regime.

Madame Leclerc's husband, we learn, has been granted control of the island of Saint Domingue because Madame Leclerc received it from her brother, Napoleon, as her 'marriage portion.' As such, both Pauline Leclerc and Saint Domingue serve as colonial properties that are exchanged between men. When General Leclerc dies of yellow fever, Madame Leclerc performs an extravagant show of mourning, cutting her flaxen hair, and quickly exits to France. Further, Clara's triumphant scene of ballroom conquest, in which she wins the eye of the new colonial commander, General Rochambeau, rapidly results in her utter disempowerment as she becomes entrapped between her husband's jealous attempts to imprison her and Rochambeau's predatory attentions. When black revolutionary forces led by General Dessalines approach Le Cap, vowing to kill all the women and children in the city, Rochambeau attempts to abduct Clara on the pretext of protecting her. Yet Clara insists that to depart from her home against St. Louis's will amounts to a death sentence: 'Here I must stay if I am sure to perish,' she asserts.[9] Ironically, then, Clara is more terrorized by her husband's death threats than by those of the approaching army.

Sansay thus displaces the violence of race revolution with that of patriarchal, domestic violence. Indeed, the 'secret history' of the revolution seems to have more to do with the story of violence internal to heterosexual marriage than with that of black on white violence. Mary writes, 'Nothing can be more brutal than St. Louis in his rage! The day of his affair with the general, he threw [Clara] on the ground, and then dragged her by the hair:— I flew to her, but his aspect so terrified me that I was obliged to withdraw: and when his fits of tenderness return he is as bad in the other extreme.' [10] Later in the novel, St. Louis threatens to disfigure Clara by rubbing acid in her face. The intimate 'horror' of such scenes within the novel tends to affectively supersede the intermittent anecdotes of revolutionary violence that are reported by Mary as occurring at a distance. Accordingly, we might say that Sansay substitutes the violence of gendered oppression

9. Sansay, *Secret History*, 65.
10. Sansay, *Secret History*, 68.

for that of race revolution. What are the political implications of this substitution? In one respect, Sansay would seem to thereby erase the politics of race from the scene of the Haitian Revolution in favor of a story of white, elite marriage. Yet a careful reading of the novel indicates that Sansay more often entwines issues of race and gender such that her accounts of domestic violence in colonial spaces function to critique a colonial fantasy of white superiority and black incapacity as well as the inequities of marriage.

Indeed, Clara's self-understanding shifts decisively at a moment when General Rochambeau's violence is revealed to extend from gender relations to race relations. Although increasingly disaffected by Rochambeau's aggressive pursuit of her, Clara's career as a coquette is brought up short in relation to scenes of racial violence. Rochambeau, Mary reports, has presided over the burning at the stake of three black revolutionaries in the public square. While she reports on the general censure of this 'cruel act,' she also indicates that this particular cruelty is but a prelude to a more disturbing one: namely, Rochambeau's attempt to extort money from a white creole named Feydon and his subsequent execution of Feydon for failing to produce the funds demanded. 'Since the death of Feydon,' Mary writes, 'the general [Rochambeau] appears no more in public. A settled gloom pervades the place, and every one trembles lest he should be the next victim of a monster from whose power there is no retreat . . . Clara is in the greatest dejection. She repents bitterly the levity of her conduct.'[11]

Clara regrets pursuing Rochambeau when she comes to see him as the embodiment of colonial policies that are fundamentally unjust and oppressive. The primary catalyst for Clara's new understanding of Rochambeau (and of colonialism more broadly) is his treatment of the white creole; however, this treatment is revealed to be of a piece with his violence toward blacks and women as well.

The category of the creole thus becomes central to the events of the novel and to Sansay's understanding of the meaning of the

11. Sansay, *Secret History*, 82.

Haitian Revolution. In the language of colonialism, creoles are individuals of European or African descent who are born in the colony; creoles are thus natives of the New World who are nonetheless not indigenous peoples. From a metropolitan colonial perspective, white creoles of the West Indies were typically viewed as degraded figures. In their distance from metropolitan culture and climate, white creoles were presumed to have imbibed a certain social degeneracy from the world of the plantation—a degeneracy that was not biologically racial (not explicitly a matter of racial mixing, for instance) but that was nonetheless often metonymically associated with discourses of racial impurity. In the novel, Clara and Mary initially embrace this account of the creole as indolent and degenerate but subsequently develop sympathy for the plight of the creole in the colonial setting and, accordingly, significantly revise their understanding of ceole character. Mary describes this shift in viewpoint as one that occurs in relation to the social disorder caused by the revolution: 'The creole ladies have an air of voluptuous languor which renders them extremely interesting. . . . Almost too indolent to pronounce their words they speak with a drawling accent that is very agreeable: but since they have been roused by the pressure of misfortune many of them have displayed talents and found resources in the energy of their own minds which it would have been supposed impossible for them to possess.'[12] In narrative terms, this shift of viewpoint regarding the creole is rendered central to the novel when Clara redefines her identity from that of a metropolitan colonial (a Pauline Leclerc figure, wife of a French planter, mistress of Rochambeau) to that of a creole refugee (an American woman in flight from anti-colonial revolution).

Significantly, the creole refugee, according to Sansay, is as much in danger of being the victim of metropolitan colonial violence as of black revolutionary violence. When bloodshed breaks out on the island, Mary writes, 'Many of the Creoles, who had

12. Sansay, *Secret History*, 56.

remained on the island during the reign of Toussaint, regret the change, and say that they were less vexed by the negroes than by those who have come to protect them. And these negroes, notwithstanding the state of brutal subjection in which they were kept, have at length acquired a knowledge of their own strength. More than five hundred thousand broke the yoke imposed on them by a few thousand men of a different colour, and claimed the rights of which they had been so cruelly deprived.'[13] This passage indicates that Mary's sympathies for the situation of the creole are related to what we might call an ontological shift in her understanding of race as well. Rather than accepting colonial doxa concerning the degeneracy of the creole and the incapacity of blacks for self-rule, she asserts that white creoles are not well-served by colonial policy and asserts, as well, that colonial policy is fundamentally flawed in its understanding of the peoples (white and black) who inhabit Saint Domingue.

To be sure, Sansay's primary interest generally lies with the situation of white women. However, because her concern is with white women from the colonial periphery of the Atlantic world, her plot focuses on the development of a creole consciousness that tends to cut across racial categories rather than reinforce them: in effect, Sansay finds the dichotomy between metropolitan and creole identity more significant than that between white and black identity. Black creoles thus become subjects of sympathy in her narrative, as do white creoles.[14] When Mary and Clara see the atrocities committed by Rochambeau against blacks and white creoles, they seek to leave the island and are ultimately able to do so because they are American women: French men are not allowed to leave the island because they are required to defend it, and, moreover, British blockades around the island prohibit

13. Sansay, *Secret History*, 60.
14. A significant instance of this is the story of Zuline, related by Mary in the novel, a creole mulatta whose efforts save a white man during the revolution. A novel titled *Zelica the Creole*, which follows the fate of a mixed race creole, was published in 1821 in London and has been attributed to Sansay, though critics are divided on the accuracy of this attribution.

French men and women from passing their lines. Americans, on the other hand, are allowed to leave, and the two sisters join a community of refugee creole women who are dispersed across the Caribbean. Traveling first to Cuba and then Jamaica, Mary repeatedly writes of creole women who have been left without property or husbands by the revolution. Yet what emerges from these tales of creole women and their daughters is something of a utopic community of independent women: 'Every talent, even if possessed in a slight degree of perfection, may be a resource in a reverse of fortune; and, though I liked not entirely [the creole ladies'] manner, whilst surrounded by the festivity and splendour of the Cape, I now confess that they excite my warmest admiration. They bear adversity with cheerfulness, and resist it with fortitude.[15] The creole women are now unattached to men or to property and what emerges in the space of this lack is a bounty of individual talent and previously untapped interior 'resources.' Creole women thus become figures of strength who are mobile and independent: no longer a form of property (like Pauline Leclerc) that changes hands between men, they are sources of value and labor unto themselves.

Ultimately disburdened of both Rochambeau and St. Louis, Clara is united with her sister in Kingston at the close of the novel, and Mary announces their plan to travel to Philadelphia to make a new home. Further, Mary ends the letter with the image of an idealized marriage and home that is premised on the figure of the independent creole woman the novel has championed. Mary's marital ideal is based on conjoining men and women of equal inner resources: 'Attachments between [equals] last through life, and are always new. Love continues because love has existed; interests create interests; parental are added to conjugal affections; with the multiplicity of domestic objects the number of domestic joys increase. In such a situation the heart is always occupied, and always full. For those who live in it their

15. Sansay, *Secret History*, 93.

home is the world; their feelings, their powers, their talents are employed.'[16] Appearing in the final pages of the novel, this marital ideal is implicitly predicated on the figure of the creole woman who is not dependent upon any resources exterior to her own, but who generates resources from within. Moreover, the creole marriage is generative of a cosmopolitan sensibility: for such a couple (who carry their valuables within them as a productive capacity) 'their home is the world'—that is, they are at home in any location in the world including the colonial periphery. In effect, Sansay's novel describes the Haitian Revolution as generative of a female creole subjectivity that will be most at home anywhere, including Le Cap, Kingston, Santiago, and Philadelphia.

In her focus on the figure of the creole, Sansay indicates that both Haiti and the United States are Atlantic colonial peripheries in which a creole politics is required to throw off the fetters of colonialism. Moreover, I would argue that Sansay was not alone in understanding the relation between Haiti and the United States in these terms. President John Adams, for instance, quickly moved to establish diplomatic relations with Toussaint Louverture when the black leader assumed control of Saint Domingue. Indeed, Adams was instrumental in passing a law known as 'Toussaint's Clause' in 1799 that established trade with Saint Domingue despite the poor state of United States-French relations at the time. As such, Adams encouraged Toussaint to break with French policy in order to trade freely with the United States. This course of action is one that repeats the story of United States commercial and political independence from European powers, and Adams urged Toussaint to follow this route in order to establish a commercial alliance of unrestricted 'creole' trade between the United States and Haiti. Northern merchants who depended on the Caribbean trade were supportive of this policy; however, southern planters objected strenuously to

16. Sansay, *Secret History*, 120.

recognizing a black leader and voiced concerns about the potential 'contagion' of antislavery revolution to the United States South. When Jefferson assumed the presidency, he abruptly reversed Adams's policies, cutting off diplomatic and commercial relations with Toussaint and offering assistance to Napoleon in removing Toussaint from power. One might speculate that for Jefferson, a Virginian slave-owner, the racial opposition of black and white loomed far larger in his understanding of the situation than did the metropolitan-creole divide that united an independent Saint Domingue and an independent United States in Adams's mind.

After Jefferson was elected, the harbor at Le Cap 'emptied of American vessels so swiftly, that Toussaint was moved to ask sarcastically, 'if the change in administrations had destroyed all the American ships.'[17] Historian Michael Zuckerman concludes, 'Color countermanded everything for Jefferson.'[18] Certainly, in the 'empire for liberty' that Jefferson imagined as the future of the United States, a racial division between blacks and whites was foundational.[19] Further, the foundational nature of a black-white divide has tended to underpin accounts of the 'imagined community' of the United States nation from Jefferson's time forward. In sum, the concept of a creole cosmopolitanism, imagined vividly by Sansay in her novel, has largely disappeared

17. Michael Zuckerman, 'The Power of Blackness: Federalists, Jeffersonians, and the Revolution in San Domingo,' in *La Révolution Française et Haïti*, 2 vols. (Port-au-Prince: Société Haïtienne d'Histoire et de Géographie [Editions Henri Deschamps], 1995), 2: 126.

18. Zuckerman, 'The Power of Blackness,' 135.

19. Famously, the passage from *Notes on the State of Virginia* in which Jefferson addresses the possibility of blacks and whites living together in the future of the United States is an apocalyptic vision of race war: 'Why not retain and incorporate the blacks into the state, and thus save the expense of supplying, by importation of white settlers, the vacancies they will leave? Deep rooted prejudices entertained by the whites; ten thousand recollections, by the blacks, of the injuries they have sustained; new provocations; the real distinctions which nature has made; and many other circumstances, will divide us into parties, and produce convulsions, which will probably never end but in the extermination of the one or the other race.' For useful discussion of Jefferson, race, and empire, see Peter Onuf, *Jefferson's Empire: The Language of American Nationhood* (Charlottesville: University Press of Virginia, 2000).

from cultural histories of the United States, as has an understanding of it as structurally related to Haiti by way of the geopolitics of Atlantic colonialism.

One way in which to understand the exclusion of the Haitian Revolution from the world stage of history is to consider its erasure from print, either by way of enforced illiteracy of New World Africans (as Gilroy suggests) or by way of forceful measures of censorship, that, as Julius Scott has shown, were indeed used in the Atlantic world to arrest the spread of antislavery revolution.[20] But a novel such as Sansay's raises a different question about the relations among print, revolution, and silence. When histories and ideas appear in print and fail to circulate, the instrumentality of print needs to be relocated in other realms, and most particularly in the realm of reception. It is difficult to give an account of how Sansay's novel was received, save to say that by and large it did not attract much attention and has not in the years since its first publication. Indeed, the novel may have fallen upon an unreceptive audience at the time of its publication because it did not provide what its title seemed to advertise—namely, an account of what Americans had come to expect as the 'horrors' or scenes of atrocities committed by blacks against whites in the Haitian Revolution that were widely reported on in the United States press from the 1790s forward.[21] In other words, the novel proposed an imagined community that bore little resemblance to

20. Julius S. Scott, *The Common Wind: Currents of Afro-American Communication in the Era of the Haitian Revolution*, Ph.D. diss. Duke University, 1986.

21. Representative newspaper references to the horrors of St. Domingo include the following two from 1802: 'With one hand the black demons of slaughter were seen holding up the writhing infant, and hacking off its limbs with the sword in the other. Those that escaped the sword were preserved to witness more horrid sensations, being dragged by the negroes to their strong places in the mountains, to serve as hostages or to glut their fury' (*Boston Gazette*, March 15, 1802, 14: 2). 'The latest accounts from St. Domingo, represent that Colony as being once more in a state of general insurrection, the negroes having risen throughout the whole interior, and commenced the repetition of those outrages which have heretofore rendered St. Domingo a scene of devastation and horror' (*Spectator*, New York, 6 [547]: 3). The latter quotation gives something of the flavor of the generic invocation of the 'horrors' of St. Domingo as familiar scenes of black on white violence.

the one that was then taking shape in the United States—a community in which a black/white opposition was increasingly deeply inscribed and a community in which the creole identity of white and black Americans had receded from view.

If we return to the question posed early in this essay—How is print related to revolution?—we can say quite clearly that Sansay's novel did not generate an acceptance of the premises of creole cosmopolitanism or an embrace of the forms of community that she asked her readers to imagine. Thus neither in terms of argument nor in terms of the procedure of generating a readership did her novel effect revolution. As such, it seems imperative that critics consider scenes of dissemination and reception in any analysis of the relation between print and revolution.[22] Nonetheless, it seems worth noting, as well, that the dissemination and reception of a given text is not necessarily temporally discrete. In other words, if Sansay's novel was not often read in 1808, it may nonetheless still be read (and taught) today as exemplary of an alternative imaginary—an imaginary that may still exist in our future insofar as we learn to read it in our past. If we learn new ways to read, we may eventually discern a variety of counter-cultures still to come in the rich archive of materials available to us from the Atlantic world in the Age of Revolutions.

22. Certainly a great deal of work in the field of history of the book is attentive to precisely these questions. Robert Darnton's model of communications circuits, set forth in 'What is the History of Books?' (in *The Book History Reader*, ed. David Finkelstein and Alistair McCleery [London and New York: Routledge, 2002], 9–26,) is particularly useful in this regard.

Llorente's Readers in the Americas

NANCY VOGELEY

JUAN ANTONIO LLORENTE is best known as the author of a history of the Spanish Inquisition, published in Paris in 1818.[1] Born in 1756 in the Rioja area of northern Spain, he died in Madrid in 1823. He was educated for the clergy and became secretary to the Inquisition, charged with gathering documentation so as to write its history. When José Bonaparte arrived in Spain in 1808 with the invasion of Napoleon's troops, he authorized Llorente to continue his work. To justify its takeover, the new French government needed to accumulate evidence of state crimes, and the Spanish monarchy's centuries-old collusion with the Church in quelling opposition was already seen as unnatural and barbaric practice in world capitals. With the promise of reform, Llorente sided with the French. He saw the French regime as permanently ensconced and as beneficial in paving the way for needed modernization. Thus Llorente and others of equal intellectual and artistic stature cooperated with the foreigners and so have gone into Spanish history as *afrancesados,* hated equally by the people who remained loyal to the Spanish monarch and by a so-called liberal faction of Cádiz merchants who stayed on in

---

1. L'Histoire *critique de l'Inquisition d'Espagne, depuis l'époque de son établissement, par Ferdinand V jusquáu règne de Ferdinand VII . . . par D. Jean Antoine Llorente. . . .* Traduite de l'espagnol . . . par Alexis Pellier (Paris: Tournachon-Molin, 1823). The first edition in Spanish appeared in 1822 in Madrid (although Alcalá Galiano claims that it, too, was really published in Paris). For background on Llorente, see *Noticia biográfica (Autobiografía),* nota crítica de Antonio Márquez, ensayo bibliográfico de Emil van der Vekene (Madrid: Taurus, 1982).

NANCY VOGELEY is professor emerita of Spanish at the University of San Francisco.

Spain to protect their interests. When, at the battle of Vitoria in 1813, French forces were defeated, these collaborators had to flee. Some went to London, but Llorente sought refuge in Paris.

Llorente's reputation has usually been restricted to Europe and tied to his history of the Inquisition. Marcelino Menéndez y Pelayo, in his study of Spanish heterodoxy, famously villainized Llorente as a Jansenist and closet Protestant, libeler of the Church, traitor to his country for having criticized the Spaniards who fought against French rule, and thief for having taken Inquisition materials out of Spain and sold them in Paris.[2]

In the United States, Llorente is a minor author, known for his Inquisition history, which was translated into English in 1826 in editions in Philadelphia (T. B. Peterson, printer) and New York (G. C. Morgan, printer). Here, however, I aim to examine Llorente's less-known, second career in Paris—a chapter that brought him near Spanish America and recast his profession as an historian. Menéndez y Pelayo acknowledges this second career by saying that when Llorente left Spain, shamed and scorned by his countrymen, he turned to 'filibusterismo americano' or the business of illegal traffic to the Americas.[3] In Paris, between 1818 and 1823, Llorente wrote a number of essays designed to interest Spanish American readers. Dealing with the writing of religion into new constitutions and Church authority as it affected increasingly civil issues such as marriage and Vatican concordats with governments they were timely advice to Americans in territories newly freed from Spain. In French and in Spanish, they were printed in Paris but also in San Sebastián in northern Spain. From there, via routes we can only guess at, they found their way to the Americas. Thus, Llorente's thinking came into Spanish America—particularly Mexico, as I will

---

2. Menéndez y Pelayo, *Historia de los heterodoxos españoles*, pról. Arturo Farinelli (1882; reprint, México: Editorial Porrúa, 1983), 264–69. Llorente first tried to sell his history of the Inquisition to an English publisher. Karen Racine has found in the Longman publishing archives at the University of Reading two letters dated 1816 (June and August) in which they considered the manuscript for translation and publication but decided against the project.

3. Menéndez y Pelayo, *Historia*, 268.

show—in the form of long, thoughtfully composed arguments. It also came in shorter forms, such as the word-of-mouth of travelers (importantly, Fray Servando Teresa de Mier, who had been in Spain and France), and in the reports of others who recast his ideas in their letters and manuscripts. But it is important to note that it also came in, not in dribbles and drabs, but in book-length essays, supported by an established press business and a Mexican censorship system which even permitted several reprints of his works.

Focus on Llorente allows examination of two considerations which I believe have not received sufficient attention. The first is the impact of French printing and transatlantic trade routes on Mexico during that country's first years of nationhood. South Americans (Miranda, Bolívar, Bello, and Rivadavia) traveled to London and were much affected by the constitutional advice of Jeremy Bentham.[4] Yet few independence-minded Mexican leaders left their country, and, instead of London friendships, books from Paris and the United States influenced their thinking.[5] Mexico declared its independence from Spain in 1821. Thus, in the period between 1821 and 1824, while South America was still fighting, Mexico was at peace, already reflecting on nation-building, and its leaders drew on those books' language for the legal justifications and premises they would write into their first constitution in 1824.[6] The second point is Llorente's assessment that Mexico

4. See Miriam Williford, *Jeremy Bentham on Spanish America: An Account of his Letters and Proposals to the New World* (Baton Rouge: Louisiana State University Press, 1980).

5. Here it must be noted that United States revolutionaries and constitutionalists had understandably repudiated English thought and turned to French writers, whom they, in turn, retailed to their neighbors, the Mexicans, in increasing trade relations in the early 1820s.

6. This fact is often unacknowledged, as all Spanish American independence movements have been subsumed under the Venezuelan story and phased into accounts of their more famous men. An example is a review by John Elliott in *New York Review of Books* (July 13, 2006, 34–36) of the biography by John Lynch, *Simón Bolívar: A Life* (New Haven: Yale University Press, 2006). For an interesting discussion of Latin American legal history, see John Henry Merryman and David S. Clark, *Comparative Law: Western European and Latin American Legal Systems: Cases and Materials* (Charlottesville, Va.: The Miche Company, 1978), in which 'Latin America' is considered to be one tradition and 'religion' in postcolonial development is treated in terms of attitudes toward the clergy—'clericals' and 'anticlericals.' In realizing the broad implications of Llorente's contribution to Mexico, I here acknowledge helpful discussion at the conference 'Liberty/Égalité/Independencia.'

needed to mark out religion's role in the new state structure. Bentham's secular utilitarianism in the formulation of legislation emphasized the greatest happiness for the greatest number of people, but Llorente's awareness of Spanish America's Catholic history—and Mexico's clerical leadership in its independence revolt—made him realize that Mexico's ongoing dependence on religion as a bulwark of public order and guarantor of personal, other-world happiness, would, first of all, have to be resolved. Unlike Bentham, whose point of departure was theoretical and who lacked much knowledge of where his ideas might be implemented, Llorente was an historian and a political realist. He had worked with fellow historians in Spain such as Juan Bautista Muñoz, who had also been charged with gathering materials for an archive and writing a review of Spain's conduct in the Americas. Thus the two men were among several who were inventing a new historiography—one which departed from old apologetic, providential histories so as to uncover past abuses and recommend reforms.[7] In this way Llorente's identification of a need to detach from old mental habits, as Mexicans wrote authority and obedience into their first constitution, is connected to his notion of history writing. Renewal could only proceed after the nation's past was laid to rest. When Spain's empire fell apart, decolonization and state planning in the Americas were natural outlets for his work.[8]

7. Llorente's early publications in Spain attest to his research into legal history: *Leyes del Fuero Juzgo; o recopilación de los Visigodos españoles,titulada primeramente 'Liber judicum'* (Madrid: Hernández Pacheco, 1792); *Noticias históricas de las tres provincias vascongadas, en que se procura investigar el estado civil antiguo de Alava, Guipúzcoa y Vizcaya y el origen de sus fueros* (Madrid: Imprenta real, 1806–8); *Discurso heráldico sobre el escudo de armas de España, leído . . . en el mes de julio del año 1808* (Madrid: imprente de T. Albán); *Colección diplomática de varios papeles antiguos y modernos sobre dispensas matrimoniales y otros puntos de disciplina eclesiástica* (Madrid: Ibarra, 1809); *Disertación sobre el poder que los reyes españoles ejercieron hasta el siglo duodécimo en la división de obispados y otros puntos conexos de disciplina eclesiástica* (Madrid: imprente de Ibarra, 1810); *Observaciones sobre las dinastías de España* (Zaragoza: Oficina de Miedes, 1813). His concern for the public's opinion of an historical institution appears in a report read to the Spanish Academy of History, *Memoria histórica sobre qual ha sido la opinion nacional de España acerca del tribunal de la Inquisición* (Madrid: imprente de Sancha, 1812).

8. Because the Spanish Conquest was based not just on a military takeover of American territory but also on the catechization of its indigenous population, Catholic faith was an essential ingredient of membership in the Spanish empire. Therefore, rejection of that membership at the time of independence meant reconsideration of that teaching. In France, parallel efforts to leave behind monarchism and embrace republicanism took the forms of 'dechristianization' and 'desacralization,' rather than 'decolonization.'

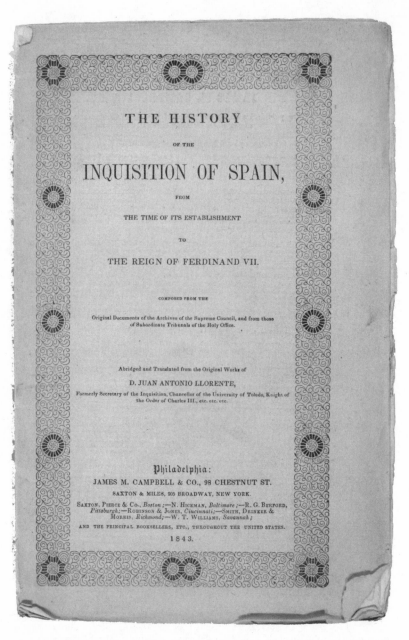

THE HISTORY

OF THE

INQUISITION OF SPAIN,

FROM

THE TIME OF ITS ESTABLISHMENT

TO

THE REIGN OF FERDINAND VII.

COMPOSED FROM THE

Original Documents of the Archives of the Supreme Council, and from those
of Subordinate Tribunals of the Holy Office.

Abridged and Translated from the Original Works of

D. JUAN ANTONIO LLORENTE,

Formerly Secretary of the Inquisition, Chancellor of the University of Toledo, Knight of
the Order of Charles III., etc. etc. etc.

Philadelphia:
JAMES M. CAMPBELL & CO., 98 CHESTNUT ST.

SAXTON & MILES, 205 BROADWAY, NEW YORK.

SAXTON, PIERCE & Co., *Boston ;*—N. HICKMAN, *Baltimore ;*—R. G. BERFORD,
Pittsburgh ;—ROBINSON & JONES, *Cincinnati ;*—SMITH, DRINKER &
MORRIS, *Richmond ;*—W. T. WILLIAMS, *Savannah ;*
AND THE PRINCIPAL BOOKSELLERS, ETC., THROUGHOUT THE UNITED STATES.

1843.

An abridgment and translation from the original works of Juan Antonio
Llorente. *The History of the Inquisition of Spain, from the time of its establish-
ment to the reign of Ferdinand VII* (Philadelphia: James M. Campbell and
Co., 1843)

My research on these essays has largely been carried out in the Bibliothèque Nationale (Paris), where they have been over-looked for various reasons: Histories of expatriate Spanish litera-ture of the period—such as the one Antonio Alcalá Galiano wrote in London—have featured the activity of Spaniards there. In contact with the British Romantics, the Spaniards defined lit-erature in terms of that poetry and ignored the political works of their fellows in France. For example, Alcalá Galiano conceded the value of Llorente's history of the Inquisition but said that its language was hardly Castilian, since its author was Basque.[9] His-torians of American constitutionalism have skipped over Llo-rente, emphasizing the influence of Rousseau's *Social Contract*, the French 'Declaration of the Rights of Man and the Citizen,' and Thomas Paine's *Rights of Man* on the men who wrote Mexico's first constitution. These works from a generation be-fore were important—as was also the groundwork done by the writers of Spain's first constitution at the Cortes de Cádiz in 1810–12, in which Mexican delegates participated.[10] Yet Llorente's outline for a religious constitution, based on his expe-rience inside Spain's Inquisition, his study of the relationship between the monarchy and the Church and various Spanish legal codes, and his witness to recent French experiments with a na-tional church and a married clergy, has generally been forgotten. So my inquiry here will extend to why appreciation of those Llo-rente essays has disappeared from history books. Preliminarily I am finding that it became convenient to say that Mexicans based their first constitution on the United States model, thus blaming Mexico's later divisions on the federalism of that plan and United States meddling. But I also guess that 'religion' is an un-resolved problem still in Mexican society and that historians

9. *Literatura española, siglo XIX*, ed. Vicente Llorens (Madrid: Alianza Editorial, 1969), a translation of 'Literature of the Nineteenth Century: Spain,' in *The Athenaeum* (London, April–June, 1834) 55.

10. For background, see the collection edited by Nettie Lee Benson, *Mexico and the Spanish Cortes: 1810–1822* (Austin: University of Texas Press, 1966).

have been reluctant to acknowledge early attempts to merge this relic of Spanish colonialism into national narratives.

Llorente—a Spaniard, Inquisition functionary, and resident in Paris where post-Napoleonic legal disputes were raging, the Pope was signing secret agreements with the French king, and notions of apostolic authority in the kingdom were replacing revolutionary gains—was uniquely qualified to appreciate the kind of decolonization that Spanish Americans were facing. If, in Anglo-America, separation from the monarch was easy (in the United States, though not in Canada), and writing a constitution to insure an individual's natural rights in society was accomplished by separating church and state so that all faiths were tolerated, in Spanish America those tasks were not as simple. Many Spanish Americans were still monarchists and deeply pious—to the point, Mexican liberals said in the period, of fanaticism. Rome still exercised control throughout the area; in fact, the Mexican novelist and political pamphleteer José Joaquín Fernández de Lizardi wrote in his last will and testament in 1826: 'I leave my homeland independent of Spain and all other crowned heads, except Rome.'[11] Lizardi even resented as reminders of Church authority the regular tolling of bells in church clocks.

The first of Llorente's post-Spain essays was printed in French in Paris, probably in 1818, by a printer just off one of the streets bordering the church of Saint Sulpice. This *Projet d'une constitution religieuse, considérée comme faisant partie de la constitution civile d'une nation libre indépendante, écrite par un Américain, publié avec une préface par Don Jean Antoine Llorente*, was attributed to an American.[12] Although Llorente took credit for the preface, he probably also wrote the whole, 164-page work. This was followed by a printing in 1819 in Paris—now in Spanish—of an almost

11. For the text, see José Joaquín *Fernández de Lizardi, Folletos 1824–1827*, María Rosa Palazón Mayoral e Irma Isabel Fernández Arias, ed., vol. 13, *Obras* (México: UNAM, 1963–97) 1037–53.

12. Printed by L.E. Herhan of Paris. Some have put this work to 1820.

identical work for which Llorente also wrote a preface addressing Americans.[13] In 1821 a printer in San Sebastián, Baroja, put out two of Llorente's works—*Apología católica del proyecto de constitución religiosa, escrito por un Americano,* for which Llorente did claim authorship, and an anonymous *Carta* specifically directed to Mexicans.[14] *Carta* is today held in the Sutro Library, a San Francisco repository of the warehouse of a Mexico City bookseller—thus attesting to its receipt there. I believe that Llorente also wrote this work because the subject matter is his and because the same printer printed both. *Apología* answers the censure of two Dominicans in Barcelona and, in addition to being printed in Spain, was also printed by two different printers in Paris in that same year (Rosa and Moreau). Paris, with its community of Spanish exiles was obviously one intended venue for this work; even the frontispiece of the San Sebastián edition says that it, too, was for sale in the Paris bookshop of Rosa 'en el Gran Patio del Palacio Real.'

Added to these six imprints are two printings of the anonymous *Aforismos políticos,* which Llorente is credited with having authored—one in 1821 in Madrid and the other in Mexico City in 1822.[15] Also relevant to Americans because they treated the legal limits of Pope and king are two studies which Llorente published in Paris in 1818—one dealing with pragmatic sanctions in France and concordats, and another, under a pseudonym, an inquiry into the Spanish king's jurisdictions.[16] In 1822 (Paris) and 1823 (Madrid), he

13. *Discursos sobre una constitución religiosa, considerada como parte de la civil nacional. Su autor un Americano. Los da a luz D. Juan Antonio Llorente* (Paris: Stahl, 1819).

14. *Carta escrita á un americano sobre la forma de gobierno que para hacer practicable la constitucion y las leyes, conviene establecer en Nueva España atendida su actual situación* (Madrid: - imprente de Ibarra, 1821).

15. *Aforismos politicos escritos en una de las lenguas del norte de la Europa por Un Filósofo [pseudo.]* . . . *y traducidos al español por Don Juan Antonio Llorente. Doctor en Cánones, Abogado de los tribunales nacionales* (México: D. Mariano Ontiveros,1821).

16. *Monuments historiques concernant les deux pragmatiques-sanctions de France* . . . *suivis d'un catéchisme sur la matière des concordats, par M. Llorente* (Paris: A. Bobée, 1818); *Consultas del real y supremo Consejo de Castilla y otros papeles sobre atentados y usurpaciones contra la soberanía del Rey y su real jurisdicción. La da á luz Don Astreófilo Hispáno* (Paris: A. Bobée, 1818).

published a treatise on the political history of the Popes.[17] In 1826 Mexican printers produced two other Llorente works in the nature of clarifying relationships between civil government and the Church. They were *Disertación sobre el poder que los reyes españoles ejercieron hasta el siglo duodecimo* (Imprenta del ciudadano Alejandro Valdés) and *Pequeño catecismo sobre la materia de concordatos*, translated from French into Spanish by José Mariano Ramírez and published by Mariano Galván Rivera.

In 1827 Mexico saw the third edition of a Llorente collection, *Colección diplomática de varios papeles antiguos y modernos sobre dispensas matrimoniales y otros puntos de disciplina eclesiástica*, published originally in Madrid.[18] So now—to sum up—we have fourteen such related items.

Two aspects of this second phase of Llorente's career should be noted. The first is how the linkages implicit in the almost simultaneous printing of his works by presses in Paris, San Sebastián, Madrid, and Mexico City (and also New York and Philadelphia) point not only to the north-south routes across the Pyrenees that we are accustomed to seeing, but also east-west transatlantic crossings. The second point is how these, now eight, editions of almost the same work—and six related essays—reveal Llorente's persistent concern for easing religion into new legal systems—and, at the other end, reception by American readers. I will not consider here the many reprintings and translations in Europe of Llorente's *History of the Spanish Inquisition*, or Llorente's role in the reprinting of Las Casas's *Brevísima relación de la destrucción de las Indias*, a publishing event that made a major contribution to Spanish American independence.[19]

17. *Portrait politique des papes considérées comme princes temporels et comme chefs de l'Eglise depuis l'établissement du Saint-Siège à Rome jusqu'en 1822* (Paris: Béchet, 1822); *Retrato político de los papas, desde S. Pedro hasta Pío VII inclusive, con espresion del principio y fin de cada pontificado y reflexiones críticas en los que dan occasion; formado con presencia de las historias eclesiásticas escritas por el cardenal Fleuri, Natal Alejandro, y otras* (Madrid: T. Albán, 1823).

18. The first two editions were published in Madrid in 1809 and 1822. In Mexico City, Imprenta de Galván was the publisher of the third edition.

19. *Oeuvres de Don Barthélimi de Las Casas, precedes de sa vie, et accompagnées de notes historiques, additions . . . par J. A. Llorente, . . . [avec] l'Apologie de l'auteur par H. B. Grégoire* (Paris: A. Eymery, 1822); *Colección de las obras del Venerable Obispo de Chiapa, don Bartolomé de Las Casas . . . Da todo á luz El doctor don Juan Antonio Llorente* (Paris: Rosa, 1822).

First, I will comment on the French press network. Although the influence of Spanish-language publishing in London on Spanish America in the years after 1814 is well-known, less known is how the French printing industry over the last decades of the eighteenth century and the early years of the nineteenth exported its production not only to Spain but also to Spain's properties in the Americas. Writing for those markets were Frenchmen such as the Abbé Grégoire, exiled Spaniards such as Jean Pierre Claris de Florián and José Marchena, and also Spanish Americans such as the Peruvian-born Pablo de Olavide. In France they translated the French Encyclopedists, Voltaire and Rousseau and also wrote original works. They relied on presses in Paris but also in Bordeaux, Montpellier, and Lyons. The Spanish Crown alternated between welcoming this literature coming out of France and cordoning off the border. In particular, the French Revolution of 1789, and then the terror under Robespierre, caused Spanish officials to try to stop the entry of materials they considered seditious. By the late eighteenth century the Inquisition was no longer the watchdog for heresy that it had been in the sixteenth and seventeenth centuries but instead a board that oversaw the literate population's reading. In 1814, when Ferdinand VII returned to Spain and reinstituted the Inquisition, French books again became suspect, only reentering in great numbers between 1820 and 1823 under Rafael de Riego's liberalism.

The publishing activity on Spain's periphery should not then come as a surprise in the midst of all this literary traffic between France and Spain. Barcelona, Valencia, Las Palmas (in the Canaries and Mallorca), and then later Cádiz, had presses which took over much of Madrid's business during the Peninsula War. In 1814 a press in La Coruña printed Rousseau's *Social Contract* for Valentín de Foronda (a Spaniard from the Basque region who had served as Spanish consul in Philadelphia for eight years). In 1821, as we have seen, a San Sebastián printer published two of Llorente's essays. This city began to assume overseas importance early in the eighteenth century when, in 1728, the Real Compañía Guipuzcoana de Caracas was given the monopoly for trade with Venezuela, and San Sebastián was designated as the port for that concession. In 1788 San Sebastián acquired rights to trade with other American ports, and in a report, dating probably from the following year, a *comisario* there wrote: 'The printed works and manuscripts that have been circulating here since July are those that are concerned with the present events of the revolutions in France and its general assembly. The city is flooded with this kind of paper, whose acquisition is made easy by its commerce, its situation near the border, and its population, composed in large part of members of that nation, who praise and proclaim these events in their conversations.'[20]

In addition to Paris, then, a Spanish-language business of printing politically sensitive literature developed in northern Spain and southern France. Printers sent their productions back and forth over the Pyrenees. From ports on the seacoast, willing ships took these materials to Spanish America, where Inquisition officials during the period of Spanish rule tried to monitor the imports.[21] In 1801 a printer in Paris had published the popular novel *Cornelia Bororquia, o la víctima de la Inquisición*, an indictment of the Inquisition, published anonymously but written by the Spaniard Luis Gutiérrez, a newspaper editor in Bayonne. Inquisition edicts in Spain and Mexico immediately banned the book. In 1815 Juan Sempere y Guarinos had published in Bordeaux his *Histoire des Cortès d'Espagne*. In 1817 Juan Meléndez Valdés died in Montpellier. In 1820 Marchena's translation of the novels of Voltaire was published in Bordeaux, and in 1821 his

20. Richard Herr, *The Eighteenth Century Revolution in Spain* (Princeton: Princeton University Press, 1958), 244.

21. See John Rydford, *Foreign Interest in the Independence of New Spain: An Introduction to the War for Independence* (1935; reprint, New York: Octagon Books, 1972), Chapter 8.

translation of Rousseau's *La Nouvelle Héloise* in Toulouse. In 1824 Francisco de Goya went to Paris and then Bordeaux, where his friend Leandro Fernández de Moratín lived, and painted his portrait and Llorente's. Moratín's works were printed in Paris in 1825, and he died there in 1828. Francisco Martínez de la Rosa published his collected works in Paris between 1827 and 1830. The *Gaceta de Bayona*, printed in Bayonne between 1828 and 1830, was directed by the Spaniards Alberto Lista, Félix José Reinoso, and Sebastián Miñano. This list of Spanish expatriates in France, while by no means complete, is an indication of the way Llorente fit into a cross-border world of Spanish and French-language printing.

This book business underlies my second point—Llorente's advice to politicians about merging the past with the future and faith with secular governmental forms. He illustrated how instituting a religious constitution might accomplish this in the 1819 text, *Discursos sobre una constitución religiosa. Discursos* suggests how Catholic readers in Spanish America might leave behind monarchical rule, with its attendant myths and securities, as they adopted impersonal republicanism with its language of law and liberty. They particularly seized on Llorente's opinion of the Inquisition as custodian of public morality. If prior licensing had worked in the past to keep out undesirable books, then, supposedly, Llorente would know how freedom of the press might work. He would know whether mandates that public utterances respect faith and the person of the king would be sufficient restraints on slander, immorality, and disorder. Americans did learn from his historical review of how the print industry in Protestant countries, by opening up the Bible to ordinary people, had affected morality and faith there; they probably were surprised that Llorente did not appear to think that great disorder had ensued. Indeed, with press controls, chaos had broken out in Catholic Spain. War raged across the peninsula, and the American colonies were rebelling. So Llorente, in rethinking why this civil disobedience had come about and how it might be prevented in the future, began by separating loyalty to king from faith. He told his readers that the king was not divinely appointed, and thus their American revolt against bad colonial government was no crime involving their souls. He revealed how, in the past, religious leaders had improperly cooperated with despots in making believe that faith also meant political fidelity. Yet, in criticizing the Church, Llorente did not advocate rejecting faith or separating religion from civil society. Instead he advised that the new American nations retain their official Catholicism and merge faith with new legal formulations.

Llorente began his preface to the *Discursos* by assuring readers in a kind of *imprimatur* that this work, which had come into his hands, did not oppose Catholic dogma. It confessed all the mysteries, sacraments, and precepts; and it recognized the necessity of obedience to the Pope (as long, he said, as the Pope did not exceed the limits of his authority). Llorente said that a Catholic, as a rational being, had not lost his 'rights of man.' He then tried to fend off accusations that the work he was introducing would be seen as going further than the civil code of the French clergy and as essentially Protestant. However, he credited Protestants with having contributed to the Enlightenment of the present day through their translations and printings. He called printing 'a divine art' and criticized Jesuits, rather than Protestants, for having divided Europe by finding heresy everywhere. He concluded his preface by saying that this review of religion's history in Europe would be useful to readers in Venezuela, the Rio de la Plata region, Chile, and 'other places looking to consolidate the independence that they desire and now partly enjoy'—i.e., Mexico—as if the summary were a cautionary tale.

In the body of the *Discursos*, the author addressed Catholic societies in which that faith had already unified the population. The common people, having been taught the faith of their fathers, were already joined together. Thus, even if a literate elite was skeptical of religion's teachings because of access to print and new philosophies, that elite should embrace the faith of the majority, considering that no other force was as capable of effecting national union. A judicial system built on religious faith, which could assure reward or punishment in an afterlife for deeds performed on earth, is far more effective than one which only relies on men's capabilities for finding out and punishing crimes, he argued. Other nations, newly formed, which did not enjoy this custom or were made up of religious diversity, might decree a purely civil code. But the spiritual dimension of life, which religion postulates, reinforces morality most successfully.

Llorente then projected how the two institutions historically supportive of a Catholic society—the Church and the monarchy— might right past wrongs. He advised Catholics to return to the early church, before it was taken over by ecclesiastical bureaucratic interests. Jesus had always said that his kingdom was not of this earth; thus bishops who attempted to interfere with men's lives were misguided. Popes must stop using excommunication to punish political actions, as, for example, the Mexican priest Miguel Hidalgo who had been excommunicated for leading the rebellion against Spain. The writer allowed that one man might continue to head up the nation, though now as a constitutional monarch.

The author then moved to issues of tolerance. If Catholicism was adopted as the official religion, what did this mean for individuals living under such a system? If the Church would back off from regulations it regarded in the past as laws and consider them only as advice—for the individual Catholic, tithing, attendance at Mass, confession, fasting, observance of holy days, and obedience to controls over marriage and divorce—and for the clergy, celibacy—the new code could proceed more easily. In fact, the author recommended that governments pass fewer laws, relying instead on exhortation and inner devotion.

Llorente's concern for the role of the clergy in Mexican society was readily apparent. Mexico had sent seventeen delegates to the Cortes de Cádiz and, of whom, thirteen were religious. Thus, post-colonial leadership had to take into account the vows of obedience which such men owed Rome. However, if friars were no longer bound to celibacy and could marry, then increasingly they would not require special privileges such as immunity and would be eligible for civil positions.

Throughout the two-hundred-page essay, Llorente is concerned with the Inquisition or a body like it. On the one hand, he repudiates the necessity of the Inquisition, saying that the Inquisition forces faith, and that man's nature requires that he be led by reason. He repeats the message of tolerance—now in the context of the peaceful compromise that Europe needed after its bloody wars. On the other hand, he recognizes that the Enlightenment, with its proliferation of skeptical and agnostic philosophies spread by print made new enemies for religion. As he puts it, the new philosophers have criticized the Church either through serious or comic modes; and their criticism has had the effect of either causing men either to laugh at religion or abandon it altogether. He shows class consciousness in recognizing that an educated elite, charged with directing the fortunes of new nations, has been unsettled by these new Enlightenment philosophies. The example of the United States constitutionalists in removing religion from civil affairs also poses a threat to Spanish Americans who may think that they should imitate it and thus relegate religion to the margins of political power.

Llorente, however, never considers tolerance to be freedom of religious faith (or 'tolerancia de cultos' as it was called); this possibility seems to have horrified most Spaniards, who could not imagine religious pluralism. For example, in 1811 the *Gaceta de Caracas* had published an essay on how an officially Catholic nation might permit the practice of other faiths. Written by someone called William Burke, the essay stirred great emotion among Venezuela's readers, who could not appreciate Burke's plea for tolerance from the perspective of a Catholic minority in Protestant England.

Why did Llorente give up the fiction that he was writing a preface for a constitutional project authored by an American and admit that he was the American? I have concluded that his assumption of an American point of view reflects, to a certain extent, an unselfish desire to suggest to Spanish Americans how to conserve religion in their constitutions while also implementing reform. His expatriate status in Paris allowed him a view from the outside, and an American identity fit his critical stance. However, I also believe that Llorente, in drawing up a model constitution, was realizing his own dreams for a Catholic Europe—indeed, the new American nations could accomplish what Catholics in France and Spain could not. Liberals in both France and Spain had had to go undercover in those years because despotic monarchies had recently been returned to power at the Congress of Vienna. But Americans were freer to interrupt history. Llorente was famous for disguise in his Paris writings, hiding behind anonymity or pseudonyms. Thus, I think that in his pleas for reform he was not only addressing Americans but also Europe and Rome. He was posing as an American so as to imagine how any traditionally Catholic society might evolve into an enlightened monarchy or even a republic. However, to convince European readers of his expertise, he needed to reveal his identity.

That Llorente's writings were widely read in Mexico is illustrated by the following examples. Llorente had a huge effect on the discussion regarding the Inquisition at the time the Cortes de Cádiz were drawing up the empire's first constitution in 1812. Although the Cortes did away with the Inquisition in that formulation, men like Antonio Ruíz de Padrón and Antonio Puigblanch, who argued for its abolition, and José Clemente Carnicero, who argued for its retention, all began their arguments by drawing on Llorente's research. In Mexico's pamphlet wars through the years 1820 to 1823, Puigblanch particularly was cited admiringly, and his long essay on the Inquisition was reprinted there in 1824.[22]

22. See Nancy J. Vogeley, 'Actitudes en México hacia la Inquisición: el pro y el contra (1814, 1824),' *Revista de la Inquisición (Madrid)* 11 (2005): 223–43.

When Agustín de Iturbide proclaimed Mexico's independence from Spain in 1821, his Trigarantine proclamation included as one of its three guarantees the preservation of the colony's Catholic faith. Thus, although Llorente's advice that Mexico produce a religious constitution seemed to be a *fait accompli* when the first constitution, written in 1824, proclaimed Roman Catholicism as Mexico's official religion, such acquiescence was not the case. Again evidence from the pamphlet wars, which shows that the question of whether to reinstate the Inquisition so as to preserve religion was a hard-fought issue, puts the lie to the appearance of unanimity. Perhaps because later historiography sought to minimize the role of the Church and the clergy then, political historians have concentrated on other, secular, aspects of the writing of this constitution, such as federalism vs. centralism, division of powers, and questions of citizenship, thereby excluding Llorente's contribution to the dialogue.

Two of Llorente's readers at this time—José Joaquín *Fernández de* Lizardi and Juan Germán Roscio—famously took his essays into account. Lizardi, in a newspaper written over the months of 1823, *El hermano del perico que cantaba la victoria*, acknowledged that he was drawing on Llorente's *Aforismos políticos*.[23] In an 1825 pamphlet, Lizardi quoted from Llorente's *Proyecto de una constitución religiosa*.[24] In a newspaper published in 1826–27, *Correo semanario de México*, he based almost all of his material on the history of the popes, on Llorente's *Retrato político de los papas*.[25] And in still another paper, in a caution which suggests either Llorente's dangerous reputation or Mexican attempts at responsible

23. Lizardi quotes Llorente: 'The republic is a form of government that excludes any arbitrariness on the part of anyone.' (La república es una forma de gobierno que excluye toda arbitrariedad de parte de quien quiera que sea.). Lizardi. *Periódicos*, María Rosa Palazón Mayoral, ed., Vol. 5, *Obras*, 45.

24. 'Observaciones que El Pensador Mexicano hace a las censuras que los señores doctores D. Ignacio María Lerdo y D. Ignacio Grajeda hicieron de sus Conversaciones Sexta, Vigésima, y Vigésima Segunda entre el Payo y el Sacristán,' Lizardi, *Folletos 1824–1827*, 13:415–535.

25. *Periódicos, Correo semanario de México*, María Rosa Palazón Mayoral, ed., vol. 5, *Obras*.

journalism, Lizardi warned a fellow writer not to plagiarize Llorente, advising instead either to cite him openly or disguise him in such a way that the source was not recognizable.[26] Another famous reader of Llorente, in whose work the influence is unstated, but still obvious, is the Venezuelan Juan Germán Roscio. In his *Triunfo de la libertad sobre el despotismo en la confesión de un pecador arrepentido de sus errores politicos, y dedicado a desagraviar en esta parte a la religion ofendida con el sistema de la tiranía*, Roscio argued much as did Llorente—advising Christians to go back to the teachings of the early Church and ignore later accretions to faith. Roscio published his work in Spanish in Philadelphia in two editions in 1817 and 1821; the Philadelphia work was bootlegged into Mexico in 1822 and reprinted twice in Mexico in 1824 and 1828.[27] Carlos María Bustamante, an influential intellectual leader in Mexico in the 1820s and a devout Catholic, was much affected by Roscio's indictment of the Spanish monarchy and criticism of the clergy.

Finally, in volumes in the Sutro collection, two copies of Llorente's *Pequeño catecismo sobre la materia de concordatos*, published in Mexico in 1826, are bound together with *Proyecto de decreto y ordenanza que consultó al supremo gobierno desde el año de 1842; la junta nombrada por el mismo para arreglar el cuerpo médico militar* (published in Mexico in 1846). Why is this coupling important? It is important, I believe, because it suggests that Llorente had currency later in Mexico, when liberal resentment of Church controls deepened. In reforms and constitutions in 1833, 1835, 1843, and then 1847, religion was a hot issue. In 1856 the *ley de desamortización*, which seized many Church properties, was passed. Internally, liberals and conservatives were divided, and externally Mexicans wondered how much they were still controlled by the

26. 'Preguntas interesantes de El Pensador a d. Rafael Dávila,' April 29, 1826, in *Folletos, 1824–1827*, 13: 761–68.

27. Thomas H. Palmer published the first edition; Mathew Carey the second. In Mexico Martín Rivera published the 1824 edition and the Imprenta de York, in Oaxaca, the 1828 edition. Evidence of its passage from Philadelphia to Mexico is contained in my forthcoming book *The Bookrunner: Philadelphia's Book Trade wih Mexico, 1822–1823*.

Vatican. Thus, Llorente's study of concordats would have mat-
tered in their constitutional deliberations.

Llorente's thinking, then, can be seen to have had an impact on
the Mexican mind in the national period. However, there appear
to be no translations of his works published in Paris in either England nor the United States. English readers seem only to have
read Llorente's Inquisition history, associating it with attacks by
novelists like Ann Radcliffe and defenses by retrograde philosophers such as Joseph de Maistre; in the United States Llorente's
history was his only work to be translated.[28] Its documentation of
religious persecution fed building anti-Spanish sentiment.
United States ships were competing with Spanish shipping in the
Caribbean; United States leaders feared Spanish movement into
the Louisiana and Florida territories they had just purchased,
and, in order to legitimize the takeover of Texas, an anti-
Spanish/Mexican, anti-Catholic campaign was necessary.

28. Charles Le Brun, an émigré writer and translator in Philadelphia, published there
in 1826 a portrait of Llorente in his Spanish-language *Retratos políticos de la revolución de
España* but this work, which compared the success of the United States revolution with the
failure of the Spanish revolution of 1820, seems to have been largely exported since it is
not part of the holdings of the Library of Congress, the Historical Society of Pennsylvania, or the American Antiquarian Society. It is to be found, however, in California collections which were gathered from Mexican sources.

Daniel Webster and the Making of Modern Liberty in the Atlantic World

SANDRA M. GUSTAFSON

Imagining Liberty in the Atlantic World

IN THE YEARS BETWEEN 1815 and 1830, concepts of modern liberty developed in the Atlantic world in a political context shaped by transnational ideals and alliances. Three sets of events from 1815 provide the parameters for my discussion of the conceptual development of liberty during this period: the Battle of New Orleans and the Treaty of Ghent, which concluded to the War of 1812; the defeat of Napoleon at Waterloo and the creation of the Holy Alliance; and the arrival of Ferdinand VII's forces of reconquest in Spanish America. These military, legal, and political events provide a framework for understanding the circulation of revolutionary ideas and the media of their circulation in the Americas and the wider Atlantic world during these years. When the meaning of liberty was articulated and contested in a web of relations between the United States and other revolutionary states, including France, Haiti, Spanish America, and Greece.

As the crisis over slavery and the Union elevated national concerns after 1830, Atlanticism became less prominent in United States politics. The intensifying nationalization of politics after 1830 reoriented core political concepts, binding the meaning of liberty more firmly to the problems of civil and human rights

SANDRA M. GUSTAFSON is associate professor of English, University of Notre Dame.

raised by the enslavement of people of African descent and the challenges of federalism that the secessionist movement brought to the fore. The adequacy of the United States Constitution as a vehicle that could fulfill aspirations for liberty and sustain a viable state was contested after 1830 in a way that it had not been in the previous decade and a half. Prior to 1830 proponents of the United States Constitution were on the offensive internationally, offering it as a model for republics throughout the Atlantic world. After 1830 those same proponents were more often on the defensive, seeking to shore up its authority within the very nation that it instituted. The shift, brought about by the dialectical emergence of Garrisonian abolitionism and intensifying Southern secessionism, can be traced in a landmark speech that Daniel Webster gave in 1830. In debate on the Senate floor, Webster responded to South Carolina Senator Robert Hayne's federalist view of the Union as a compact of sovereign states, offering instead a national model of the Union as an embodiment of liberty. Webster's stirring formulation in this speech became his motto for the remainder of his career: 'Liberty and union, now and forever, one and inseparable.'[1] Twenty years later, in his gorgeously Unionist Seventh of March speech, Webster supported the Compromise Measures of 1850, including the poisonous Fugitive Slave Law, thereby turning long-time admirers such as Ralph Waldo Emerson into harsh critics. Rather than joining liberty and union, Emerson felt, Webster had sacrificed liberty to union.

Webster continues to be known principally as the aesthetician of the Union. Prior to 1830, however, Webster focused more on the other half of the 'Liberty and Union' slogan, and he did so in a manner that tied United States history firmly to its Atlantic context. In five major orations delivered between December 1820 and August 1826, Webster addressed Atlantic world revolutionary history, and in the process shaped concepts of modern liberty.

---

1. 'Second Reply on Foot's Resolution,' in *The Works of Daniel Webster*, ed. Edward Everett (Boston: C. C. Little and J. Brown, 1851), 6 vols. 3: 270–342; quotation on p. 342.

These speeches elevated Webster to international celebrity as a man of letters and champion of liberty. His speeches were attended by political luminaries, reprinted on three continents, and read in politically influential circles. Running through all five of these speeches is a conception of modern liberty based on an Anglo-American tradition that focused on the circulation of knowledge, the broad distribution of property, the absence of established religion coupled with the moral authority of Christian values, and strong institutions to support the types of social order that Webster believed were integral to true liberty. In these speeches he also developed a historical narrative of national origins and a core set of phrases and images that provided an aesthetic and affective base for commitment to the nation as the best and safest guarantor of liberty. Like Edmund Burke, whom he cited in his speeches and with whom he was constantly compared, Webster believed such affective and aesthetic grounds to be a more effective means of uniting and energizing a state than the rational assent model favored by social contract theorists such as John Locke.

Three of those speeches were commemorative addresses monumentalizing successive moments in United States history that were for Webster the sources of a modern concept of liberty. They included the Plymouth oration (1820), a celebration of New England's 'core values' and institutions, attended by the old revolutionary and former president John Adams, who had been an early proponent of this view of New England; the Bunker Hill Monument oration (1825), which was attended by another luminary of the American Revolution, the Marquis de Lafayette, whose continued role in Atlantic world politics helped Webster transform the dedication of a monument on a local battlefield into a world-historical event; and the eulogy on Presidents Adams and Thomas Jefferson (1826), when in the presence of Adams's son, President John Quincy Adams, Webster surveyed the contributions of the two late presidents to national and international politics. In these speeches Webster sought to transform the thriving New England tradition of commemorative address into a genre that signified beyond the region or the nation, and he succeeded well. Let me cite one prominent example. Lafayette, who had a continued presence in French politics as a reformer and a liberal during the 1820s, informed Webster that the Bunker Hill address 'has been translated in French and other languages, to the very great profit of European readers.'[2]

Webster's commemorative speeches triangulate between region, nation, and the revolutionary Atlantic world, with the nation as the central object of definition. Webster's Atlanticism emerges more sharply as a discrete concern in the two major deliberative orations that he performed in the House of Representatives. Webster's internationally famous speech in favor of the Greek revolutionaries (1824) and his celebrated oration in support of Simón Bolívar's Congress of Panama (1826) define a modern form of liberty rooted in Enlightenment universalism, produced by the circulation of knowledge, and embodied in tradition. Webster was already a recognized lawyer and former representative from New Hampshire when he was elected to Congress from Massachusetts, and he chose the Greek rebellion as the focus of his maiden speech in order to make a statement about the ideological role that the United States should play in the emerging world order. Six years later he supported Bolívar's Panama Congress over the objections of Andrew Jackson and Southern leaders who feared Spanish American interest in Cuba and the spread of the antislavery thought that Bolívar had absorbed from the Haitian Revolution and made a centerpiece of his theories of post-independence nationalism. Webster felt it was imperative to support 'the spirit of liberty on this side of the Atlantic.'[3] These two Congressional speeches relate Webster's emerging national vision to an understanding of the international

2. Fletcher Webster, ed., *The Private Correspondence of Daniel Webster*, 2 vols. (Boston: Little, Brown, 1857), 1:400.
3. 'The Panama Mission,' in *Works of Daniel Webster*, 3:178–217; quotation on p. 202.

community that profoundly shaped his thinking about the United States as a model for and arbiter of liberty. On the floor of the United States House of Representatives Webster transformed revolution and counter-revolution in the Atlantic world into a grand drama of modern liberty.

Let me briefly sketch the Atlantic-world stage that Webster played upon. In the United States, the second defeat of Britain secured political independence and ushered in a period often called 'the Era of Good Feelings,' when an absence of significant oppositional politics produced something approaching a one-party state. Thomas Jefferson's strategic weakening of the executive branch of the government during his presidency contributed to a political system in which Congress bore substantial power. The 'great triumvirate' of John Calhoun, Henry Clay, and Daniel Webster emerged into roles of national influence, each strongly representing one of the three major regions of the country (Calhoun the South; Clay the West; Webster the North).[4] The political roles of the great triumvirate were enhanced by their reputations as talented and distinctive orators. During these years congressional deliberations played a defining role in national governance, and the eloquence of these representatives was central to the civic culture of their era. Their major orations drew large crowds, were printed in the newspapers, as separates, and in anthologies, and circulated via personal correspondence. The growth of media networks—performance venues, the press, the postal service and the roads, canals, and later railroads that serviced it—was at the top of a national political agenda dominated in these years by what were known as 'internal improvements,' development projects that took priority for Webster and many of his colleagues over national expansion.

Abolition had not yet emerged as the defining movement within antislavery. In 1820 the Missouri Compromise temporarily settled

4. Merrill D. Peterson, *The Great Triumvirate: Webster, Clay, and Calhoun* (New York: Oxford University Press, 1997).

the question of slavery in new territories, and for the next decade antislavery efforts had an Atlantic world focus, driven by the African colonization movement and efforts to ban the slave trade. Founded in 1817, the American Colonization Society sought a solution to the problem of African slavery that led in 1822 to the foundation of Monrovia (later renamed Liberia) as a destination for the resettlement of former slaves. Led by Great Britain, international antislavery efforts also focused on the abolition of the slave trade. Only after 1830 did antislavery efforts in the United States increasingly focus on the specific national dimensions of slavery.

The anti-colonial and republican movements in the Caribbean and Latin America also focused attention on Atlantic world politics. Revolutionary struggles for Spanish American independence extended from 1808 until 1826. During these years 'the Liberator' Simón Bolívar helped lead anti-colonial resistance movements in the northern part of the continent; experimented with federalist and republican forms of government in Gran Colombia, the state that encompassed substantial portions of Venezuela, Panama, Ecuador, and Colombia; and organized an inter-American congress in Panama.[5] Bolívar complained of European and North American indifference to his people's struggles. 'America stands together because it is abandoned by all other nations,' he complained in his 'Jamaica Letter' of 1815, characteristically referring to Spanish America as 'America.' It would have made more sense, he felt, if 'Europe herself, as a matter of common sense policy, should have prepared and executed the project of American independence.'[6]

When Europe did become involved, however, it was not on the side of 'America.' The Holy Alliance of European monarchies was ostensibly created to promote the expressly Christian values of justice, love, and peace in Europe, but its emphasis quickly became

5. John Lynch, *Simón Bolívar: A Life* (New Haven: Yale University Press, 2006).

6. 'Reply of a South American to a Gentleman of this Island' ['Jamaica Letter'], *Selected Writings of Bolívar*, comp. by Vicente Lecuna, ed. Harold A. Bierck, Jr., trans. Lewis Bertrand, 2 vols. (New York: The Colonial Press, 1951), 1: 103–22; quotations on p. 121 and p, 107.

SPAIN.

AN

ACCOUNT
OF THE
PUBLIC FESTIVAL
GIVEN BY
THE CITIZENS OF BOSTON,
AT THE EXCHANGE COFFEE HOUSE,
JANUARY 24, 1809,
IN HONOR OF
SPANISH VALOUR & PATRIOTISM.
WITH THE
REGULAR AND VOLUNTEER TOASTS,
AND ALL THE
ORIGINAL SONGS AND ODES
SUNG ON THE OCCASION.

IN WHICH IS ALSO INTRODUCED
A BRIEF SKETCH OF SPAIN,
GEOGRAPHICAL, HISTORICAL AND POLITICAL.

....
SPAIN is not a *dead* but sleeping *Lion.*
....

Copy Right of the "SKETCH" and "NATIONAL ODE," having been secured by the author
agreeable to Act of Congress, they are here published by permission of Mr. PAINE

PRINTED
BY RUSSELL AND CUTLER,
AND FOR SALE AT THEIR PRINTING-OFFICE IN CONGRESS-STREET,
BOSTON.

[1809]

Spain. An Account of the Public Festival Given by the Citizens of Boston, at the Exchange Coffee House, January 24, 1809, in Honor of Spanish Valour & Patriotism. With the Regular and Volunteer toasts, and All the Original Songs and Odes Sung on the Occasion (Boston: Russell and Cutler, [1809]).

the protection of sovereign power and the prevention of revolution. In his speeches from these years, Webster repeatedly focused on the threat that the alliance posed to the spread of liberty. He noted with alarm that alliance powers promulgated the doctrine of Laibach, also known as the Troppau Protocol, which called for the suppression of revolutionary movements in Europe.[7] The protocol was brought to bear on the resistance movement in Greece, which in 1821 flared into full-scale war for independence from the Ottoman Empire and became an international cause célèbre. The Alliance intermittently threatened to intervene in Latin America as well, and Webster warned that the Allied Powers viewed even the United States itself as 'in a state of rebellion or of anarchy.'[8]

During these years the United States and Great Britain were frequent allies on behalf of Atlantic world republican independence movements and against the counterrevolutionary power of the Alliance. In 1822 President James Monroe recognized five of the new Spanish American republican governments, and Britain warned that it would do the same if independence was challenged. The next year threats that France and Spain, backed by the Holy Alliance, were attempting to retake South America led Monroe to declare hemispheric solidarity in his State of the Union address, articulating what later became known as the Monroe Doctrine. Bolívar testified to the significance of the Anglo-American alliance when in 1826 he proposed an 'Americas' league to the representatives at the Congress of Panama. Bolívar suggested Britain as the head and protector of the newly independent states and the United States as a partner, albeit a dangerously close and powerful partner which he wanted to keep on the

---

7. The Troppau Protocol (1820) asserts that 'States, which have undergone a change of government due to revolution, the result of which threaten other states, ipso facto cease to be members of the European Alliance, and remain excluded from it until their situation gives guarantees for legal order and stability. . . . If, owing to such alterations, immediate danger threatens other states the powers bind themselves, by peaceful means, or if need be by arms, to bring back the guilty State into the bosom of the Great Alliance.' Carlton J. Hayes, *A Political and Cultural History of Northern Europe*, 2 vols. (1916; New York: Macmillian Co., 1932) I: 733

8. 'The Revolution in Greece,' in *Works of Daniel Webster*, 3: 60–93; quotation on p.71.

periphery of his projected economic and military league to prevent its swallowing its southern neighbors. It was this series of events that led Webster in his House speech to assert that Monroe's declaration was met by 'the free people of the United States' with 'one universal feeling of the gratified love of liberty.'[9]

Making Modern Liberty

What did Webster mean by liberty? And what specifically is *modern* liberty? Contemporary philosophers recognize two traditions of political thought that correspond to different meanings for the term. In 1958 Isaiah Berlin famously defined positive and negative variants of modern liberty. 'Negative liberty' is delimited by the answer to the question, 'What is the area within which the subject—a person or group of persons—is or should be left to do or be what he is able to do or be, without interference by other persons?' This is a Cold War version of the classical liberal definition of liberty principally identified with Anglo-American political philosophy as articulated by John Locke and John Stuart Mill, and further refined by John Rawls and Berlin himself. It is distinguished from a form of liberty associated with Rousseau and Jacobinism and linked, in Berlin's thought, to the totalitarian and fascist movements of the twentieth century. This 'positive liberty' is defined by the answer to the question 'What, or who, is the source of control or interference that can determine someone to do, or be, this rather than that?'[10] A common shorthand for distinguishing positive and negative liberty shared by many political philosophers is to trace negative liberty to the Glorious Revolution and the American Revolution and positive liberty to the French Revolution. This distinction can be boiled down, too simply and yet influentially, to Locke versus Rousseau, or to property and civil protections on the one hand, and the general will and human rights as a basis for state intervention on the other.

9. 'Panama Mission,' in *Works of Daniel Webster*, 3: 203–3.

10. Isaiah Berlin, *Liberty*, ed. Henry Hardy (New York: Oxford University Press, 2002), 169.

The idea that there is a distinctly 'modern' concept of liberty emerges in the writings of a contemporary of Webster's, the Swiss liberal Benjamin Constant, who in his 1816 essay 'The Liberty of the Ancients Compared with that of Moderns' recast the negative Lockean and positive Rousseauian definitions of liberty in developmental historical terms.[11] The terms 'negative' and 'positive' liberty suggest a conceptual mapping of differences; 'Anglo-American' and 'French' liberty suggest a national explanation of differences; 'Lockean' and 'Rousseauean' liberty suggest lines of philosophical development initiated by major thinkers. By designating many of the same concepts as a sequence, or a historical development, rather than as parallel conceptual tracks, Constant suggested that progress necessitates the embrace of 'modern' liberty. He argued that two features of modern political life distinguish ancient from modern liberty: these are representative government and commerce. Ancient liberty was participatory and political in nature; modern liberty consists of the protection of individual liberties and the growth of private pleasures through commerce, a system necessitated by the growth of large republics and made possible by the development of representative systems. Constant insisted that 'we can no longer enjoy the liberty of the ancients, which consisted in an active and constant participation in collective power. Our freedom must consist of peaceful and private independence.'[12] The French Revolution went awry, Constant argues, because Rousseau and his followers tried to imitate the ancients. 'Social power injured individual independence,' he concludes.[13]

Webster shared Constant's aversion for the French Revolution, but he differed from Constant both in his specific objections and in his historical teleology. Whereas the liberal Constant described the flaws of the French Revolution as an excess

11. Benjamin Constant, 'The Liberty Of The Ancients Compared With That Of The Moderns' in *Political Writings*, trans and ed. Biancamaria Fontana (Cambridge: Cambridge University Press, 1988), 309–28.

12. Constant, 'Liberty of the Ancients Compared with that of the Moderns,' 316.

13. Constant, 'Liberty of the Ancients Compared with that of the Moderns,' 320.

of social power at the expense of personal freedom, Webster described the contrast between the American and French Revolutions as a difference between 'guarded, regular, and safe' development and the 'unfortunate but natural' outcome of 'an irregular and violent impulse.'[14] Here he echoed Edmund Burke's conclusion in his 1775 speech on conciliation with America that the Americans had 'the advantages of order, in the midst of a struggle for liberty.'[15] The conciliation speech was an important precursor text to Webster's Plymouth oration. Crucially, where Burke presented the American Revolution as an extension of the British constitution, Webster claimed that the American colonies did much more than simply reproduce the values and institutions of the mother country. In ancient Greece, Webster observed, colonies merely mimicked the 'parent city,' leading to 'those mutual dissensions and conflicts which proved so fatal.'[16] The settlers of British North America sought not just to replicate the metropolis. Rather they aspired 'to erect systems of more perfect civil liberty, or to enjoy a higher degree of religious freedom.'[17] In an 'age of progressive knowledge and improvement,' the settlement of North American colonies not only 'enlarge[d] the natural boundaries of the habitable world' and 'extend[ed] commerce and increase[d] wealth among the human race.' It also produced 'moral effects,' and affected 'the state of human knowledge, the general tone of human sentiments, and the prospects of human happiness.' In short, the European discovery and settlement of the Americas gave 'civilized man' 'a new range for his thoughts, new objects for curiosity, and new excitements to knowledge and improvement.'[18] It is this progressive

---

14. 'The Bunker Hill Monument,' in *Works of Daniel Webster*, 1: 57–78; quotation on p. 72.

15. Edmund Burke, *On Empire, Liberty, and Reform: Speeches and Letters*, ed. David Bromwich (New Haven: Yale University Press, 2000), 88.

16. 'First Settlement of New England,' in *Works of Daniel Webster*, I: 1–54; quotation on 16.

17. 'First Settlement of New England,'in *Works of Daniel Webster* 1:17.

18. 'First Settlement of New England,' in *Works of Daniel Webster* 1:17.

quality that elevated modern over ancient colonization and explains for Webster the advances of modern over ancient liberty.

Webster's signature rhetorical gesture was to set out theoretical opposites in order to resolve them in the institutions of the American state. In his speeches tradition is set against revolution—except in the United States, where revolution originated from traditional institutions and therefore is readily absorbed into them. Reason is opposed to feeling, but not when political reason calls forth appropriate feelings of sympathy and identity with people resisting oppression. Performance is distinct from print, unless the oration is printed and circulated via personal correspondence to influential members of the audience, such as John Adams and the Marquis de Lafayette, who are themselves prominently featured in the printed text. The institutions of knowledge mediate the opposing terms and relate them to the overall development of the United States as well as to the communications networks of the Atlantic world.

At Bunker Hill, Webster described the expansion of knowledge and the growth of an Atlantic world:

> Knowledge has, in our time, triumphed . . . over distance, over difference of languages, over diversity of habits, over prejudice, and over bigotry. . . . The whole world is becoming a field for intellect to act in. Energy of mind, genius, power, wheresoever it exists, may speak out in any tongue, and the *world* will hear it. . . . There is a vast commerce of ideas; there are marts and exchanges for intellectual discoveries. . . . Mind is the great lever of all things . . . and the diffusion of knowledge . . . has rendered innumerable minds, variously gifted by nature, competent to be competitors or fellow-workers on the theatre of intellectual operations.[19]

Central among the intellectual advances that Webster cited was the development of political thought, which fed directly into advances in 'human liberty and human happiness.'[20]

19. 'The Bunker Hill Monument,' in *Works of Daniel Webster* 1:71.
20. 'The Bunker Hill Monument,' in *Works of Daniel Webster* 1:72.

Liberty was a sentiment as well as a product of knowledge for Webster, who observed to Lafayette that 'A great chord of sentiment and feeling runs through two continents, and vibrates over both.'[21] As Burke's American heir, Webster brought the full repertoire of affective rhetorical techniques to bear in the service of a tradition of revolutionary enlightenment. Feeling, he insisted, is a force of historical change. His goal in his commemorative speeches was to give 'right direction to sentiments, and open proper springs of feeling in the heart.'[22] 'Let us feel deeply how much of what we are and of what we possess we owe to this liberty, and to these institutions of government,' he urged in his speech on Adams and Jefferson. Feeling must sustain the institutions of liberty: 'If we cherish the virtues and the principles of our fathers, Heaven will assist us to carry on the work of human liberty and happiness.'[23] In his speech on the Greek Revolution, Webster observed that words could produce feelings that would change history. Moral causes had replaced military power. Public opinion triumphed over brute force. Webster urged his Congressional colleagues to provide 'a manifestation of our sympathy with a long oppressed and now struggling people,' arguing that 'the Greeks address the civilized world with a pathos not easy to be resisted.'[24]

In Webster's view, as knowledge circulates and as feelings of sympathy for oppressed peoples grow, liberty spreads. Webster's claims resemble key features of Jürgen Habermas's description of 'publicity' as a facilitator of modern concepts of freedom. The similarities between Webster and Habermas are particularly apparent in Webster's celebration of Greek reading societies and other modes of knowledge production and circulation that fuelled their revolutionary resistance to the Ottoman Empire. He praised the

---

21. 'The Bunker Hill Monument,' in *Works of Daniel Webster* 1:71.
22. 'The Bunker Hill Monument,' in *Works of Daniel Webster*, 1:62.
23. 'Adams and Jefferson,' in *Works of Daniel Webster*, 1:147.
24. 'The Revolution in Greece,' in *Works of Daniel Webster*, 3: 92.

Greek leaders for their ability to build institutions of knowledge such as schools, colleges, libraries, and the press and located the origin of the Greek resistance movement in an 'improved state of knowledge' and the growth of literature.[25]

Greece mirrored the United States' revolutionary experience, Webster claimed, but Spanish America was different. 'They are but pupils in the school of popular liberty,' he observed of the sister republics to the south, attributing their slow progress to differences of 'race' and political and religious experience.[26] Yet, Webster insisted, the United States had been a primary influence in their reform efforts. 'They have looked steadily, in every adversity, to the *great Northern light,*' he claimed.[27] Here Webster clearly overstated his case. Bolívar, for one, was openly skeptical of the United States as a political model for Latin American republics. 'As long as our countrymen do not acquire the abilities and political virtues that distinguish our brothers of the north,' he wrote, 'wholly popular systems, far from working to our advantage, will, I greatly fear, bring about our downfall.'[28] Great Britain was his favored constitutional model, with its hereditary senate as a guarantor of liberty against the dangers of popular demagoguery.

Webster's description of the new knowledge produced in the North American colonies stood in sharp contrast to Bolívar's expressions of frustration at the limited knowledge he was able to produce about Spanish America. The 'facts about America and her development' were 'shrouded in mystery,' he wrote in his 'Jamaica Letter.' 'Who is capable of compiling statistics of a land like this?'[29] Bolívar was unable to give a satisfying answer to a correspondent's questions because he 'lack[ed] documents and books' and because he had only 'limited knowledge of a land so vast, so varied, and so little known as the new world.'[30] Bolívar

25. 'The Revolution in Greece,' in *Works of Daniel Webster,* 3:79, 85.
26. 'The Panama Mission,' in *Works of Daniel Webster,* 3:215.
27. 'The Panama Mission,' in *Works of Daniel Webster,* 3:217.
28. *Selected Writings,* 1: 115.
29. 'Jamaica Letter,' 109.
30. 'Jamaica Letter,' 103.

warned the delegates to the Second National Congress of Venezuela in Angostura that, 'subject to the threefold yoke of ignorance, tyranny, and vice, the American people have been unable
to acquire knowledge, power, or [civic] virtue.'[31]

On the matter of civic order, Bolívar sided with Rousseau, who
urged the controlling force of society and the popular will over the
individualism and liberalism that Constant advocated. In his Jamaica Letter, Bolívar expressed skepticism over the capacity of
Spanish Americans for full liberty, asking, 'Is it conceivable that a
newly emancipated people can soar to the heights of liberty and,
unlike Icarus, neither have its wings melt nor fall into an abyss?'[32]
Four years later, advising the legislators at Angostura about the
new constitution that they were about to form, he warned that
'absolute liberty invariably lapses into absolute power' and advocated forms of 'popular education' that would include newly
created institutions modeled on the Athenian Aeropagus and the
Roman censors and domestic tribunals.[33] These ancient institutions were designed to enforce moral order, which Bolívar felt was
critical in a state where the people had been denied the opportunities for self-governance enjoyed in the British colonies of North
America. Like Rousseau, he wished to import ancient institutions
of social order to sustain the republic and enforce virtue.

For Webster, as for Bolívar, modern liberty required subjects
prepared to exercise it. The New England free school served
much the same function as the Aeropagus and the tribunals,
though it had the virtue in Webster's eyes of being an inherited
local institution and thereby a traditional form of authority—
and not one imported from the past. In the Plymouth address,
Webster described the free school in terms that Michel Foucault
would have found refreshingly frank: 'We regard [education] as a
wise and liberal system of police, by which property, and life, and
the peace of society are secured. . . . We hope for a security beyond

31. 'Jamaica Letter,' 176.
32. 'Jamaica Letter,' 115.
33. 'Jamaica Letter,' 192.

the law, and above the law,' he continued, 'in the prevalence of an enlightened and well-principled moral sentiment.'[34] The free school was an American export that Webster urged upon his international audience. In contrast to Bolívar's lack of information about Spanish America in the Jamaica Letter, Webster was able to offer comparative statistics on literacy rates in England (one child in fifteen could read and write), Wales (one child in twenty), France (one child in thirty-five), and New England, where literacy, the fruit of institutions established by Massachusetts Bay colony law in 1647, was close to universal. Webster linked the Christian faith of the Puritans closely with both literacy and citizenship, observing that 'whatever makes men good Christians, makes them good citizens.'[35] The institutions of literacy and Christianity characterized modern liberty for Webster and distinguished the Puritans from the 'barbarians' who inhabited the continent before them.

Along with education, Christianity, and the circulation of knowledge, property was the fourth support of modern liberty for Webster. He contrasted the feudal model of property that still encumbered Europe with the broad distribution of property in America where, he claimed, the Puritans who landed at Plymouth encountered a Lockean new world in which 'the whole soil was unreclaimed from barbarism.'[36] Native Americans served Webster principally as a foil, representing for him the condition of peoples without the institutions of modern liberty, and have consequently been displaced. For Bolívar, in contrast, indigenous Americans and non-white creoles marked the central challenge of the new Spanish American republics. While Bolívar did seek ways to redistribute land and wealth, he presented that project as a component of the larger effort to create a broadly based social equality, built on laws and institutions that could mediate between the strongly discriminated racial groups that characterized postcolonial society. Few differences are more marked than these in the political thought of

34. *Works of Daniel Webster* , 1: 41–2.
35. *Works of Daniel Webster,* 1:44.
36. *Works of Daniel Webster*, 1:35.

the two men. The racial hierarchies that were a consistent preoccupation of Bolívar's were all but ignored by Webster. Suppressing the persistent indigenous presence, and restricting his references to an African American presence to his discussion of the slave trade, Webster portrayed an 'America' that was New England writ large.

Nowhere in these speeches did Webster look abroad and find an example that the United States could profit from, in the manner of Robert Dahl in his recent book *How Democratic Is the American Constitution?*[37] In his subsequent career, Webster was an important figure in the formation of international law, but the nearest he came to an embrace of some non-United States–based political form here was his support for Bolívar's Congress of Panama. It is worth remembering that this was a controversial project that was greeted with hostility by Webster's Southern colleagues in Congress because they feared Bolívar's example on the issue of race and slavery.

Webster presented a world that had many alternatives to New England institutions of modern liberty—but none of which was good. He summed up his celebration of New England as a crucible of modern liberty with a warning:

> We are bound to maintain public liberty, and, by the example of our own systems, to convince the world that order and law, religion and morality, the rights of conscience, the rights of persons, and the rights of property, may all be preserved and secured, in the most perfect manner, by a government entirely elective. If we fail in this, our disaster will be signal, and will furnish an argument, stronger than has yet been found, in support of those opinions which maintain that government can rest safely on nothing but power and coercion.[38]

Webster feared the political and military threats to the Americas that were posed by the counterrevolutionary forces of the Holy

37. Robert A. Dahl, *How Democratic is the American Constitution?* (New Haven: Yale University Press, 2002).
38. 'First Settlement of New England,' 1: 44–45.

Alliance. He feared the forces of social disorder that in his view had destroyed the French Revolution and threatened to cripple the new Spanish American states. He also feared the moral threat posed by the persistence of the African slave trade, and he offered an impassioned plea for New England to be 'purified' from it. As in John Winthrop's day, and in our own, Webster saw the city upon a hill being threatened by forces both external and internal.

Webster's fears for the United States experiment seem idle at best and egregiously jingoistic at worst—and, applied to the world as it is now, they surely are. But a moment's thought suggests the obvious fact that Webster had real cause to worry. The looming conflicts about slavery and the federal system would require a civil war to resolve. I sometimes describe Webster as being like Shakespeare, because both writers are full of clichés. My point is that he told an influential story in which modern liberty was a product of United States institutions. This story has achieved such wide circulation that it is easy to lose sight of its historical moment, but that moment is crucial to its significance. A national narrative such as Webster's can block the emergence of new forms of liberty. Seen in the Atlantic world context of his own time, however, Webster can still offer perspectives on our world today.

Closing the Last Chapter of the Atlantic Revolution: The 1837–38 Rebellions in Upper and Lower Canada

MICHEL DUCHARME

HALF A CENTURY AGO, two historians, Robert Palmer and Jacques Godechot, proposed that the late-eighteenth-century revolutions of the Atlantic World be integrated into one analytical framework. They argued that the American Revolution of 1776, the Dutch uprising of the 1780s, the unrest in the Austrian Low Countries after 1787, the French Revolution of 1789, and all of the European revolutions of the 1790s were, in fact, a single phenomenon. It was, in their view, as if one single, great revolution had shaken the Atlantic world between 1776 and 1800.[1]

1. Robert R. Palmer and Jacques Godechot's proposal first appeared in 'Le problème de l'Atlantique du XVIIIème au XXème siècle,' in *Storia Contemporanea, Relazioni del X Congresso Internazionale di Scienze Storiche* 6 vols. (Florence: G. C. Sansoni Editore, 1955), 5: 219–39. Each wrote a history of the Atlantic Revolution: Robert R. Palmer, *The Age of the Democratic Revolution. A Political History of Europe and America, 1760–1800*, 2 vols. (Princeton: Princeton University Press, 1959); Jacques Godechot, *Les Révolutions (1770–1799)* (1963; reprint, Paris: Presses Universitaires de France, 1986), 99–177.

MICHEL DUCHARME is an assistant professor of history at the University of British Columbia. The ideas discussed in this paper were first developed in his Ph.D. dissertation, 'Aux fondements de l'État canadien. La liberté au Canada de 1776 à 1841' (McGill University, 2005). The author wishes to thank Anna de Aguayo (Dawson College, Montréal) for her useful comments and editing work and the Social Sciences and Humanities Research Council of Canada (SSHRC) and the Fonds pour la Formation de Chercheurs et l'Aide à la Recherche (FCAR) for their support.

Even if we can appreciate the transnational ambition of their analysis, we must recognize that this description of the so-called 'Atlantic Revolution' was really quite limited in scope, as it focused only on the United States and Europe.[2] Not a single word was said about Saint Domingue, although its unrest and revolts of the 1790s eventually led to the creation of Haiti in 1804. In fact, if we exempt the United States, it was as if the entire New World had gone missing from this Atlantic Revolution. In recent decades, historians, including many participants in this conference, have tried to correct this deficiency. They successfully integrated the nineteenth-century Central and South American revolutions by exploring Spanish and Portuguese colonial histories.[3] Finally, it can be said that the historical analysis of the Atlantic Revolution covers all Europe and America, between 1776 and 1840. Or can it? There is, in fact, one country's history that continues to be left out of the Atlantic framework: Canada's.

When Canadian historians have studied Canadian history at the time of the American and French revolutions, very few have tried to integrate it into an Atlantic framework. The only conference to deal with the relationship between Canada and the Atlantic Revolution was held in 1969, at the Université de Montréal. The conference proceedings were later published in the *Annales historiques de la Révolution française* (1973). Then, during the 1970s and 1980s, Jean-Pierre Wallot showed some interest in this framework. In 1995, Allan Greer encouraged others to study the

2. Many American and European scholars have followed the path opened by Palmer and Godechot. See, among others: Bernard Bailyn, *The Ideological Origins of the American Revolution* (Cambridge: Belknap Press of the Harvard University Press, 1967); Gordon Wood, *The Creation of the American Republic, 1776–1789* (1969; reprint, Chapel Hill: University of North Carolina Press, 1998); J. G. A. Pocock, *The Machiavellian Moment* (Princeton: Princeton University Press, 1975), 333–552; Simon Shama, *Patriots and Liberators: Revolution in the Netherlands, 1780–1813* (1977; reprint, London: Harper Perennial, 1992); J. G. A. Pocock, 'The Dutch Republican Tradition,' in *The Dutch Republic in the Eighteenth Century: Decline, Enlightenment and Revolution*, eds. Margaret Jacobs and Wijnand W. Mijnhardt (Ithaca: Cornell University Press, 1992), 188–93; Stephen Small, *Political Thought in Ireland, 1776–1798: Republicanism, Patriotism and Radicalism* (Oxford: Oxford University Press, 2002); Annie Jourdan, *La Révolution, une exception française* (Paris: Flammarion, 2004).

3. See, among others: David Patrick Geggus, *Haitian Revolutionary Studies* (Bloomington: Indiana University Press, 2002); Lester D. Langley, *The Americas in the Age of Revolution, 1750–1850* (New Haven: Yale University Press), 1996. Jaime E. Rodríguez O., ed., *Mexico in the Age of Democratic Revolutions: 1750–1850* (Boulder: Lynne Rienner, 1994).

1837–38 Canadian rebellions as part of an Atlantic revolution, without venturing to do it himself. In 1998, Jean-Pierre Boyer, a communications professor at the Université du Québec à Montréal, tried to integrate Québec in the Atlantic framework in an essay published at the end of a French translation of Thomas Paine's *The Rights of Man*.[4] However, most French-speaking Québec historians, such as Yvan Lamonde, Gérard Bouchard, and Louis-Georges Harvey, preferred to study Québec history in its North American context, which they called 'l'américanité,' rather than in its Atlantic context.[5] In English Canada, historians were perhaps a bit too eager to promote what distinguished Canada from the United States to really try to integrate the Canadian past into the Atlantic framework. So, for instance, English Canadian historians writing on that period focused their attention on the arrival of the Loyalists after the American Revolution so as to establish the emergence of a distinct Canadian identity.[6]

4. Jean-Pierre Wallot, 'Révolution et réformisme dans le Bas-Canada (1773–1815),' *Annales historiques de la Révolution française*, 45: 213 (1973): 344–406; Jean-Pierre Wallot, 'Frontière ou fragment du système atlantique: Des idées étrangères dans l'identité bas-canadienne au début du XIXe siècle,' *Canadian Historical Association Historical Papers* (1983): 3–14; Allan Greer, '1837–1838: Rebellion Reconsidered,' *Canadian Historical Review* 76 (1995): 1–18; Jean-Pierre Boyer, 'Le Québec à l'heure des révolutions atlantiques,' in Thomas Paine, *Les Droits de l'Homme*, ed. Jean-Pierre Boyer (Sillery, Québec: Septentrion, 1998), 355–424.

5. For 'l'américanité', see: Yvan Lamonde, 'American Cultural Influence in Quebec: A One-Way Mirror,' in *Problems and Opportunities in US-Quebec Relations*, eds. Alfred O. Hero, Jr. and Marcel Daneau (Boulder, Colo.: Westview Press, 1984), 106–26; Gérard Bouchard and Yvan Lamonde, eds., *Québécois et Américains: La culture québécoise aux XIXe et XXe siècles* (Montréal: Fides, 1995); Louis-Georges Harvey, *Le Printemps de l'Amérique française: Américanité, anticolonialisme et républicanisme dans le discours politique québécois, 1805–1837* (Montréal: Boréal, 2005). Gérard Bouchard has integrated this 'américanité' in a broader framework: the new societies. See *Genèse des nations et cultures du nouveau monde. Essai d'histoire comparée* (Montréal: Boréal, 2000).

6. For recent works on the loyalists, see: Ann Gorman Condon, *The Envy of the American States: The Loyalist Dream for New Brunswick* (Fredericton, N. B.: New Ireland, 1984); Wallace Brown and Hereward Senior, *Victorious in Defeat: The Loyalists in Canada* (Toronto: Methuen, 1984); Christopher Moore, *The Loyalists: Revolution, Exile, and Settlement* (Toronto: Macmillan, 1984); Walter Stewart, *True Blue: The Loyalist Legend* (Toronto: Collins, 1985); Neil MacKinnon, *This Unfriendly Soil: The Loyalist Experience in Nova Scotia, 1783–1791* (Montréal and Kingston: McGill-Queen's University Press, 1986); J. M. Bumsted, 'The Loyalist Question on Prince Edward Island, 1783–1861,' *Island Magazine* 25 (1989): 20–28. On the loyalist myth, see: Jo-Ann Fellows, 'The Loyalist Myth in Canada,' *Canadian Historical Association Historical Papers* (1971): 94–111; Norman Knowles, *Inventing the Loyalists: The Ontario Loyalist Tradition and the Creation of Usable Pasts* (Toronto: University of Toronto Press, 1997).

It is true that the British North American colonies that eventually became Canada did not join the thirteen colonies in their revolution. It is also true that these same colonies did not take the opportunity to declare their independence during the French Revolution, or during the subsequent French Revolutionary War. This is not to say that the American and French revolutionary and republican ideals did not spread throughout the colonies during the 1780s and '90s. This is especially so in the portion of the province of Québec that became Lower Canada in 1791. Fleury Mesplet, for instance, a French printer who had come from Philadelphia to Montréal in 1776, remained in the city after the withdrawal of American troops in May 1776.[7] Between 1785 and his death in 1794, he indirectly promoted republican ideals through his bilingual newspaper, *La Gazette de Montréal/ The Montreal Gazette*. The promotion of republican and revolutionary principles was not only the work of people within the colony. In June 1793, Edmond-Charles Genêt, the French minister in Philadelphia, strongly urged Canadians to join the French struggle for freedom in an appeal entitled, *Les Français libres à leurs frères les Canadiens*.[8] His appeal failed to rouse his 'brothers' in the colony.

So it appears that republicanism, the main ideology behind the Atlantic Revolution, did not represent a serious threat in the northern British colonies at the end of the eighteenth and beginning of the nineteenth century. The question arising is thus: Did republicanism or any of the key principles that inspired the Atlantic revolutionaries have any impact on Upper and Lower Canada—now Ontario and Québec? Some distinguished scholars have argued over the years that it had a 'negative' impact, Canadian history

7. For the biography of Mesplet, see: Jean-Paul de Lagrave, *Fleury Mesplet, 1734–1794: Diffuseur des Lumières au Québec* (Montréal: Patenaude, 1985); and Patricia Lockhart Fleming, 'Cultural Crossroads: Print and Reading in Eighteenth- and Nineteenth-Century English-Speaking Montreal,' *Proceedings of the American Antiquarian Society* 112 (2003): 231–48.

8. Genêt's text is reproduced in Michel Brunet, 'La Révolution française sur les rives du St-Laurent,' *Revue d'histoire de l'Amérique française* 11 (1957):158–62.

being the result of a counterrevolutionary experiment.[9] It would be interesting to discuss this question, but I will confine my paper to exploring the direct or 'positive' influences of republicanism in Lower and Upper Canadian history between 1776 and 1838. I will argue that republicanism did indeed have a major 'positive' impact on these colonies, although much later than in other countries around the Atlantic.

Canada during the Atlantic Revolution (1776–1828)

In 1791, a few years after the British acknowledged American independence in the Versailles Treaty, the British government granted a new constitution to the province of Québec. It was called the Constitutional Act in Canada, but known as the Canada Act everywhere else. One of the conscious goals of the British government in adopting the Constitutional Act was to stop the dissemination of republican principles in the province. To achieve this, the British parliament split the province into two distinct colonies: Upper Canada (now Ontario), which was mainly settled by refugees from the United States or, as we know them, 'Loyalists,' and Lower Canada (now the province of Québec), comprised of French Canadians with a vocal English-speaking minority. Thus, the Crown made sure that the Upper Canadian Loyalists could no longer complain that they were living in a French colony, while French Canadians in Lower Canada could feel less afraid of being outnumbered in their colony, could continue to live under their own civil laws, and could have free exercise of their Roman Catholic faith. This division also allowed for the granting of rudimentary parliamentary institutions to the two new colonies. The British government organized these colonial governments along the principles of 'mixed' government—a

9. Seymour Martin Lipset, *Revolution and Counterrevolution: Change and Persistence in Social Structures* (New York: Basic Books, Inc., 1968), 31–63; and from the same author, *Continental Divide: The Values and Institutions of the United States and Canada* (New York: Routledge, 1990), 1–56, 59–60; Jerry Bannister, 'Canada as Counter-Revolution: The Loyalist Order Framework in Canadian History, 1750–1840,' lecture, The Liberal Order in Canadian History Conference, McGill Institute for the Study of Canada, March 3, 2006.

system in which the king (represented by the governor or the lieutenant-governor) had the executive power and in which provincial legislatures (composed of the governor, an appointed legislative council, and an elected legislative assembly) had the legislative power. The system of government conferred on Canadians in 1791 followed the usual British political system and practices, as far as colonial status would allow.

Since one of the objectives of the British government was to prevent republicanism from becoming a real threat in the province of Québec—and thereby preventing the colony from falling into an American-style revolution—the Constitutional Act can be seen to have been a great success. It effectively prevented the spread of republican practices into the colonies. Looking at their new legislative assemblies, Canadians thought they were enjoying an excellent form of government. The fact that the assembly shared the legislative power with a British governor and an appointed legislative council did not seem to bother anyone at first.[10] On the one hand, French-speaking Lower Canadians were too busy trying to exercise their new rights in the parliamentary system to pay attention to such 'details.' On the other hand, Upper Canadians were too busy trying to wrestle a life out of the Ontario forests to really criticize their constitution.

If the last decades of the eighteenth century were more or less quiet in Upper and Lower Canada, things changed during the first decade of the nineteenth century. In both colonies, reform movements appeared in 1805–6, although the Lower Canadian movement was better organized, more coherent, and more efficient than its Upper Canadian counterparts. While these movements were created at the same time as the Central and South

10. Samuel Neilson, a Whig reformer, and Fleury Mesplet, a republican, welcomed the Constitutional Act by publishing the same text promoting the new constitution in their respective newspapers: *La Gazette de Québec/ The Quebec Gazette* (February 23, March 1, 8, and 15, 1792) and *La Gazette de Montréal/ The Montreal Gazette* (March 15 and 22, 1792). Its author, Solon, was Jonathan Sewell, the future chief justice of Lower Canada (1808–38): John Hare, *Aux origines du parlementarisme québécois 1791–1793* (Sillery, Québec: Septentrion, 1993), 46, 131.

American colonies were fighting for their independence, their objectives were very different. On the whole, Canadians did not fight to obtain independence or articulate republican demands, though there were a few exceptions in Upper Canada.

Most of these reformers did not question their belonging to the British Empire or the legitimacy and form of their government. Until 1828, their demands, inspired by their reading of Locke, Blackstone, and De Lolme, aimed at gaining, for the assembly, genuine control over the executive power through a kind of ministerial responsibility, through impeachment trials, or through budgetary management, all three of which were political mechanisms that had allowed the eighteenth-century members of the British House of Commons to exercise power over the government.[11] In the end, we can say that republicanism did not have a direct or positive impact in the colonies before 1828.

Republicanism in Upper and Lower Canada (1828–38)
Until 1828, Upper and Lower Canadian reformers, as their label implies, were not demanding revolution. But results count, and after more than twenty years of political struggles in both colonies, they had achieved nothing. By 1828, the reformers understood that they needed tougher vocabulary if they were to convince the British to reform the Canadian system.

---

11. In Lower Canada, Pierre Bédard was the first to ask for the introduction of a kind of ministerial responsibility in the colony in his newspaper *Le Canadien* between 1806 and 1810. In Upper Canada, this claim was first articulated by William Baldwin in 1828–29 in a petition to the king and then in a letter to the Duke of Wellington: 'Petition To the King's Most Excellent Majesty,' reproduced in *Appendix to Journal of the House of Assembly of Upper Canada*, 1835, 1st session of the 12th Provincial Parliament (January 15 –April 16, 1835), 1: 51; 'William Warren Baldwin to the Duke of Wellington, January 3rd, 1829' in *Documents Relating to the Constitutional History of Canada 1819–1828*, eds. A. Doughty and Norah Story (Ottawa: J. O. Patenaude, 1935), 482. Lower Canadian reformers asked for the creation of a system of impeachment trials against judges and civil servants during the 1810s. In Upper Canada, Baldwin mentioned the installation of such a system in his 1828 petition to the king. During the 1800s, in Upper Canada, and the 1820s, in Lower Canada, reformers saw the vote on supplies as their only means to influence the executive power. The confrontation between the Lower Canadian House of Assembly, on the one hand, and the governor and the upper house of the Legislature, on the other, on this issue during the 1830s paralyzed the political life in Lower Canada.

And this is how colonial reformers rediscovered the power of the republican discourse. Republican rhetoric not only gave them stronger arguments against the status quo, but it also encouraged them to question the legitimacy and the organization of the colonial political structure. After 1828, republicanism as discourse and ideology became the main source of inspiration for Lower Canadian Patriots and Upper Canadian radicals. From that moment until 1838, Canadian colonies went through a political process that corresponded to the criteria of the Atlantic Revolution. The Upper and Lower Canadian unrest of the 1830s, and its culmination in the 1837–38 rebellions in both colonies, must be considered, in my view, as the last chapter of the Atlantic Revolution, a chapter that did not end happily for Canadian republicans.

During the 1830s, all colonial republicans invoked the ideas, examples, and authority of well-known Atlantic republicans. By making these references, they were trying to gain respectability, credibility, and legitimacy. It is interesting to note that they did not often refer directly to Greek or Roman republicanism. Unlike the American patriots, the Canadian republicans did not try to connect their movement to ancient times. They were instead consciously trying to connect it to the Atlantic republican tradition that had developed during the eighteenth century. During the 1820s, their inspiration came mainly from the United Kingdom and, during the 1830s, from the United States and, to a lesser extent, from Ireland. Canadian republicans sometimes mentioned and celebrated Central and South American revolutions in their newspapers, but they were not particularly inspired by these events. Rousseauian-style rhetoric about the social contract was widely used, especially in Lower Canada, but its author was rarely mentioned or quoted extensively, nor were other French republicans. The painful memory of the Terror and the ultimate failure of the Revolution, heralded by the Restoration, led the Lower and Upper Canadian republicans to turn to Anglo-American references.

The American example was seen as useful, during the 1830s, for at least two reasons. Firstly, the American Revolution was a success and its republic an emerging power. Secondly, the Canadian republicans hoped that, by presenting their cause in a distinctly American manner, the Americans would eventually side with them, should a conflict arise between them and the British.

In 1835 Louis-Joseph Papineau, the Lower Canadian French-speaking Patriot leader, argued that if the British parliament tried to dominate Lower Canada as it had tried to dominate the thirteen colonies during the 1770s, many a new Jefferson or Washington would rise in Lower Canada.[12] In Upper Canada, William Lyon Mackenzie, an important radical leader, sometimes referred to Scottish heroes, such as William Wallace, Archibald Campbell (the first Marquess of Argyle), and William Russell to promote Canadian autonomy.[13] But, as in Lower Canada, it was the American Revolution and the American republic that was his real source of inspiration. In his *Sketches of Canada and the United States* (1833), Mackenzie did not hide his admiration for America's independence and institutions.

In 1836–37, the American Revolution was clearly used to encourage Canadians to fight for their rights. It had by then become 'the' example to follow. In Lower Canada, the Patriots organized a boycott of British products during the summer of 1837, just as the American patriots had done during the 1770s. In October 1837, they organized a 'militia' called *Les Fils de la Liberté* (the Sons of Liberty).[14] A most important public assembly was held in October 1837, a few weeks before the rebellion, which saw the adoption of many resolutions. Interestingly, the first of these was to translate the second paragraph of the American Declaration of

12. Papineau, 'Nécessité de nommer un délégué de la Chambre d'Assemblée à Londres' (House of Assembly, November 17, 1835), in *Un demi-siècle de combats: Interventions publiques*, ed. Yvan Lamonde and Claude Larin (Montréal: Fides, 1998), 367.

13. *Constitution*, October 19, 1836.

14. See the 'Adresse des Fils de la liberté de Montréal aux jeunes gens des colonies de l'Amérique du Nord,' October 4, 1837, reproduced in *Assemblées publiques, résolutions et déclarations de 1837–1838*, ed. Jean-Paul Bernard (Ville St-Laurent, Québec: VLB éditeur, 1988), 216.

Independence, beginning with 'We hold these truths to be self-evident, that all men are created equal.'[15] At this same public assembly, a few of the Patriots urged violent actions against the state, although Papineau, their leader, was not in favor of it. He fled the colony a few weeks later, just before the rebellion. In Upper Canada, Mackenzie defended the right of Canadians to choose their form of government as a 'right [that] was conceded to the present United States at the close of a successful revolution.'[16] He went as far as to reprint, in the summer of 1837, in his newspaper the *Constitution*, Thomas Paine's pamphlet, *Common Sense*, first published in 1776 to promote American independence.[17] Mackenzie also wrote in his newspaper, in July 1837: 'Canadians! It has been said that we are on the verge of a revolution. We are in the midst of one; a bloodless one, I hope, but a revolution to which all those which have been will be counted mere child's play.'[18] By November, he published a short text entitled *INDEPENDENCE* in which he openly promoted rebellion.

The desire of Canadian republicans to connect their movement to the Atlantic Revolution, especially in its American incarnation, was clearly apparent during the 1830s.

Republicanism in the Canadas: the Ideology

Lower Canadian Patriots and Upper Canadian radicals not only appealed to the example of the republican thinkers of the Atlantic world but also adopted their ideals and principles. Therefore, they were Atlantic revolutionaries.

For Lower Canadian Patriots and the Upper Canadian radicals, as for all other republicans, freedom and equality were very closely linked. For them, individuals needed to be equal in order to be free. When republicans talked about equality, they were not talking only about equality under the law or equality of rights;

15. This resolution was reprinted in *La Minerve*, October 30, 1837.
16. *Constitution*, August 2, 1837.
17. *Constitution*, July 19 and 26; August 2 and 9, 1837.
18. *Constitution*, July 26, 1837.

they were also talking about moral equality and a certain amount of material equality. This is why both Papineau in 1823 and Mackenzie in 1833–34 were shocked by the inequalities they saw in the United Kingdom during their visit in the metropolis.[19] Not that the Canadian republicans were social levellers; they never intended to level fortunes. But they thought that it was impossible for individuals to be free (to participate equally in political life) if there was too great a disparity between citizens, because the rich could bribe the poor and establish a form of clientelism. Amury Girod, a Swiss immigrant who came to Lower Canada in 1831, took the side of the Patriots during the 1830s, and fought as a 'general' in Saint Eustache in 1837, considered that 'la propriété est une des causes premières de tout bien et de tout mal dans la société. Si elle est également distribuée, les connaissances et le pouvoir le seront aussi [. . .] la liberté en sera tôt ou tard le résultat immanquable.'[20] Mackenzie thought much the same, and he quoted Abbé Raynald: 'People of America ! [. . .] Be afraid of too unequal a distribution of riches, which shows a small number of citizens in wealth, and a great number in misery—whence arises the insolence of the one and the disgrace of the other.'[21]

In order to ensure the economic and social equality of citizens, these republicans envisioned a society of small landowners, all independent of one another. Mackenzie himself said: 'Agriculture, the most innocent, happy and important of all human pursuits, is your chief employment—your farms are your own—you have obtained a competence, seek therewith to be content.'[22] This economic independence would ensure political independence. For

19. Even if Papineau was not a republican in 1823, he was shocked by what he saw in Britain. See the letters he wrote to his wife between April 5 and September 22, 1823: Louis-Joseph Papineau, *Lettres à Julie*, eds. Georges Aubin and Renée Blanchet (Sillery, Québec: Septentrion, 2000), 72–91. For Mackenzie, see *Colonial Advocate*, June 27, 1833.

20. Amury Girod, *Notes diverses sur le Bas-Canada* (Village Debartzch: J. P. de Boucherville, 1835), 63. Translation: 'Property is the cause of all good and all evil in society. If it is equally distributed, knowledge and power will be also . . . . Liberty will sooner or later be the inevitable result.'

21. Mackenzie, *Sketches of Canada and the United States* (London, E. Wilson, 1833), 60.

22. *Colonial Advocate*, September 9, 1830.

most Canadian republicans, life in Canada was already characterized by social equality. Their main goal was to reform political institutions to fit this social reality. In this context, colonial republicans were very suspicious of accumulation of wealth, of capitalism,
of primogeniture, and of bank monopoly, which they considered
detrimental to equality among citizens and might allow corrup-
tion to destroy freedom.

Canadian republicans incorporated these principles into a sophisticated set of political proposals. Considering the importance that they were giving to equality, they structured their political institutions around the idea of political equality. For them,
the right of the citizens to participate in the political process was
their first and most important right. The importance given to
political participation implied that citizens should have the right
to elect their representatives. These representatives were the
only ones who could legitimately adopt laws for the well-being
of all. In this context, the Patriots and the radicals concentrated
their claims around the constitution of legislative power during
the 1830s. Their efforts had two objectives. The first was to im-
prove the representativeness of the Legislative Assembly in
Upper Canada. In this colony, unlike Lower Canada, the radicals
could not gain control of the Assembly, except between 1834 and
1836. It was clear to them that if they could not obtain a majority
of the seats in the Assembly, the problem lay not in themselves
but in the way that representation was framed.[23] In both colonies
the efforts of colonial reformers aimed at making the legislative
councils of the colonies elective, not composed of appointed
members of the elite. During the 1830s, colonial republicans did

23. Mackenzie began to contest the state of representation in Upper Canada in
1831. A committee of inquiry was created the same year with Mackenzie as its chair. Its
report was introduced in the House on March 16, 1831. Its conclusions were predict-
able: 'the imperfect state of the representation in the House of Assembly is and has
been the cause of much evil to the Community.' (*First Report on the State of the Representation of the People of Upper Canada in the Legislature of that Province* [York: Toronto Office of the Colonial Advocate, 1831], 4). Major reforms were necessary, but this report
notwithstanding, no major changes were brought to the representation in Upper Canada before the 1837 rebellion.

not concede any legitimacy to the appointed legislative councils, the upper houses of the Upper and Lower Canadian legislatures. While a few demanded outright abolition of these bodies, most wanted to make them elective. This was the Lower Canadian Patriots' main demand. Thirty-four of the 'Ninety-Two Resolutions' (the charter of Lower Canadian republicanism) adopted by their Assembly in February 1834 concerned this reform (resolutions 9–40, 51, 54).[24] Upper Canadian republicans also fought for this reform, though not with the same energy as the Lower Canadians. In its *Seventh Report on Grievances* of 1835 (the charter of Upper Canadian republicanism), a committee of the House of Assembly, chaired by Mackenzie, presented the 'elective institutions [as] the only safeguards to prevent the Canadas from forming disadvantageous comparisons between the condition of the colonists and the adjoining country.'[25]

By contesting the authority of the legislative councils, the colonial republicans were contesting the existing constitutional order of the two colonies, based on the British principle of mixed government. They were demanding the reconfiguration of power relations in both Canadas according to a model of state legitimacy drawn from republican principles. They were asking the British government to acknowledge the sovereignty of the people rather than the sovereignty of parliament.

In this context, though, as in the past, Canadian republicans were loathe to criticize the legitimacy of the British monarchy or the governor's presence in the colony. If they did not do so, it was because they thought that once the legislative power was made to really represent the 'people,' the legislature could then impose its will on the governor. The governor would then be transformed into the first of all civil servants, with no independent voice. The People would become, effectively, The Crown.

24. *Journals of the House of Assembly of Lower Canada*, Fourteenth Provincial Parliament, Fourth session (January 7–March 18, 1834), 311–35.

25. 'Seventh Report on Grievances,' *Appendix to Journal of the House of Assembly of Upper Canada*, Twelfth Provincial Parliament, First Session (January 15 –April 16, 1835), 1:11.

The republican discourse in both Canadas during the 1830s focused primarily on the concept of political liberty, not on those of individual rights or civil liberties. In a larger sense, Canadian republicans wanted to impose virtue. In Canada, as elsewhere in the Atlantic, virtue was one of the key words in republican rhetoric. This word had at least three meanings. First, a virtuous citizen was a citizen who was independent socially and economically: this independence was the best guarantee that he could not be corrupted and that he would be independent politically. Secondly, to be virtuous implied an ethic of simplicity and frugality. Thirdly, virtue meant the willingness of a citizen to defend the common good instead of his own personal interests; in this sense, virtue meant patriotism. Because the Canadian rebels adopted this vision of a virtuous society, they cannot be seen as classical liberals, as some have argued. They were not demanding more civil freedom, nor autonomy from the State. They aimed instead to control the state.

The Rebellions and their Failure

The republican discourse in the Canadas during the 1830s echoed the discourses that American, Central American, Caribbean, French, and British republicans had articulated earlier in the Atlantic Revolution. The political struggles of the 1830s in the two Canadas and the rebellions of 1837–38 can be best explained by the challenge that republicanism represented for the colonial constitution. Republicans were contesting the premises upon which the authority of the colonial state rested.

In Lower Canada, for instance, by 1836–37, it had become clear to the Patriots—who controlled the Assembly—as it was also to their opponents—who controlled the Legislative Council—that their struggle could only be settled outside the framework of existing colonial institutions. The Patriots did not recognize the legitimacy of the Legislative Council, and their opponents rejected most of the reforms proposed or adopted by the Patriot Assembly. By 1837, under such conditions, neither

NOTES OF AN EXILE

TO

VAN DIEMAN'S LAND:

COMPRISING INCIDENTS OF THE CANADIAN REBELLION IN 1838, TRIAL OF
THE AUTHOR IN CANADA, AND SUBSEQUENT APPEARANCE BEFORE HER
MAJESTY'S COURT OF QUEEN'S BENCH, IN LONDON, IMPRISONMENT
IN ENGLAND, AND TRANSPORTATION TO VAN DIEMAN'S LAND.

ALSO,

AN ACCOUNT OF THE HORRIBLE SUFFERINGS ENDURED BY NINETY POLITICAL
PRISONERS DURING A RESIDENCE OF SIX YEARS IN THAT LAND OF
BRITISH SLAVERY, TOGETHER WITH SKETCHES OF THE ISLAND,
ITS HISTORY, PRODUCTIONS, INHABITANTS, &c. &c.

Slaves can breathe in England.

BY LINUS W. MILLER.

FREDONIA, N. Y.:
PRINTED BY W. McKINSTRY & CO.

1846.

Fig. 1. A first-hand account of the rebellion and its aftermath. Linus W. Miller, *Notes of An Exile to Van Dieman's Land* (Fredonia, N. Y.: W. McKinstry & Co., 1846).

See page 205.

Fig. 2. The character standing on the deck is hatless, referring to a point in the story in which his hair has been shaven off to show his status as a prisoner.

camp could negotiate with the other. Paralysis of legislative power was the result.

Lower Canada's Patriots launched an attack on the state in November 1837. Three battles ensued. After an initial victory at Saint Denis, the British won at Saint Charles and Saint Eustache. In December 1837, Upper Canada's radicals then began their drive to overthrow the colonial government. The two rebellions were crushed, as was a second Lower Canadian uprising in November 1838 and the unrest at the Upper Canadian border with the United Sates. In 1837–38, superior British military might decided that the Canadas would not be republics. Just as the 1776 Declaration of Independence and the subsequent British military defeat heralded the beginning of the Atlantic Revolution, the failure of the Canadian rebellions and the victory of British forces and Canadian volunteers, sixty-two years later heralded its true end.

Conclusion

Political life in Upper and Lower Canada became very difficult from 1828 onwards, especially in Lower Canada, where the Patriots controlled the Legislative Assembly for a decade—something the Upper Canadian radicals were never able to do. By the fall of 1837, the Patriots of Lower Canada and the radicals of Upper Canada had launched an assault on the legitimacy of the colonial state in British North America. These two groups were not simply seeking to overthrow the existing government. At a more fundamental level, they were trying to refashion the existing constitutional order of the colonies and to reconfigure power relations in both Canadas, according to a model of state legitimacy drawn from republican principles. In accordance with their republican ideals, the Patriots and the radicals fought for, among other things, the ultimate sovereignty of the people, primacy of legislative power over executive power and the economic and political independence of all citizens. In this way, the Canadian rebellions participated in the larger revolutionary movement that was fundamentally reshaping the Atlantic World at the end of the eighteenth and the beginning of the nineteenth century. Although the Canadian uprisings occurred much later, they were not ideologically different from the upheavals that preceded them. Had they succeeded, they would have been known as the Canadian Revolution.

It is because these movements failed to overthrow the state— their leaders being better at articulating speeches and making constitutional claims than at organizing a rebellion, that the Patriots and the radicals are not often connected to the wider political and intellectual currents that were reshaping the Atlantic World at the time, even though they were clearly inspired by them and aimed to create republics in Canada. The 1837–38 rebellions may have been a failure, but they were very closely related to the complex story of the Atlantic Revolution at the end of the eighteenth and the beginning of the nineteenth century. They are best understood as its last chapter.

Index

A

Adair, John, 36
Adams, Hannah, 102
Adams, John, 76; 150, 151; 177, 186, 187
Adams, John Quincy, 177
Alcalá Galiano, Antonio, 160
Amaru, Túpac, 43, 45; 119, 121, 129
Anna, Timothy, 126
Armitage, David, 10; 63
Arouet, Francois Marie, 164, 165

B

Baillio, Jean 'Juan', 81
Barbé-Marbois, François, 81
Barlow, Joel, 11, 31, 32; 97, 98, 99, 107, 108, 109, 110, 111
Barlow, Ruth, 97
Battlori, Miguel, 125, 129
Bauer, Ralph, 12
Beauspoils, 32
Beccaria, Cesare, 70, 71
Bello, Andrés, 157
Bemis, Samuel Flagg, 23
Bentham, Jeremy, 157, 158
Berlin, Isaiah, 183
Biassou, Georges, 91, 92
Biassou, Jean-François, 89, 91, 92
Blackstone, William, 199
Blount, William, 20, 21, 24, 25, 26, 27, 30, 38, 39
Boisbrun, Claude, 89
Boisrond-Tonnerre, Louis Félix, 95
Bolívar, Simón, 7; 77; 81; 99; 125; 157; 178, 180, 182, 183, 188, 189, 190, 191
Bonaparte, José, 155
Bonaparte, Joseph, 49

Bonaparte, Napoleon (emperor of France), 13, 333, 39; 49; 93; 98; 141, 142, 143, 145, 151; 155
Bonaparte, Pauline, 144, 145, 147, 149
Bouchard, Gérard, 195
Bowles, William Augustus, 16, 25
Boyer, Jean-Pierre, 12, 13, 14; 155
Brackenridge, Hugh Henry, 31
Brading, David A., 125
Brigham, Clarence S., 8
Brissot de Warville, Jacques Pierre, 31
Burges, James Bland, 123
Burke, Edmund, 132; 177, 185, 187
Burke, William, 124, 169
Burr, Aaron, 16, 21, 24, 25, 26, 27, 30, 39; 142, 143
Bustamante, Carlos María, 168
Byers, James, 25

C

Calhoun, John, 179
de Cambefort, Joseph-Paul-Augustin, 89, 91
Campbell, Archibald, 421
Carey, James, 21, 24
de Caritat, Jean Antoine Nicolas, 31
Carroll, John, 103, 112
Chaison, Joanne Danaher, 9, 12
Channing, William Ellery, 101
Charles III (king of Spain), 128
Charles IV (king of Spain), 44, 49
Charles X (king of France), 114
Chisholm, John, 20, 21, 24, 25, 27, 230
Chotard (aîné), 80
Christophe, Henry, 112
Claris de Florián, Jean Pierre, 160
Clark, George Rogers, 22, 31, 39
Clavigero, Francesco S., 130

Clay, Henry, 179
Clemente Carnicero, José, 170
Condorcet, Marquis de. *See* Jean Antoine Nicolas de Caritat.
Constant, Benjamin, 184, 185, 189
Costi, 33
Cromwell, Oliver, 11

D

Dahl, Robert A., 191
Dalrymple, John, 30
Davidson, Cathy, 141
Delahaye, Jacques, 89
Delemeau, Jean, 46
De Lolme, Jean Louis, 199
Descourtilz, Jean Theodore, 81
Dessalines, Jean-Jacques, 83; 142, 145
Dickinson, John, 67, 70
Diderot, Denis, 86
Dillon, Elizabeth Maddock, 11; 118; 'Caribbean Revolution and Print Publics: Leonora Sansay and the Secret History of the Haitian Revolution,' 133–53
Dinsmore, James, 25
Dragonetti, Giacinto, 70, 71
Drexler, Michael, 141
Dubois, Laurent, 92
Dubois, Madame, 108
Ducharme, Michel, 11; 'Closing the Last Chapter of the Atlantic Revolution: The 1837–38 Rebellions in Upper and Lower Canada,' 193–206

E

Earle, Rebecca, 54
Emerson, Ralph Waldo, 172

F

Ferdinand VII (king of Spain), 33; 164; 175
Fernández de Lizardi, José Joaquín, 161, 171, 172
Fernández de Moratín, Leandro, 166
Flores Estrada, D. Alvaro, 49
de Foronda, Valentín, 164

Foster, Hannah Webster, 121
Foucault, Michel, 190

G

Galván Rivera, Mariano, 163
Garcia de Sena, Manuel, 77
Garcilaso de la Vega, El Inca, 129, 131
Geggus, David, 10; 'Print Culture and the Haitian Revolution: The Written and the Spoken Word,' 79–96
Genêt, Edmond-Charles, 16, 21, 23, 25, 30, 31; 196
Gilroy, Paul, 135, 136, 152
Girod, Amury, 203
Godard, Jean Baptiste, 89
Godechot, Jacques, 193
de Goya, Francisco, 166
Greer, Allan, 194
Grégoire, Henri-Baptiste, 11; 85; 97–115; 164
Gros, 87
Gustafson, Sandra M., 7, 11; 19; 'Daniel Webster and the Making of Modern Liberty in the Atlantic World,' 175–92
Gutiérrez, Luis, 165
Gutierrez de Lara, Don Jose Bernardo Maximiliano, 16, 19, 33, 34, 35, 36

H

Habermas, Jürgen, 134, 135, 137, 140; 187
Hamilton, Alexander, 58, 67
Hampe-Martinez, Teodoro, 48
Harvey, Louis-Georges, 195
Hawkins, Benjamin, 25
Hayne, Robert, 176
Hench, John Bixler, 11
Hidalgo y Costilla, Miguel, 333; 168
Hobbes, Thomas, 43
Hofstadter, Richard, 29
Houston, Sam, 38, 39
Hunt, Lynn, 63
Hurd, Nathaniel, 67

I

Imlay, Gilbert, 31
de Iturbide, Agustín, 171

J

Jackson, Andrew, 140; 178
James II (king of England), 23
Jeannot, 89, 91
Jefferson, Thomas, 17; 63; 99, 104, 107, 111; 151; 177, 178, 187; 201
Juan, Jorge, 130

K

Kemper, Reuben, 19, 34, 35
King, Rufus, 121, 122, 124, 125, 126
Klein, Lawrence, 29

L

Lamonde, Yvan, 193
de Las Casas, Bartolomé, 101, 112, 124; 163
Leclerc, Charles Victor Emmanuel, 93; 141, 142, 145
Leclerc, Pauline Bonaparte, 144, 145, 147, 149
Leisler, Jacob, 23
LePlongeon, Augustus, 8
de Limonade, Julien Prévost, 112, 113
Lista, Alberto, 166
Llorente, Juan Antonio, 11; 155–73
Locke, John, 177, 183, 184, 190, 199
Lopez, Narciso, 13
Loughran, Trish, 72
Louis XVI (king of France), 46
L'Ouverture, Toussaint, 81, 83, 86, 87, 92; 142, 148, 150, 151
Lyonnet, Pierre, 32

M

de Mably, Gabriel Bonnot, 32
Mackenzie, William Lyon, 201, 202, 203, 205
Madiou, Thomas, 95
Madison, James, 17, 18, 33, 34; 57, 67, 70
Magee, Augustus W., 16
Mahy de Cormeré, Guillaume-François, 80
de Maistre, Joseph, 173
Mangourit, Citizen, 32
Manigat, Leslie, 95
Marchena, José, 164, 165

Mariano Ramírez, José, 163
Marie Antoinette (queen of France), 44
Marquis de Lafayette. See Marie Joseph Paul Yves Roch Gilbert du Motier.
Martínez de la Rosa, Francisco, 162
Mary II (queen of England), 23
Mather, Cotton, 25
McEvoy, Carmen, 48
McGee, Augustus William, 33, 36
Medina, José Toribio, 8
Meléndez, Mariselle, 10, 12; 'Fear as a Political Construct: Imagining the Revolution and the Nation in Peruvian Newspapers,' 41–55
Meléndez Valdés, Juan, 165
Menéndez y Pelayo, Marcelino, 156
Mereghal, Servaign, 32
Merry, Robert, 30
Mesplet, Fleury, 176
Mier Noriega y Guerra, José Servando, 100; 157
Milfort, Le Clerc, 29
Mill, James, 124
Mill, John Stuart, 183
Miñano, Sebastián, 166
de Miranda, Francisco, 31, 22; 120, 121, 122, 123, 124, 125, 126; 157
Monroe, James, 35; 103; 182, 183
Monteagudo, Bernardo, 50, 51, 52
Montesquieu, Charles, 33; 35, 77
Morel, Esteven, 33
Morgan, G. C., 152
du Motier, Marie Joseph Paul Yves Roch Gilbert, 177, 178, 186, 187
Muñoz, Juan Bautista, 158
Muthu, Sankar, 69

O

O'Fallon, James, 36
de Olavide, Pablo, 164
Onuf, Peter, 36

P

Paine, Thomas, 31, 32; 66, 67, 70, 71, 72, 74; 126; 160; 185, 202
Palmer, Robert, 193
Papineau, Louis-Joseph, 201, 202, 203
Penny, Jaclyn Donovan, 12

Pereyra, Carlos, 126
Peterson, T. B., 156
Pétion, Alexandre, 12
Pitt, William, 45; 67; 120
Pope, Elizabeth, 12
Puglio, James, 32
Puigblanch, Antonio, 120

Q

Quitmann, John, 39

R

Racine, Karen, 11
Radcliffe, Ann, 173
Rawls, John, 183
Raynal, Guillaume-Thomas François, 86; 203
Reinoso, Félix José, 166
Rhea, John, 18
de Riego, Rafael, 164
del Río, García, 51, 52
del Rio, Guillermo, 48
Rivadavia, Bernardino, 157
de Robespierre, Maximilien Marie Isidore, 164
Robin, Corey, 42
Rocafuerte, Vincente, 77
de Rochambeau, Donatien Marie Joseph, 142, 145, 146, 147, 149
Rogers, John, 25
Romayne, Nicholas, 20, 21, 26, 27
Rosas Lauro, Claudia, 43, 46
Roscio, Juan Germán, 171, 172
Rousseau, Jean-Jacques, 156, 164, 166; 183, 184, 189; 200
Rowson, Susanna, 140
Ruíz de Padrón, Antonio, 170
Rush, Benjamin, 66, 67, 71, 72
Russell, William, 201

S

Salisbury, Stephen, 8
Sansay, Leonora, 11; 137, 133–53
Sansay, Louis, 142
Sarmiento, Domingo F., 131

Sayre, Stephen, 32
Scott, Julius S., 152
Sempere y Guarinos, Juan, 165
Sepinwall, Alyssa Goldstein, 11; 'The Abbé Grégoire and the Atlantic Republic of Letters,' 97–115
Sevier, John, 38
Shaler, William, 34, 35, 36
Shelby, Isaac, 24
Shields, David S., 7, 10, 12; '"We declare you independent whether you wish it or not": The Print Culture of Early Filibusterism,' 13–40
Simmons, Merle E., 122, 123, 124, 125
Skipwith, Fulwar, 18
Slauter, Eric, 10; 'Written Constitutions and Unenumerated Rights,' 57–78
Sloat, Caroline F., introduction, 7–11
Smith, Nigel, 29
Smith, Robert, 17
Stolley, Karen, 11, 12 'Writing Back to Empire: Juan Pablo Viscardo y Guzmán's "Letter to the Spanish Americans,"' 117–32

T

Thomas, Isaiah, 7
Thornton, William, 76
Ticknor, George, 105
de Toledo, Alvarez, 34, 36
Trouillot, Michel-Rolph, 133, 135

U

Udney, John, 119, 120
Ugarte, Rubén Vargas, 125
de Ulloa, Antonio, 135

V

Valdés, Alejandro, 163
Vaughan, Benjamin, 325
Viscardo y Guzmán, Juan Pablo, 11; 17–32
Vogeley, Nancy, 11; 'Llorente's Readers in the Americas,' 155–73
Volnay, Constantin François Chasseboeuf, 32
Voltaire. See Francois Marie Arouet.

W

Wahrman, Dror, 61
Wallace, William, 201
Wallot, Jean-Pierre, 194
Warner, Michael, 74, 75
Washington, George, 13, 22, 24, 38; 201
Webster, Daniel, 11; 175–92
White, Ed, 140
Wilkinson, James, 21, 24, 31, 39
William III (king of England), 24

Wilson, James, 58
Winthrop, John, 190
Wood, Gordon S., 36; 75
Wykoff, William, 17

Z

Zavala, Silvio, 123
Zuckerman, Michael, 151